THE REFORM OF PRISONERS 1830–1900

WILLIAM JAMES FORSYTHE

CROOM HELM
London & Sydney

© 1987 W. J. Forsythe
Croom Helm Ltd, Provident House, Burrell Row,
Beckenham, Kent BR3 1AT
Croom Helm Australia,
44 – 50 Waterloo Road, North Ryde, 2113, NSW

British Library Cataloguing in Publication Data

Forsythe, W. J.
 The reform of prisoners 1830 – 1900.
 1. Punishment — Great Britain — History —
 19th century   2. Corrections — Great Britain
 — History — 19th century
 I. Title
 365'.7'0941   HV9646

ISBN 0 – 7099 – 4918 – 9

Printed and bound in Great Britain by Mackays of Chatham Ltd, Kent

Contents

Acknowledgements

I would like to thank the following people for their help in the preparation of this work:

Dr Margaret Hewitt, for her continuing and enthusiastic interest in the project;

Alex Allan, for her abiding enthusiasm and the typing of the manuscript;

Heather Eve of Exeter University Library for her inexhaustible patience with my requests that obscure texts be obtained through inter-library loan;

My Father, for searching out the autobiographies of long-forgotten Victorian prisoners, and my Mother for her great interest in the project;

Dr Barry Turner, Professor Bob Leaper, Bill Jordan and Dermot Walsh of Exeter University Sociology Department, who have given me great support and encouragement during the last ten years.

Abbreviations in References

PP	Parliamentary Papers
PRO	Public Record Office
RCGPP	Report of the Commissioners for the Government of the Pentonville Prison
RCP	Report of the Commissioners of Prisons
RDCP	Report of the Directors of Convict Prisons
RDMCP	Report on the Discipline and Management of the Convict Prisons
RInsP	Report of the Inspectors of Prisons
SC	Select Committee

To my wife Patricia
and my daughter Nuala
with love

Introduction

The Reformatory Endeavour

During the last few years scepticism has grown in Britain regarding reformatory ways of dealing with offenders, and indeed many who are not outrightly hostile to such endeavours have come to believe that the penal system ought mainly to concentrate on other purposes such as deterrent impact, incapacitation or efficient containment according to regulation. The shift away from what are usually called rehabilitative or therapeutic approaches[1] represents a striking change in attitude, for throughout the quarter-century up to 1975, a great deal of attention was paid to the maintenance and advancement of such methods of working with offenders. This may be easily illustrated by reference to the increase in the number of probation officers, extensive changes in law regarding disposition of juvenile offenders, the emergence of new therapeutic or training prisons such as Grendon Underwood, the Barlinnie Special Unit or Coldingley, and the growing emphasis on non-custodial, residental or semi-residential rehabilitative provision for probationers, released prisoners and other groups of offenders seen to possess special problems.

Since 1975, however, although the skeleton of the penal system remains, as it was established before that date, there has been an erosion of belief in the reformation of the offender and the consequent diminution of general criminality, given the resource of powerful state institutions and a faith in the progress apparently guaranteed by the application of human energy, reason and knowledge. Earlier optimism has begun to give way to either distrust of such endeavours or reduced expectations of their successful outcome. Accordingly, that approach has been assailed by intellectuals suspicious of the deeper purposes of reformatory systems, portraying them as serviceable instruments of 'a whole encircling industrial order';[2] by philosophers and writers, who have questioned the deeper purposes of such attempts within the total institution in particular;[3] and by many others who view an emphasis on such work within the penal system as part of a wider softening of penal rigour as a result of a plethora of false and utopian social theorising during the years since the end of the

1

Second World War. Many people working in the penal system itself are, partly in consequence, experiencing a growing uncertainty regarding their obligation or capacity to catalyse changes in prisoners' self-perception and their attitudes to others, and to alter behaviour among offenders. Such reduced confidence in reformation may be detected in the fields of youth custody, probation supervision and prison. Now the reformatory ideal is on the defensive, faced with querulous demands from some for the plain unvarnished fairness of a sentencing system based on some calculation of harm done, and with an impatient belief among others that reformatory endeavours are at least inconclusive and at worst harmful.[4]

In respect of prisons this change of attitude is especially marked. In 1979, for example, the May Committee of inquiry into the United Kingdom Prison Services sharply remarked that 'the rhetoric of treatment and training has had its day and should be replaced'. The committee was concerned to preserve what seemed to them to be 'admirable and constructive' endeavours with prisoners but in general expressed strong doubts that substantial personal change within individuals was a major realisable goal of the prison system.[5] Two years later, even among those administrators fairly well disposed to reformatory prison discipline, there was evident a weary sense that the prison system 'has become decreasingly able to meet virtually any of the objectives . . . other than simple incapacitation', and that 'the words of Prison Rule 1, that the purpose of the treatment and training of convicted prisoners should be to encourage and assist them to lead a good and useful life, are at present simply a pious aspiration'.[6] Thus it has doubtless appeared to many who, like myself, worked in the penal system during the 1960s and early-1970s, that this aspect of prison discipline has receded rapidly. What seemed an important and permanent feature of policy and practice, requiring only more personnel, money and knowledge for the realisation of its wider claims, has swiftly become seen as a vague and shadowy thing no longer at the centre of concerns, perhaps inappropriate. And it was out of a curiosity concerning the deeper reasons for and meanings of such a fundamental change that this book was conceived.

This study is of the growth of reformatory theory as a basis of prison discipline during the early-nineteenth century and of its subsequent decline after 1865, when the reformatory ideas upon which prison administration had previously been substantially based, were attacked and discredited by men who had come to distrust many of the ideas at the heart of the earlier structure. It was written because I felt that much might be learned from that past decline of reformation, particularly in respect of the different theories of criminal behaviour and penal purpose which emerged in the dispute. I felt, too, that such a study might provide an insight into wider contemporary philosophical developments, for certainly prisons, like other aspects of government, reveal a great deal about the shifting viewpoints of the society around them. In addition, by 1885, reformation in its previous form had been discredited and there was therefore an opportunity to construct a full account of this change, the conceptual bases of which were most precisely debated and documented so that it was possible without difficulty to excavate the more general ideas advanced by those who defended that approach or pressed for its decline.

It is perhaps necessary at the outset to make three points clear. First, there is not necessarily a correlation between an increase of mercy or leniency extended to prisoners and the growth of the reformatory ideal. It is indeed the case that reformatory systems can result in longer periods of incarceration than those systems which are predominantly deterrent. For example, in the later-twentieth century a child who has committed an offence might, for reasons of rehabilitation, be placed in an institution for 'disturbed' or 'deprived' children for a number of years; whereas for that same offence an adult might have received, say, two months' imprisonment. Secondly, it is of course true that the reformatory purpose is unlikely to form the sole basis of a prison regime and will usually coexist with such purposes as retribution, deterrence and incapacitation, although its weight within a prison system at any point of history will vary. It is worth noting that very few reformists in history have seen deterrence as of no importance in a prison system and, often in a theological context, they may see retribution as a part of reformism or indeed consider retribution as being highly important in a prison system quite independent of their reformism. Thirdly, it ought to be said that although the word 'reformatory' is commonly used in respect of specialist residential institutions for Victorian children who had collided with the criminal law, these institutions were but one aspect of the reformatory endeavour and indeed (not being viewed as prisons either contemporarily or subsequently) are not considered in this study.

Although the methods of reformists have varied greatly from one era to another, they have had certain features in common in their approach. At the heart of all penal reformatory endeavour there is always a notion of reclamation of the individual; 'faulty' parts of the attitude of the individual prisoner towards himself, towards others and towards the wider society may be changed at more than a mere calculative level. Fundamental and permanent alteration may consequently be achieved in those aspects of behaviour which are criminal or seen as crime-linked, and a re-union with law-obedient society can be brought about. In addition, the treatment of the prisoner by penal officials is held to be very important in securing this change. They must exemplify desired attitudes and behaviour in their conduct and conversation with him, so that a prisoner sees the desired qualities in action, experiences their effect upon him and wishes to emulate and learn from such self-evidently valuable qualities. In this connection there is a strong notion not just of distant example but of trust and close engagement, an idea that an official superior can win the attention and commitment of the prisoner through sympathy and consideration as well as through fairness and firmness in his dealings with him. Thirdly, the reformatory approach is neces-sarily associated with a search for aspects of the individual and his social surroundings which have some apparent connection with his crimes; this connection will have its theoretical foundation in well-established bodies of theological or more general philosophical theory about the mainsprings of human behaviour. Fourthly, there is a concern that the actions planned and undertaken should be based on the knowledge gained of the individual. There is within the reformatory concept a tendency towards individualised adjustment of action in accordance with the perceived needs of the individual and the difficulties which he has to overcome; this may also include adjustment of the actual time spent in prison on the basis of the apparent receptiveness, capacity or resistance of the prisoner. Fifthly, there is usually a recognition that certain 'groups' or 'types' of prisoner are less likely than others to change attitude and behaviour, together with a definition of these. Lastly, reformists set high store by instruction in certain skills and know-ledge which are believed likely to increase the capacity of the prisoner to maintain himself and his newly acquired attitudes in the face of personal, social or economic demands on leaving the prison.[7] In summary, therefore, penal reformists share some of the general aspirations common to later-twentieth-century psycho-therapeutic engagement with the individual — the 'combatting [of] his sense of isolation, reawakening his hopes, supplying him with new information as a basis for . . . learning, stirring him emotionally and encouraging him to apply what he has learned'.[8] Indeed, penal reformists usually suggest that the kind of changes they desire will involve emotional discomfort as complacency and hostility give way to commitment to new attitudes and behaviour.

Consequently, in every penal reformatory endeavour there are general beliefs about what is desirable in human attitude and behaviour, theories which explain the failure of prisoners to attain that standard, and prescriptions of methods to enable such accomplishment to occur. Thus the beliefs that the practice of, say, group therapy or the enforcement of solitude are an essential component of a reformatory attempt would be linked to some wider context or notion of a reality which transcends the individual and provides a general basis for approach in the light of the implied value, nature and potential of man. For example, in the late-1830s, penal administrators based a new reformatory method on a theological analysis of human value, nature and potential. By contrast, in the 1960s, ideas about the reform of offenders generally derived from a prevailing influence of secular psycho-social explanations of human behaviour, together with a notion of 'cure' or 'growth' within a nourishing framework of dedicated professionals, co-ordinating between disciplines, located within substantially resourced formal institutions of the state, sustained by an optimism about social environmental change and human potential.

To many of those who administer or inhabit British prisons much of what follows will seem familiar, for, despite changes in language, method and theory, two of the most striking features of the prison system during the last two centuries have been the importance of the reformatory claim in penal development and the intractability of the problems which it has defined as requiring solution. As Michael Ignatieff has pointed out, these two aspects of penal history need to be recognised because frequently institutional structures have been strengthened on the basis of such claims.[9] Indeed, it would seem in the light of this, that the present decline of reformation is but temporary and that it will become again a preoccupation among penal strategists. For that reason, if for no other, its history needs to be studied.

There is, however, a more purely historical reason for this undertaking. In the past two decades there have appeared a number of books written by historians and philosophers who were concerned to revise the somewhat optimistic evolutionary approach to the history of therapeutic and correctional institutions in France and Britain which had thitherto prevailed. Of these, Michel Foucault is perhaps the best known and he saw the nineteenth-century prison as a formidable part of the apparatus of a strengthening tyranny in what he called 'the carceral city',[10] a kind of inhuman disciplinary society which he plainly believed was coming to dominate man in modern times. The high intelligence and penetrating insights of this philosopher have exercised a substantial influence upon the view of the rise of the prison among West European historians generally. In Britain, one notable writer, Michael Ignatieff, has recently unambiguously and plausibly linked the nineteenth-century prison to the growth of an increasingly controlling state, seeking effective ways to subdue radical dissent from or inarticulate resistance to values and laws which themselves served to facilitate the rise of industrial entrepreneurialism.

These works depicted the reformatory emphasis of the early-nineteenth-century prison as an important part of a far-reaching strategy to exclude offenders from their surrounding society by subjecting them to various structures of 'repression, rejection, exclusion, marginalisation', and to 'insidious leniencies, unavowable petty cruelties, small acts of cunning, calculated methods, techniques, sciences that permit the fabrication of the disciplinary individual'.[11] Foucault himself pointed up the legitimation of power implied by the use of such institutional reformatory or curative actions. Greater enforcement was justified as benevolent, desirable and beneficial, in part by the artificial stimulation of fears about the increase of disorder, dissidence or crimes, and further by the steady 'normalisation' of mechanisms of power and 'abnormalisation' of the attitude or conduct to be erased. Therefore disconnections were achieved by the severance of the criminal held in large secretive prisons away from the deferent, obedient, industrious poor, who were thereby subtly influenced to perceive the deviator from legality as alien. The result was to reduce the likelihood of a hostile united lower order, as well as achieving the truncation of personality and the objectification of madness or criminality as a disease or malfunction exterior to normality. The mad learned that their madness was a detached, menacing phenomenon which had to be placed in the hands of rational men of knowledge rather than regarded as a natural and profound part of self; the criminal was assaulted at the level of soul, taught to abominate those feelings and habits pointedly associated with his crime. Thus was entailed a new kind of tyranny: a subjugation of those parts of man previously accepted as 'the dark side of human awareness'[12] to the new disciplinary and intellectual structures. Based upon purposefully constructed and disseminated information, these structures purported to be validated by objective rationality whose operators, being themselves children of an age of reason, sought to reconstitute man as a stifled persona according to the image of a new social order in disregard of whatever actual human need he possessed. All reformist approaches were essentially aspects of the pursuit of power through the mounting of reverberating discourse which demanded ever-increasing regulation. It did not appear surprising to Michael Ignatieff that prisons so closely resembled factories for 'penal and industrial discipline developed along the same trajectory', both requiring colonisation of the minds of the poor 'into that caricature of ascetic rectitude that the rich adopted as their self image'.[13]

Although the label 'revisionist' is somewhat misleading in that Foucault and Ignatieff differed in their approach to their subject, it is nevertheless clear that both writers were distrustful of those who were engaged in reformatory endeavours and consistently doubted that these were in any serious way dedicated either to the human value of their charges or the importance of the social inclusion of prisoners. Admittedly, Ignatieff has recently reconsidered the views which he expressed in his first work and has acknowledged some difficulty with his earlier assumption that there was a widespread penitentiary practice in mid-nineteenth-century prisons.[14] In this reconsideration he has clearly responded to a number of 'counter-revisionists' who have accused him and Foucault of mistaking reformist propaganda for actual development. However, his distrust of reformation remains for he still doubts the determination and genuineness of these reformists. Now he represents them as some sort of 'symbolic system . . . in which the reform of the guilty criminal was held to reveal the triumph of good over evil, conscience over desire, in all men and women. If there was a social message in the ideal of reform it was that the institutional salvation of the deviant acted out the salvation of all men and women, rich and poor alike'. This process reflected the strong hold which 'the drama of guilt and repentance held for the Victorian imagination'.[15]

Victorian prison reformists have been viewed with suspicion by a long line of writers stretching back as far as Charles Dickens[16] and Thomas Carlyle,[17] and Ignatieff might be seen as but a recent inheritor of a literary tradition in which either the inhumanity or the moral duplicity of such officials have figured highly. It therefore seems necessary to look again at these reformists' motives and actions. Consequently, suspicious of the hostility which the reformists aroused and doubtful of the counter-revisionist assertion that their influence upon practice was slight,[18] I have sought to re-examine the entire business of Victorian prisoner reformation as it was expounded and practised in prisons. This should help to determine whether an alternative assessment might be made to the recent revisionist works which have been both so widely acclaimed and so vigorously condemned,[19] and which might also call into question the stereotypical picture bequeathed to us by Dickens and others.

Evangelicals and Associationists

Penal reformatory endeavours in the late-eighteenth and early-nineteenth centuries were almost entirely underpinned by two general systems of thought, each of which offered an internally consistent explanation of the formation of criminal attitude and conduct, such attitude and conduct being unquestionably acquired environmentally and post-natally. Every major reformatory endeavour between 1775 and 1860 was based upon one or other where it was not the product of an integration of the two approaches.

The first of these was evangelicalism. By 1820, evangelicals had constructed a general analysis of social change in an industrialising era which was essentially conservative in its emphasis upon a divinely ordained stratified society, cemented by ties of deferent obedience among the poor and solicitous charity among the wealthy, and insisting upon the value of every human being in the eyes of God. Pointing to what they conceived to be man's natural inclination to sinfulness and disobedience, evangelicals argued that the economic changes in Britain and political ideas emanating from France were destroying the ancient stable basis of society — what Perkin later described as 'a society distributed in small units, a society of villages and small towns in which everyone knew everyone else', characterised by 'the social control of the ordinary squire over his tenants and villagers'.[20]

Evangelicals maintained that a moral cataclysm was coming to pass whose symptoms were the rapid spread of irreligion, immorality and crime among the poor, especially those massed in the great cities which were brought into being by the economic and demographic changes of the late-eighteenth and nineteenth centuries. Early evangelicals such as William Wilberforce therefore castigated all sections of society for this spread of sin and unbelief but in particular they campaigned to convert two groups to their theology of a passionate, zealous enthusiasm for the doctrines of 'the corruption of human nature, the atonement of the Saviour and the sanctifying influence of the Holy Spirit'.[21] These were the clergy and the aristocracy, whose spiritual vitality and energetic philanthropy were in evangelical terms essential to the achievement of a reaction to the social tranquility which they believed that God intended for mankind and which had prevailed hitherto.

In all their work evangelicals has as their objective the capture of souls. With extraordinary success, often in league with the newly emerged evangelical wing of the Quakers, they attacked all evils which in their terms distanced men from their Creator, whether these were individual acts (prostitution, begging, drunkenness) or institutionalised systems (the Caribbean slave trade, widespread capital punishment, promiscuous public relief through the old Poor Law). By 1825 they had established themselves as a most formidable influence in church and society in Britain, forming close ties with the wealthy and influential, who sensed in their message an antidote to the diseases of Jacobinism, dissidence and disobedience.

The implications of all this for the social treatment of prisoners were obvious to all who shared that thirst for Christianity as a living force which thunderously reflected God's deepest purposes for human beings and which possessed the beauteous universal truths of God to be proclaimed to all men. First, the state must regard its captives primarily in the light of their significance in the eyes of God. Officers and magistrates responsible for the prison were expected to bend all their efforts towards establishing the presence of living Christianity within the prison as a constant feature of all that they did and taught. Secondly, they must seek out the particular aspects of spiritual and moral defectiveness of each prisoner and must seek to rectify these, not merely by their own example and faith — which were of course essential as conveyors of regeneration — but also by programmes of action which would involve the supply of knowledge and understanding previously lacking and which would be adapted according to the spiritual and moral state of the individual. Thirdly, they had to recognise that certain groups or individuals would be so deeply mired in sin that they would in all likelihood pose grave problems for the reformer. Nevertheless, he was to persist in his work in sure faith that to God all things are possible. Fourthly, in order to prepare men to live industriously and dutifully, the prisoner should be provided with a stock of skills. The exact nature of these would require detailed investigation for each individual so that the moral and spiritual vitality derived from the rest of the work would not be checked by helplessness in the economic market on release. Indeed a virtuous, sober and frugal life based on industrious labour was entirely with the grain of evangelical thought which emphasised the different functions of men within God's stratified society and the importance of obedient, watchful and faithful living.

Evangelicals and other Christian thinkers were convinced that criminals must experience suffering at the hands of the earthly powers for two reasons. The first was a belief that all punishment must inflict pain because in a Christian society the institutions of that society must as far as possible reflect the behaviour of God. Just as God on the last day would inflict pain in accordance with his perfect judgement, so it must follow that pain was the natural sequella of sin on earth. This notion of natural consequence of sin was deeply held by evangelicals who saw it as part of a grand design of human affairs. Indeed the infliction of pain was to them, as to Bishop Butler in the eighteenth century, an inescapable part of penal discipline irrespective of any deterrent impact.[22] However, evangelicals primarily viewed the infliction of pain as means towards the eventual regeneration of the criminal. Pain endured allowed expiation of past sin to begin, and through the lonely personal suffering of the offender the prospect of an atoning leap of faith towards Christ became more likely. They emphasised the regenerative aspect of retribution and consistently warned that pain inflicted purely for deterrence and without a spiritual aim merely hardened the heart against the punisher and the society which legitimated his actions. The aim of the pain and its precise shape must be such as to induce sinners 'to throw themselves with deep prostration at the foot of the cross, there to obtain pardon and find grace to help in time of need'.[23]

The vision was therefore essentially one of a voluntarist conservative Christian philanthropic society in which the poor — grateful, obedient heaven-bound — would look up with gratitude to their superiors, forever engaged in charitable dynamic Christian action on their behalf and maintaining vital sincere relationships with them. Although the extraordinary energy of evangelicals was a substantial force in the creation of a more centralised and regulatory state in mid-nineteenth-century Britain and although evangelicals relied upon the institutions of the state, such as its laws or ships of war, to prevent cruelty to the mad or to annihilate the slave trade, they were only interested in a more efficient state as a base for a passionate, God-inspired appeal to the outcast and sinner. Initiatives in social policy were significant only in so far as they allowed fuller access of energetic zealous Christian visionaries to the hearts and minds of the poor so that the torpid, vicious, sinful deterioration of man might be reversed and the poor be deeply stirred in spirit by the love and care displayed by their regenerated superiors. As one labourer was heard to remark at the evangelical Lord Shaftesbury's funeral, 'Our earl's gone. God A'mighty knows he loved us and we loved him. We shan't see his likes again',[24] an oft-quoted example of the simple, dutiful, grateful and obedient labouring man, paternally nurtured and supervised, proceeding through his life in gratitude and goodness.

The notion of an ever-active God lighting the fires of spiritual revolution amidst his creatures through the crusades of the reborn was in marked contrast to the other major thesis which also implied a self-contained and coherent idea of the reformation of erring human beings and which had been built up during the one and a half centuries prior to the mid-nineteenth century. This thesis derived its starting point from the rapid development of natural science of the seventeenth century during which the mechanical nature of heavenly and earthly phenomena was investigated so that 'Newton's laws of motion put the capstone on the idea that the universe was a grand machine . . . God the master engineer constructed a perfect machine and left it running'.[25] From this concentration on the laws of motion and behaviour of natural phenomena it was a short step to investigation of man as a piece of divinely devised equipment which obeyed certain laws to be discovered by patient exploration.

Accordingly by the end of the eighteenth century there had developed a psychological thesis known as associationism which purported to explain the formation of human attitude and conduct in terms of the impact of experience upon the individual. Taking as a starting point John Locke's notion of the human mind at birth as a blank sheet or *tabula rasa*, philosophers such as David Hume and David Hartley constructed a body of psychological theory of great complexity and variety. In essence, the argument contended that human attitude was formed through the association between sensations and experience. Although the impact of experience was believed to be particularly strong in childhood, the process persisted throughout life; thus to David Hume human personality could be explained entirely by reference to the experiences which had given rise to sensations, which in their turn had created attitudes. Consequently, to the associationist the criminal was one who had learned through earlier experience that crime produced pleasure, and repetition produced more pleasure. The first task of the reformer of prisoners was to substitute a measured quantity of pain over a period of time sufficient to reverse the attitude to criminal action and the vices believed to be associated with it, hence obliterating the desire for repetition. The second objective was to provide rewards sufficient to implant desires for other (virtuous) actions previously detested or avoided.

Whilst John Locke had earlier applied his own associationist ideas to educational method, Jeremy Bentham placed associationist reasoning at the foundation of the multi-purpose institution which he invented in the late-eighteenth century and called Panopticon. One of the purposes of this was the reformation of prisoners and Bentham intended that, by the measured and prolonged infliction of pleasure and pain within a carefully regulated regime, behaviour patterns would be systematically altered. By a combination of rewards and punishments, the lazy would become models of industry, the defiant turn docile, the criminal become law abiding. Bentham was clear that such a reformatory endeavour would require substantial time and patience for its success as he believed that it was the steady accumulation of experiences with their attendant sensations which produced durable attitudes and persistent conduct. Therefore the erasure of earlier established patterns of conduct and their replacement by opposite tendencies could only be achieved slowly.

However, he was confident that this mixture of pleasure and pain would eventually result in a happy situation in which 'things which had been originally objects of desire become objects of aversion and, on the other hand, things which had been objects of aversion . . . become objects of desire'.[26] Furthermore, as associationists generally argued, repetitive infliction of the pleasure or pain at length wholly destroyed the original tendency, in that 'propensities suppressed are weakened and by long continued suppression killed'.[27]

Associationist theory was, then, an elaborate, coherent and self-contained basis for reformatory practice. The individual tendencies of prisoners would need to be taken into account and the regime tailored to each. Staff would need to inspect closely the progress of each prisoner's reformation and new skills would need to be taught them so that the newly acquired attitude to work, for example, would bear fruit after release. Certain groups were deemed easier to reform than others, in particular the young, whose experience of crime as pleasurable was seen as smaller than that of older offenders. Where reformation had failed to result, the notion of indeterminancy of sentence could be applied: Bentham, for example, believed that those who failed to maintain themselves after release should be held in a subsidiary panopticon for the rest of their lives.[28]

This behaviourist thesis, rooted in the psychological assumptions of the late-eighteenth and early-nineteenth centuries, formed the second theoretical base of reformatory method before 1865. In practice it was not necessarily divorced from evangelicalism for, as explained, the idea of pain as a consequence of sin was an essential part of evangelical theology. Yet although systems of reformation in Victorian England drew liberally from both theoretical approaches, they were in their pure theoretic form distinct from one another: the one appealed to the spirit soaring upwards towards man's redeemer, the other to the less ethereal and, many argued, more realistic known laws of the psychology of humankind.

References

1. 'Reformation: (a) Improvement in form or quality, alteration to a better form, correction or removal of faults or errors; (b) The action of reforming . . . another's conduct or morals. Reformist: One who advocates reform. Rehabilitate: (a) To re-establish a person's good name . . . by authoritative pronouncement; (b) To re-establish the character or reputation of a person; (c) To set up again in a proper condition. Therapeutic: Of or pertaining to the healing of disease.'

2. M. Ignatieff, *A Just Measure of Pain*, Macmillan, 1978, p. 215.

3. M. Foucault, *Discipline and Punish*, Penguin, 1977.

4. P. Bean, *Punishment: A Philosophical and Criminological Inquiry*, Robertson, 1981.

5. *Report of the Committee of Inquiry into the United Kingdom Prison Services*, HMSO, Cmnd 7673, 1979, paras 4.27 and 4.28.

6. *Report on the Work of the Prison Department*, HMSO, Cmnd 8543, 1981, para. 16.

7. This reformatory model draws from N. Tutt, 'Justice or Welfare', *Social Work Today*, vol. 14, no. 7, 19 October 1982, pp. 6–10.

8. S. Bloch (ed.), *An Introduction to the Psychotherapies*, OUP, 1979, p. 14.

9. M. Ignatieff, *A Just Measure of Pain*, pp. 218–20.

10. M. Foucault, *Discipline and Punish*, p. 308.

11. Ibid.

12. A. Giddens, *The Constitution of Society*, Polity Press, 1984, p. 158.

13. M. Ignatieff, *A Just Measure of Pain*, pp. 215, 214.

14. M. Ignatieff, 'State, Civil Society and Total Institutions: a Critique of Recent Social Histories of Punishment', in S. Cohen and A. Scull (eds), *Social Control and the State*, M. Robertson, 1983, pp. 75–105.

15. Ibid., p. 92.

16. C. Dickens, *American Notes*, Chapman Hall, 1910, pp. 117–30.

17. T. Carlyle, 'Latter Day Pamphlets', *Centenary Edition of the Works of Thomas Carlyle in Thirty Volumes*, vol. XX, Model Prisons, Chapman & Hall, 1898, pp. 48–86.

18. M. E. De Lacy, 'Grinding Men Good? Lancashire's Prisons at Mid Century', in V. Bailey (ed.), *Policing and Punishment in Nineteenth Century Britain*, Croom Helm, 1981, pp. 182–216.

19. For a recent negative view of M. Foucault's historical method, see K. Jones and A. J. Fowles, *Ideas on Institutions*, Routledge & Kegan Paul, 1984, pp. 27–46.

20. H. Perkin, *The Origins of Modern English Society*, Routledge & Kegan Paul, 1969, pp. 51, 42.

21. W. Wilberforce, *A Practical View of the Prevailing Religious System*, 13th edn, Cadell, 1818, p. 271.

22. J. Heath, *Eighteenth Century Penal Theory*, OUP, 1963, p. 11.

23. W. Wilberforce, *A Practical View*, p. 107.

24. E. Hodder, *The Life and Work of the Seventh Earl of Shaftesbury*, Cassell, 1886, vol. III, p. 520.

25. T. H. Leahey, *A History of Psychology*, Prentice Hall, 1980, p. 89.

26. J. Bentham, ed. J. Bowring, *Deontology or the Science of Morality*, from the MSS of Jeremy Bentham, Longman, 1834, vol. 1, p. 144.

27. J. Bentham, *Panopticon or Inspection House*, Postscript Part 2, in J. Bowring (ed.), The Works of Jeremy Bentham, Tait, 1834, vol. 4, p. 140.

28. Ibid., p. 169.

1

The Application of Reformatory Theory to Prisoners c1815–1840

The Growth of Spiritual Reformism up to 1835

Throughout the first three decades of the nineteenth century almost all English and Welsh prisons were administered by local sheriffs and magistrates in the case of shire county prisons, and by a mixture of magistrates and councillors in the case of borough prisons. In Scotland almost all prisons were under the administration of the Royal Burghs. Criminal offenders were found in two different sorts of prison:- the gaols of a county or borough whose theoretical purpose was to hold prisoners until due process of law removed them (e.g. acquittal, execution or transportation); and the Houses of Correction, which were prisons of sentence originally erected for petty offenders against vagrancy, moral or petty criminal legislation in late-Tudor and early-Stuart times. Although this distinction between 'remand' and 'sentence' functions had become somewhat blurred, it is the case that the great majority of prisoners sentenced to prison were placed in Houses of Correction. It is also notable that the great majority of sentences were for relatively short periods (almost invariably less than two years, most usually under six months) because more serious offenders were dealt with in other ways, commonly by transportation. The central state itself was concerned with criminal prisons in two principal ways. First, by legislation parliament sought to set minimum standards, although the localities retained considerable discretion in deciding upon interpretation and implementation; and, secondly, as a result of a very complicated and tortuous process of negotiation, discussion and delay reaching back to the late-1770s when transportation had been temporarily interrupted

15

by the American Revolution, a penitentiary for up to a thousand longer-term prisoners governed by a state-appointed committee had become fully operational at Millbank in 1821. However, prison discipline before 1835 was mainly the province of the local dignitaries and indeed there was no mechanism for sustained central scrutiny or supervision of these in England, Wales and Scotland. There was only, after 1823, a requirement for the county and larger borough institutions of England and Wales to report about their regimes to the Home Secretary annually, whilst assize judges had earlier been required to confirm the lawfulness of prison rules.

During this pre-Victorian period reformists devised techniques for prisoner reform which were substantially based upon the Christian notion of spiritual revival. These reached their apogee in the mode of prison discipline known as the separate system. Their object was explicitly to alter the relationship of the prisoner to other human beings and himself at a level which was more profound than mere calculation of pain likely to be incurred if action was undertaken. Primarily they sought to introduce the prisoner to the reality of God, the salvation offered through Christ and the urgent necessity for surrender to God's will. Such theorists and practitioners were easily able to appeal to the well known and influential opinions of a good number of late-eighteenth-century reformers, legalists and administrators, but they added to these an unmistakeable evangelical edge as well as a refinement of method. They speedily adopted as a starting point the authoritative work of John Howard, the famous explorer of prisons in the late-eighteenth century. He had complained that although magistrates had reconstructed many prisons according to his model of sanitary, roomy, healthy institutions, inspected by magistrates and administered by salaried staff, they had as yet scarcely touched upon 'that still more important object, the reformation of morals in our prisons.'[1] Howard had by no means been the only influential voice calling for a substantial reformist base to prisons during the late-eighteenth century. The jurist Sir William Blackstone had urged the establishment of penitentiaries designed 'to accustom them to serious reflection and to teach them both the principles and practice of every Christian and moral duty',[2] whilst Jeremiah Fitzpatrick, Inspector General of the Irish prisons, had claimed that no penal undertaking was more valuable than 'establishing penitentiaries for the reform of the obdurate and villainous, for preserving the morals, as yet untainted of the giddy and

unthinking, for implanting a detestation of vice and respectful submission to the laws' — the kind of penitentiary prison recommended by John Howard and the 1779 Penitentiary Act.[3] From an
early period, therefore, the claims made that prisons, if properly
arranged, had the capacity to achieve substantial reform of their
inmates were frequent and depended upon most optimistic
assumptions which deeply appealed to the generation of evangelical and Quaker prison reformers which followed Howard's
death.

A particular pressure towards the reformatory view of prisons
between 1815 and 1835 was the influence of the Society for the
Improvement of Prison Discipline and the Reformation of
Juvenile Offenders, whose zeal was most marked in the prison
discipline debate. This society was typical of the large number of
Evangelical societies established to combat certain social evils or
promote particular reforms. On its committee sat well known
Quakers such as Joseph Fry (Elizabeth's husband), William Allen,
Samuel Gurney, Thomas Hancock and Samuel Hoare. There
were also many evangelical members of the Church of England,
such as Thomas Fowell Buxton, Lord Suffield, William Crawford,
John and Walter Venning and Francis Cunningham. Some of
these were related by marriage (Buxton married one of the
Gurneys as did Samuel Hoare). In addition to these groups were
numbered several notable liberal parliamentary campaigners,
including Stephen Lushington (a capital punishment abolitionist
and anti-slave-trader), Henry Grey Bennet (a parliamentarian
who pressed for reform of London prisons) and other distinguished
philanthropists like Edward Foster, the botanist and founder of the
Linnean Society, and J. L. Goldsmid, a Jewish financier and
penal reformer. The society cultivated the engagement of the
highest echelons of society, having at one time the Duke of
Gloucester as a patron, and at whose meetings Lord John Russell,
Lord Calthorpe (also an evangelical) and the Earl of Derby were
on occasion present. In the early-1820s among the Vice Presidents
were listed a duke, a marquis, numerous earls, three bishops, a
number of other members of the Lords and sixteen members of the
Commons.

This society promoted spiritual and moral reformism as an
important basis of prison discipline by means of closely argued,
very detailed and lengthy published reports. It was plainly most
influential as a result of the way in which the highest in the land
were drawn into its reforming activities so that the Evangelical

17

notion of a charitable cementing of society was emphasised. The actual gathering of information and preparation of reports, though, naturally fell on the shoulders of the committee members, especially Samuel Hoare who remained chairman throughout the history of the society, and the secretary William Crawford. Policy with regard to new penal developments or the content of evidence to be offered to parliamentary committees was often decided by Hoare. However, there was no variation in the emphasis on prisons as 'a school of moral discipline' in which would be created 'religious and moral principles . . . sober and industrious habits', for 'wherever the attempt has been made . . . with energy and perseverance success has invariably followed . . . in a great number of instances offenders, even the most hardened, who have for a reasonable time been subjected to a well regulated system of discipline do abstain from further violation of the law'.[4] Indeed, until prison reform was incorporated by the State in 1835, the most notable force for such reform and the strongest advocate of the reformation of prisoners was this society, apart only from the founding father of penal reform, John Howard, whose works were studied and discussed long after his death in 1790.

By the late-1820s it had become widely accepted that the prisons of Britain ought as a matter of primary duty to seek the moral reformation of the prisoner. John Joseph Gurney remarked that 'prisons ought to be so conducted as to produce reform' for 'the reformation of criminals is the true object'[5] of prisons. The evangelical William Roscoe urged a system of discipline which 'would not be relaxed till it had effected an entire change in their morals and manners',[6] whilst slightly earlier James Bicheno, another noted Prison Discipline Society member, asserted that 'the reformation of the criminal should be the motive, the object and the measure of all our exertions'.[7]

From the early period of John Howard all reformists were struck by the probability that within prisons as they were constituted at the end of the eighteenth century there existed very powerful influences which operated to prevent the reconstitution of attitude and belief which they sought. In particular writers increasingly pointed to the unrestrained intercommunication between prisoners which occurred in unreformed prisons because they believed that, left to their own devices behind the walls of a prison, prisoners would divert each other from reform. They would glorify the stumbling blocks which prevented the flow of God's grace such as drinking, gaming and sexual adventures, and would either teach each other criminal skills or at least reinforce criminal attitudes by encouraging or rewarding the exhibition of defiance, hardihood and contempt towards God and law. This anxiety began to be expressed during the late-eighteenth century; the pious reformist London merchant Jonas Hanway frequently emphasised the corruption which occurred in prisons.[8] The early-nineteenth century prison explorer James Neild excoriated the promiscuous association, drunkenness and vice in prisons which 'disqualify the mind for the humiliation consonant to the place'[9] and a London physician commented that in Newgate the prisoners 'may get drunk when they please'.[10]

By far the majority of prison discipline theorists held that the unreformed prisons resulted in 'the corruption of the morals of almost all' because the prisoners were herded together and left to their own devices.[11] This concern that a countervailing force existed to prevent reformation within prisons became by 1820 one of the foundations of all arguments that prisons ought to be remodelled. It was feared, with George Onesiphorus Paul, that these were no more than a 'seminary of vice and a certain intro-duction to the most infamous practices',[12] whilst the evangelical William Roscoe pointed out that unless administered according to strict regulation a prison was 'a scene of debauchery, idleness and profanity, an epitome of human wretchedness, a seminary of crimes'. In her rules for the government of Newgate prison female ward, Elizabeth Fry expressly prohibited 'begging, swearing, gaming, card playing or immoral conversation'[13] in an attempt to gain some control over 'the ferocious manners and expression of the women towards each other and their abandoned wickedness'.[14]

Having identified this contamination within prisons, Christian reformists then began to set out the ways in which attitude was to be changed. One idea which had appeared in the late-eighteenth century was that prisoners must be placed in such a situation that they were compelled to reflect upon their lives and upon the causes of their present incarceration and degradation. This reflection, it was believed, was most profound if the individual was removed from the distractions of association with other criminals and the noise and bustle of communal life within prison. The enforcement of at least partial solitude was held by Jonas Hanway, John Howard[15] and Samuel Denne writing in the early 1770s[16] to be essential for promoting such reflection. Later well known penal reformers such as George Onesiphorus Paul[17] lauded the tendency of solitude to create a sense of guilt and awareness of folly, what

William Roscoe later called 'self reproach, contrition and shame'.[18]

Before 1830, however, most spiritual reformists were intent upon gaining a presence in the classified association system which had come to characterise the larger prisons by 1825. This had also resulted from the emphasis upon prisons as places of contamination and had been a less expensive and less radical response to that problem than the insistence on solitude. Consequently prisoners were classified in groups according to their sex, pre- or post-conviction status and the seriousness of their crime, on the basis that the worst evils revealed by Howard and his successors would thereby be prevented. Young offenders would be kept out of reach of older habitual offenders, unconvicted from convicted, women from men, and this system had become the basis of public policy towards prisons. The aim of spiritual reformists was to ensure that a potent religious influence existed in prisons so as to create, as far as possible, the introspection and sense of sin which were essential preconditions of regeneration, means by which 'many an evil spirit may be exorcised'.[19] During the early-nineteenth century these reformists steadily gained ground in their arguments for a firm religious and moral discipline in classification prisons[20] without which reformation was unattainable,[21] for the Gospel 'alone can effectually teach men to deny all ungodliness and worldly lusts',[22] instituting 'the terrors of a future state . . . essential to the reformation of men who have accustomed themselves to brave the powers of this world'.[23] The intention was to reform the criminal associated in his classified group by means of instruction in Christian truth, moral homilies, exhortation and admonitions, and lengthy and earnest discourse, for 'as the Gospel is the only means by which a sinner can be converted into a saint, so is it the most likely way of inducing a profligate to become a moral man', and indeed religion 'is the most powerful engine that can be applied to the human mind'.[24]

The work of the chaplain as the Christian minister to a lost flock became indispensable to this reformatory theory and was described in terms which left no doubt that great spiritual change would result from it. In evangelical fashion he would 'inculcate line upon line and precept upon precept . . . that nature when left to her own direction is wretched and miserable and poor and blind and naked' for 'a pious clergyman would have it in his power to be of infinite service to society by teaching the fundamental doctrines of religion'.[25] However, it was intended that such clergy should aim at much more than mere instruction of the mind in established truths; they were to penetrate the feelings in such a way as to move the whole nature of the hearer inexorably towards religion as his only sure and certain hope for the future and the centre of his affections. In the first place spiritual reformists dwelled at length on the need for 'kindness, gentleness and true humility . . . serenity and firmness . . . the spirit not of judgement but of mercy . . . Christian kindness'[26] as they sought to establish a regime which stimulated gratitude and receptiveness in the minds of the prisoners.

The aspiration did not of course exclude the belief of spiritual reformists that prisons should be places of severity and rigour but they were divided in their attitude to the widespread introduction of the treadmill (or treadwheel) in prisons between 1815 and 1825. The treadmill was a large cylindrical drum revolved by the pressure exerted by rows of prisoners stepping upwards onto it in unison. Although some of these machines ground corn or raised water, most had as their purpose merely the economical infliction of deterrent penal labour. Yet some reformatory purpose was urged by adherents of the mill such as physical and psychological inurement to labour, and indeed the Prison Discipline Society gave support to it initially. Notwithstanding this there was sharp controversy about the use of the mill in the early 1820s and many reformists distrusted it as 'a species of torture', 'a system of hopeless and hardening terror . . . a bulwark against all moral and religious feeling' creating 'a feeling of misery, resentment . . . the energies of his mind are exerted to resist coercion'.[27]

Consequently, spiritual reformists from an early stage recognised a tension between the possibility that severity would excite hostility and the need to win the trust and close attention of prisoners. William Roscoe[28] and James Bicheno[29] both pointed out that cruelty or harshness were not conducive to true repentance; the aim was to touch the feelings with tenderness and compassion as well as to discipline with firmness and rationality. As Elizabeth Fry reported: 'yesterday we were some hours at Newgate with the poor female felons . . . I heard weeping and I thought they appeared much tendered'.[30] The sorrow experienced was intended to be part of the regeneration rather than the distant infliction of pain, and the mercy of Christ to the repentant was to be emphasised. As John Clay, in the very early days of his ministry at Preston House of Correction, told his captive audience: 'take upon you the gentle and saving yoke of Christ

21

for he is merciful and to your God for he will abundantly pardon
. . . if however, prisoners, you are in the smallest degree anxious
to procure the forgiveness and favour of your maker recollect that
you must learn to love Him . . . if a man would hope to enjoy anything like happiness in this world he must be a religious man — he
must be a Christian.'[31] By such earnest pleas it was hoped that the
pains of imprisonment would no longer serve to excite resentment
and a lust for vengeance but would be the first part of expiation of
wrong done by suffering endured. By spiritual comfort and con-
frontation chaplains would unmistakeably convey to prisoners that
they were not outcast human refuse but souls beloved of God for
whom the patient shepherd was seeking. In this search he would
engage their deepest sorrows and guilts, although he could work
effectively only when the stumbling blocks to grace and truth such
as free access to drink or dance halls had been, as in a prison,
removed.

This emphasis on the chaplain as a spiritual torch within the
prison was a consistent feature of spiritual reformist literature in
the 1820s although the idea had its critics. In similar vein, reformists demanded that all the staff of prisons should be remarkable for
their Christian qualities so that the work of each would reinforce
the effect of his colleagues, providing a uniform emphasis on hope,
dignity, love and salvation to characterise the entire institution.
Not only must a chaplain 'feel deeply concerned for the welfare of
his charges' but officers were to be sober and earnest, while the
governor was to serve as 'a moral functionary'[32] who must 'guard
himself against every impulse of anger or personal resentment'.[33]
Throughout his imprisonment the prisoner was to have dealings
only with humane, benevolent and Christian men and women who
would 'as much as possible substitute mild entreaty and persuasive
arguments for a system of terror',[34] people of 'humane but firm
disposition, individuals well recommended as sober, honest,
steady and if possible of some education'.[35]

It was clear to reformists, on both spiritual and associationist
grounds, that criminals were neither identical in their wickedness
nor did they possess the same tendencies which brought them into
conflict with the criminal law. Plainly, therefore, differing
approaches would be necessary with individuals, and the reformists
displayed in their writings an interest in the earlier habits and
attitudes of prisoners as well as with the individual surrounding
influences of their lives which had some apparent connection with
crime. To some it seemed that imprisonment for a first offence was

a major cause of future crime because the young offender was thrown amongst hardened criminals who would influence his impressionable young mind towards further crime: 'early imprisonment therefore is the great and primary cause from which crime originates. From this source most of the evils flow which affect the youthful offender and at the earliest age lead him into those paths of vice from which there is afterwards no escape',[36] for 'here he finds able and willing tutors in all the varieties of crime and the very foundations of virtue are utterly sapped and destroyed. The spirit of proselytism flourishes in its greatest vigor amongst the vicious . . . the prisoner enters a boy in years and a boy in vice; he departs with a knowledge of the ways of wickedness which thrice the time spent elsewhere could scarcely have conferred upon him.'[37] Others detailed 'those evil habits which idleness has occasioned',[38] whilst some explained criminality in many as stemming from a lack of clear distinction between right and wrong behaviour together with defective parental care which had resulted in a failure to know right conduct or in actual encouragement in 'habits which become fixed and radicated forming a part of their very nature'.[39] Other commentators referred to the lack of employment and consequent poverty as 'the parent of crime'.[40] Thus the things which were commonly urged to account for a predisposition to crime were the irreligion which resulted when the young 'have actually been tutored by worthless parents in schools of idleness and nurseries of vice',[41] the corrupting effect of imprisonment in unreformed prisons and environmentally-induced poor moral habits and attitudes.

From an early stage of Christian reformist theory it was argued that prisons had to buttress the experience of Christian regeneration with skills and influences which would assist the individual prisoner steadfastly to resist temptation when released from the institution and no longer subject to the instruction of his mentors. Although it was widely anticipated that religious conversion would be the major reformatory objective, it was generally recognised that prisoners needed to be taught specific skills to enable them to maintain themselves after release. Mrs Fry, for example, taught her women knitting and needlework, and magistrates from Somerset regaled parliamentary committees with accounts of prisoners who had been taught carpentry and cabinet making,[42] advancing great claims for the value of such training.

Reformists were under no illusions that their efforts would invariably be successful and at this early stage some of them began to argue for adjusting the period of incarceration to ensure that some reformation had been achieved. William Roscoe even argued that no prisoner should be released until he had learned some 'art, trade or profession'.[43] A strong interest developed in continuing reformatory influence after release by, for example, the idea of placement of young prisoners in 'refuges' where they would be 'trained up in the habits of industry, instructed in moral and religious duty and after a time provided with suitable situations'.[44] There they would remain 'until satisfactory hopes of reformation have appeared'.[45] Even when officials had discovered 'the character, temper and moral constitution' of each prisoner and had adjusted treatment to suit each, it was clear that there would still be the 'obstinate and arrogant';[46] some groups seemed especially prone to fail to reform, for example those trained up in large cities as thieves from infancy.[47]

The strong tradition of prisoner reform based upon evangelical theory by 1830 not unexpectedly attracted opposition from those who did not share the belief that prisoners might be spiritually redeemed and socially rehabilitated by these means or that prisons should have as a primary function these aims. In particular those who held deterrence or retribution to be the major purposes of a prison criticised the Prison Discipline Society and other notable reformists for undermining these purposes. For example, in a well known article in the Edinburgh Review, Sydney Smith attacked reformation as the basis of prison,[48] suggesting that the main aims of punishment might be deflected by such solicitude and he demanded entirely deterrent prison regimes.[49] In addition, although by 1825 elements of reformatory discipline were plainly evident in most English counties, reformists were themselves aware that prisons were not in fact administered wholly according to their vision and that they were under attack from opponents. They imagined that, given a perfect prison, their success would be undeniable and would overwhelm competing arguments. In their search for the inherent defects obstructing this success they alighted upon classification.

Spiritual Reformism Perfected — The Separate System

By 1830 under the 1823 General Gaol Act[50] the classificatory system had become very widespread in local prisons. As explained earlier, contamination would be reduced by, for example, segregating groups of misdemeanants and felons[51] and placing them in different parts of the prison, each group having its own exercise space, day rooms, sleeping accommodation and labour areas. Yet, towards the end of the 1820s, it became clear to a number of parliamentary select committees that during the previous quarter-century there had apparently occurred a huge increase in crime.[52] Some witnesses who argued the deterrent or retributory primary function before these parliamentary committees took advantage of this to urge a return to unmistakeable severity in prisons with substantial use of the treadmill: 'I think there is now a greater dread of it and that it produces more order and regularity into the gaol'.[53] Reformist witnesses contended that, even given classification, contamination continued in prisons. For example, it might be the case that a man was convicted for a misdemeanour and placed amongst apparently less serious offenders but it might well be that he had previously committed felonies undetected or indeed been so convicted unknown to the prison; therefore by classification he was entirely erroneously placed in the apparently less criminal class and was free to corrupt unchecked. Clearly the reformists knew that they had to refine their model of prison discipline if they were not to be overwhelmed by those who sought a deterrent or retributory primary objective for prisons. They thus developed a new system of discipline which they called the Separate System.

The history of this system has been elaborately detailed elsewhere[54] and it need only be noted that it was developed from some of the early reformist writers such as Jonas Hanway, was first implemented in 1829 at Philadelphia Penitentiary in America, was detailed in a lengthy British report by William Crawford (an evangelical member of the Prison Discipline Society who had been sent by the new Whig government to investigate American prisons),[55] and became by 1840 the most coherent and persuasive reformatory model of a prison regime. It claimed to answer all the problems which were inherent in classification and furthermore claimed that all the methods developed by earlier reformists, such as earnest pious discourse, instruction, skill training and enforced reflection, would not only be most effective if practised within this new system but were too diluted to be effective within the classification system.

The separate system was initially set out in the 1834 report by Crawford but the concept was expanded in more detailed reports by William Crawford and the ex-chaplain of Millbank Penitentiary, Whitworth Russell. The later reports were published

25

between 1836 and 1838, after both men had been appointed
Inspectors of Prisons for the Home Counties under the 1835
Prisons Act.[56] First, they launched an attack on classification,
whether or not this was accompanied by a veto on verbal communication between prisoners.[57] They pointed out that it was
impossible to prevent contamination or to secure any depth of
moral or spiritual change within a system which allowed prisoners
to congregate together, for 'the mere aggregation of individuals is
known to inspire sentiments of confidence and hardihood. But
when this association ripens into intercourse, the consequences
become extremely pernicious. A single irredeemable convict is
able to taint the whole confederacy, to repress any rising thought
of amendment, to sear the conscience and to fix the wavering spirit
in the ways of guilt.'[58] Every reformist endeavour, no matter how
spirited and co-ordinated, was thereby doomed to fail in an
associated system where the 'comparatively innocent are seduced,
the unwary are entrapped, and the tendency to crime in offenders
not entirely hardened is confirmed by the language, the suggestions and the example of more depraved and systematic
criminals.'[59] Religious impressions were almost instantly dis-
pelled, all moral discussion mocked, the example of staff scorned
and the entire body of prisoners criminalised by the contagious
power of vice and defiance which could never be counteracted as
long as prisoners remained in association, whether classified or
not.

Crawford and Russell went on to argue that the prisoner must
be entirely deprived of the company of other criminals during his
sentence and that this could only be done by incarceration in single
cells and by arrangements which would preclude any possibility
even of a gesture or sign from one to another. The prisoner during
his sentence would seldom leave his cell and on those rare
occasions would be most carefully prevented from contact with
others. Only then, they urged, would the true reflection which
must precede repentance become possible, some sixty years after
Howard, Denne and Hanway had begun to discuss it. Making the
widest claims they insisted that separation 'inevitably tends to
arrest the progress of corruptness. In the silence of the cell contamination cannot be received or imparted . . . day after day with
no companion but his thoughts the convict is compelled to reflect
and listen to the reproofs of conscience. He is led to dwell upon
past errors and to cherish whatever better feelings he may at any
time have imbibed.'[60]

In this way separation could prepare a rich soil for the plough of the spiritual reformist. Because the prisoner was isolated and helpless there was no need for frequent disciplinary punishment, 'the dominion of the lash', which merely stimulated 'vindictive feelings', themselves grave impediments 'to those moral and religious means which experience has proved most efficacious in the recovery of the human character'.[61] All would be silent and reflective, confronting their own folly and viciousness, reflecting upon the inexorable path from disobedience and sin to prison, expiating in their misery the offence to God and man and beginning, in their dim perception of righteousness and repentance, their atonement with Christ. Above all it was the helplessness of the prisoners which was attractive to Russell, accustomed to the lewd jests and defiant hoots of Millbank prisoners in the chapel there. 'All artificial supports are now withdrawn and the culprit is made to feel the reality of his condition and the fearfulness of that prospect leads him to think of righteousness, temperance and judgement to come . . . in short upon the offender in his separate cell all the moral machinery of the system is brought to bear with as much force and effect as if the prison contained no other culprit but himself.'[62] Isolated in this unfamiliar and lonely environment, the mind would begin to dwell upon past errors, betrayed parents, wasted opportunities, lost domestic happiness so that gradually conscience would dominate consciousness, drawing the prisoner to recognise the cause and fact of his downfall.[63]

When the prisoner had perceived that by no manipulation could he alter the conditions of his sentence and that process of sombre introspection and sorrow had plainly begun, the agents of reform could then begin their work. The prisoner would soon beg for work as a relief from monotony and he would be taught a trade and given occupation, therefore learning to associate work with pleasure. He would receive daily visits from the officials of the prison, most notably the chaplain and governor. These would come to be anticipated joyfully as a relief from solitude, so their earnest piety and moral homilies would be especially powerful in their impact. Out of loneliness and boredom the prisoner would plead for activities which would lead him towards reformation and he would derive the greatest pleasure from the redemptive programmes. What had previously been disliked and shunned would now become the cause of enjoyment and relief.[64]

Within the cells there would be considerable activity as rational, benevolent, dedicated prison officials taught, exhorted, admonished, and catechised the prisoners. The cleansed minds of the latter would now be effectively addressed, their motives entirely harnessed to the great goal of reform and their souls revived and drawn to Christ. Prisoners would be forced to nothing except seclusion — all the rest they would desire themselves because of their reduction to utter monotony and heartfelt repentance by the early stages of the discipline. No longer would chaplains have to try to force Christ upon unrepentant and deriding groups of convicts. Now such men would beg for the bread of life as their only comfort, hope and faith, ready to be permanently altered by the teaching and warning of their philanthropic custodians.[65]

The separate system surfaced in England at a time which was propitious for its adoption. In the first place the Whig governments, which were led by Grey or Melbourne for all but a few months of the decade after 1831, were responsive to the intellectual and moral thrust among the newly enfranchised middle classes towards rationalistic social administrative systems which would apparently effectively reform the morals of the poor, whether in a quite different way through Chadwick and Nassau Senior's New Poor Law or in a spiritual way in new prisons. This decade was one in which a rise in the interventionist tutelary role of the central state occurred, involving a sharp increase in those activities of central government aimed at gathering social knowledge or influencing locality. Doubtless this in part resulted from the fear that many disaffected and wicked men were on the march against the newly reformed constitutional order now fiercely defended by middle class men, for the decade began with the Captain Swing riots and ended with Chartism. Whatever the reasons, however, many were quick to accept a system which promised so much in the way of docility, reverence and repentance, just as at the same time all the assumptions about the demoralisation of the poor upon which the Poor Law Amendment Act was based were accepted with little question. This new system was just one of a number of ideas and institutions which offered some hope that rational, benevolent and efficient state activity might fill the space evacuated by the old rural paternalistic squirearchic social structure and might win over the poor to gratitude, receptiveness and duty.[66] Indeed, the Chairman of the Prison Discipline Society, Samuel Hoare, swiftly embraced the new separate system and, confronted with extensive evidence from Crawford and Russell, the House of Lords Select Committee on Gaols and

Houses of Correction which reported in 1835, concluded that the separate system was the most desirable scheme of prison discipline and came out strongly in its favour. The Lords suggested that prison inspectors be appointed to report about prisons direct to the Home Secretary, and this was put into effect in 1835. Crawford, Russell and Frederic Hill[67] (all separatists although Hill later renounced it) were selected for the inspectorate, to which were also joined Francis Bisset Hawkins (replaced by a separatist John Perry in the early 1840s) and Captain John Williams, both of whom were to emerge as sceptics. However, for the time being Crawford and Russell held the two prominent positions within the English inspectorate and Hill the post of the Scottish inspector. Within a very short time in both countries a prolonged official campaign to turn the prison system over to separation began. Reformists apparently possessed an answer to those who doubted the effectiveness of spiritual reformism and they were assured of the support of statesmen who for the first time accepted a reformist view of the prison system, itself faced with further demands as a result of rising crime rates and the reduction of transportation.

As will be seen there were many vigorous opponents of separation. However, the notion that a prison could reform its inmates was being canvassed with extraordinary energy and dedication by 1835. Elizabeth Fry's brother-in-law, the prison reformer Thomas Fowell Buxton, continued his work unchecked by the deaths of three daughters and his eldest son within the space of six weeks in 1820 ('the darlings and delights of our life . . . our most choice and comely blossoms') whilst J. J. Gurney spoke of the dawning of a new age of 'sound Whiggism', during which constitutional reform, spirituality, efficiency, knowledge and progress would march hand-in-hand to overthrow the 'wicked innovations and licentious change' of radicalism on the one hand and apathetic custom-dominated Tory contempt for change on the other.[68] Spiritual reformism and its ultimate product, separation, were only small parts of an optimistic aspiration in which the progress made by each generation would form the starting point for its successor and in which the appeal to the reason and spirit of the individual would be continuous.

Sceptics and Silentists

Turning now to the associationist base of reformatory theory it is not proposed to recapitulate the details of Bentham's long struggle to establish the Panopticon because these have been exhaustively discussed elsewhere[69] and because, with a handful of exceptions,[70] the plan of his model prison had been rejected by 1815. However, it is clear that the idea of separation was attacked, firstly by those who rejected outright the emphasis on prisons as primarily reformatory and, secondly, by those who advocated a rival model of prison discipline which based its more modest reformatory claims upon assumptions which were explicitly associationist.

Many agreed with Middlesex magistrate Peter Laurie who asserted that separatists were ingenuous concerning the nature of criminal wickedness, adding that the cellular isolation demanded by the system was ineffective and cruel. Sarcastically remarking of prisoners that 'perhaps the most eligible business would be to bring them up for deputy prison inspectors, a craft which appears to be easily acquired, extremely profitable and requiring neither the experience of ages or the wisdom of Solomon',[71] he argued that the environment within which most criminals lived invariably influenced the great majority of them towards crime after release. Others emphasised, along with Lord Brougham, the Edinburgh Review tradition that prisons must primarily be places of bleak deterrent rigour, whilst some, after experience of the separate system, became doubtful of its claims. Daniel Nihill, one of Whitworth Russell's protégés and the governor-chaplain of Millbank, wearily remarked that 'prisons are, after all, very inadequate instruments for the prevention of crime' and ought rather to be 'the instruments of propagating through the country a salutary dread of the consequences of crime', for 'the separate system . . . cannot admit of society and is therefore void of the moral probation resulting from it.'[72] A prison officer in harsher vein argued that 'placing a prisoner in Pentonville for three or four years [*under separate confinement*] will tend to make a man a confirmed idiot rather than a good and useful member of society' and wondered what value there might be in instructing criminals in the 'exact position on the maps of Jerusalem, Canaan, Mount Ephraim, Mount Gilead [or] the Land of Nod'.[73]

There was, however, a rival school of prison discipline which possessed an identifiable reformist base and which might appeal more to those who advocated penal rigour and deterrence or who prided themselves upon their pragmatic knowledge of men as they really were rather than what visionaries desired them to be. The silent system, like separation, was imported from America where it had been developed at Auburn and Sing Sing penitentiaries in New York State.[74] Its most notable advocate and practitioner, as Governor of Coldbath Fields House of Correction for Middlesex County, was George Laval Chesterton, who stood in direct and public opposition to Russell and Crawford, and was supported by Peter Laurie and the Middlesex bench. Chesterton himself had joined the Royal Artillery in 1812 and served in both the Peninsular War and that against the United States in 1814. Subsequently he enlisted to fight against Spanish colonial rule under Bolivar in South America. After a period of great privation and danger he became so deeply impressed 'with the singular interposition which . . . had snatched me from overshadowing evil'[75] that he returned to England and resolved to be ordained. After a period in which he 'became dispirited and despaired of my capacity to struggle with the world'[76] he was persuaded by John Ousby, Chaplain of Coldbath Fields, to apply for the post of governor, which he secured in 1829, abandoning his preparation for ordination.

In the first place Chesterton declared that spiritual reformism in general and the separate system in particular were predicated upon an utopian view of criminals and of the working of God in the lives of men. Many criminals were habitual offenders, 'pests and outcasts' from 'the lowest neighbourhoods' and 'foetid localities' of the cities.[77] These had no 'desire or intention to forsake their guilty courses' and, indeed, 'love the vices in which they have revelled and pertinaciously resolve to adhere to them', having an 'inextinguishable taste for riot, lasciviousness and intemperance'. Regarding many, he stated unequivocally: 'your lordships may depend upon it, it is almost impracticable to reform them. There is no fact of which I am more satisfied than that where they have once embraced theft as a craft it is entirely hopeless.'[78] Such people had experienced a pleasure from crime which from an early age had been repetitive and their entire intention was to return to it as soon as possible. This predilection had been environmentally created by vicious or criminal parents and associates and they had learned from experience a wilful defiant attitude to all who checked their desires, being 'creatures swathed in vice, nurtured in the foulest degeneracy' and deriving from theft 'its own especial excitement'.[79] By attributing to these the natural sympathy of character upon which separation could work the separatists were thus showing 'doctrinaire sentimentality'[80] and imposing a system which might well during its operation reduce rogues to tears and contrition. But this 'mental depression derived from physical prostration' was 'direful torture'[81] and 'a culpable deception',[82] the despair to which it reduced them being merely temporary. On release, they would return to their old habits which were 'really inferior to most of the brute species'.[83] Evangelical separation was theologically mistaken for, despite 'redeeming grace', God did not suddenly, by 'supernatural invocation', free offenders from their persistent defiance of Him.[84]

Chesterton therefore dismissed the 'pretensions of visionary minds . . . the ultra zeal of the separatists'[85] and he rejected their system as unnecessarily cruel. He desired to cleanse the 'Augean stables'[86] of the unreformed prison by prohibiting all conversation or communication between prisoners. They would remain in classified association and be subjected to hard fare and treadmill labour. But there *was* a pure reformatory aspect to this 'silent system'. Firstly, Chesterton reasoned that the 'better men'[87] would deeply value their freedom from the tyranny and contamination of the others, and so would experience 'the poignant sting of guilt'.[88] The rest, however, would defy the system and for perhaps the first time in their lives would encounter immediate pain as a result of prison punishment for breaking the silence. In their 'contest with external things'[89] the pain inflicted would be both automatic and of increasing severity the longer the defiance lasted. By these means 'forced into reflection . . . they become penitent and submissive. The lesson is not lost upon them and in process of time their dispositions are so obviously improved as to attest the valuable benefit of the treatment they had received.'[90] As Chesterton put it in regard to a man sent to Coldbath Fields after violence to staff at Pentonville: 'I put him immediately into association but I gave him a very friendly caution as to his conduct. I had been informed that he had used threats of violence . . . and I first told him of our power to repress any violence and the very heavy punishment that would await him if he attempted it. Then I pointed out to him the duty incumbent on him to behave peaceably and quietly and submissively. The man fell at once into an orderly frame of mind and has continued in the best frame of mind ever since.'[91]

This reformatory theory depended upon a less optimistic view of reformatory possibility, prided itself upon its pragmatic recognition of men as they really were, and sought repetition of pain in the face of disobedience to create a desired association. The silentists clearly aimed to instruct men in the true principles of their self interest within an artificially created penal environment. They carefully defined the pains to be inflicted so as to render objects of present aversion (industriousness or obedience to superiors) objects of desire in the future and, by repetition, new tendencies or behaviours could be stimulated and perpetuated. Those who showed special effort and obedience were given star badges, financial rewards and 'an occupation which tends to interest the mind'.[92] Thus 'after a short period of submission to the discipline and instruction of a well ordered prison a softening influence seems imperceptibly to improve the expression of the features of many an hitherto neglected child of misery . . . patience, submission, industry and creditable emulation become daily strengthened'.[93] Captain Williams, Inspector of Prisons for the North and East had no doubt that this system taught prisoners 'habits of self control' and 'obedience and industry'.[94]

The silent system depended for its reformist claims upon an associationist view of human behaviour as learned consequentially and experientially according to God's model for human life and it sought to change attitude and behaviour at more than a level of mere calculation. Prisoners would learn new attitudes by repeated impact and habitual desired conduct would be stimulated in an artificial penal environment in which the rational and benevolent firmness of disciplined staff would be most important. On entering Coldbath Fields, Chesterton's first task was to destroy the tyrannical and corrupt cabals of staff which had previously dominated the prison. The particular habits (idleness, lying), attitudes ('innate love of thieving for its own sake', optimistic expectations of 'better luck next time') and other characteristics of criminals (lack of 'intellectual vigour')[95] were subjects of close attention of silentists. Concluding that although a certain number of prisoners had become fixed in their associations between crime or idleness and pleasure (for example, most vagrants who were 'idle, drunken, dirty . . . sunk in swinish abasement'),[96] they found that others were less confirmed in their attitudes and conduct. The false associations that had begun developing amongst those who were of a more 'reflective mind'[97] or not entirely habituated to crime might be erased and new durable connections instilled by a carefully planned regime of punishments to discourage disobedience or criminality. With these reformables, desired associations would be strengthened by carefully selecting them out for more favourable and reward-based treatment, for full associationist reformation could never be achieved 'exclusively by coercion'[98] which, without incentives, would result in despair or torpor. Although it is not the case that the silent system was predominantly a reformatory system of prison discipline (being indeed most substantially based upon the notion that the reform of many criminals was exceedingly difficult and that deterrence was a more achievable aim), it is clear that a pure reformatory theory existed within it and Chesterton especially had hopes that offenders with some previous education would be amenable to the rational rewards and punishments designed to habituate them to more enlightened self-interest within the system.

Although both separation and silence sought to enlist what Wilberforce called the 'passions' or 'affections' of listless or vicious men by emphasising the pleasant and enjoyable associations now aroused by such things as religion and labour,[99] it is clear that the two systems differed substantially. The silent system emphasised associationism as the core of the reformist endeavour and its advocates insisted that this was in accordance with God's consequential laws of conduct/attitude-formation. Separatists insisted upon the evangelical notion of a God who intervened in sudden and dramatic ways through His earthly servants to interrupt the laws of consequence to achieve reformation. Separatists also put much more emphasis upon individual instruction and close engagement than silentists.

By 1840 there existed two systems of prison discipline, one of which was predominantly spiritual reformist and the other possessing characteristics of plain associationist reform. Indeed, although there is no doubt that many embraced these systems for reasons other than their promise of reformation — for example because separation made a prison easier to manage or because silence was cheaper than its rival — a time had undoubtedly arrived in which the endeavour to reform criminals was more precisely analysed than ever before in terms of spirit, divine working, human reason and associationist environmentalism. Certainly concerning separation there was an unmistakeable optimism about the improvability of human attitude and behaviour which had penetrated deeply the minds of many of those who wrote about and governed British penal policy. As John Buckle, the separatist Recorder of Worcester put it: 'the superior efficacy results from this, that it is essentially a moral punishment acting on the mind which is the seat of crime. The feeling of loneliness is itself a feeling of intense privation; add to this the self-reproach which nature has attached to vice; conceive the feelings of loneliness in the midst of self-reproach with your crimes face to face and you will understand the nature and moral force of separate confinement.'[100]

Political Concerns and Administrative Changes
1834 – 1840

As already indicated, between 1834 and 1840 there occurred considerable change in the administrative relationship of central government to local prisons and it is important in conclusion to discuss this. In the first place at a parliamentary level important debates took place in the House of Lords where the influence of separatist reformatory theory especially grew as a result partly of the evidence before the 1835 Select Committee of the Lords and partly because a number of Whig peers consistently supported the two Melbourne governments in their promotion of a uniform and reformatory prison system. Among these were the veteran Norfolk prison reformer Lord Suffield, who had long campaigned against the slave trade and the Game Laws (died 1835); Lord John Russell, Melbourne's Home Secretary; and the President of the Council Lord Lansdowne, another slave trade abolitionist, Catholic emancipationist and one who was especially concerned to promote moral education among the poor as an antidote to Chartism. However by no means all the peers who led the campaign for reformatory prisons were so politically committed. The Chairman of the 1835 Lords' Committee, the Duke of Richmond, for example had only broken from Wellington and the Tories because he believed them to be wavering in their opposition to Catholic emancipation, whilst Lord Wharncliffe, another disenchanted Tory and also a persistent supporter of separation,[101] had become estranged from his Tory colleagues owing to his acceptance of the Reform Bill.

It had been during Melbourne's Home Secretaryship in Lord Grey's period of office during the early 1830s that Crawford had been dispatched to America and it does seem, despite cross-party support for reformatory prisons, that this item of social policy was promoted by the Whig governments of Melbourne. Although some of the major parliamentary proponents of reformatory prisons were, obviously, members of the government, support for this idea was not confined to one political group — nor was the opposition. Vociferous parliamentary opponents of reformatory prisons throughout the 1830s and 1840s were two lawyers: Lord Grey's Lord Chancellor Lord Brougham, who regarded 'the distinction between separate and solitary confinement' as 'most flimsy, shadowy and unsubstantial', and Lord Lyndhurst, Lord Chancellor under Wellington who, during Peel's brief ministry in the winter of 1834–5, held separation to be 'harsh, unnecessary and severe'.[102]

The case urged before both Houses was that Parliament had a duty 'to endeavour to reform those individuals who violated the law of the country'.[103] This was deemed to be especially urgent with regard to young offenders of whom 'by a well regulated system of instruction and discipline a great portion . . . could be saved'.[104] To opponents who pointed up the potential cruelty of separation, the government spokesmen in particular dwelled upon the insistence of separatists that prisoners be placed in light warm cells, receive frequent visits from officers and the chaplain, and spend their time in valuable pursuits such as reading and voluntary occupations.[105] They emphasised the success of separation in America where 'every improvement in prison discipline had proceeded upon the principle of the separation of the prisoners — a provision which was most essential in any system of prison discipline'.[106] Ultimately, despite objections that the powers of local magistrates would be curtailed by new penal disciplines emanating from the Home Office[107] and despite the determined opposition of Brougham and Lyndhurst, the Act to give indisputable legality to separation as a system of reformatory treatment passed in August of 1839.[108]

At an administrative level the results of the earlier 1835 Prisons Act were unmistakeable. The five prison inspectors set to work to influence the localities and the Home Office used both their powers of inspection and their duty to advise local magistrates and the Home Secretary. The duty of certifying new prison rulebooks and architectural innovations in local prisons given to the Home Secretary in the same Act devolved upon Crawford and Russell, who thus became involved in advising their superior about matters which were far outside their own geographical area. Consequently the presence of all the inspectors, but especially the two Home District ones, in prison discipline became most important by 1840 with a substantial amount of work undertaken by them.

First, they led the attack on unsuitable local practices. Captain Williams in the North and East complained that the chaplain at Oakham County Gaol was lax in his attendance at the prison in the winter of 1837–8,[109] while Whitworth Russell in 1839 angrily asserted that the chaplain of Giltspur Street Prison in London had been drunk whilst delivering a sermon at Newgate.[110] Secondly, the vetting of rules sent in for certification quickly became a large part of Russell and Crawford's work and brought with it many difficulties. Amendments had to be inserted in the regulations proposed for Ipswich County Gaol, new plans for Worcester were unacceptable, a special visit had to be made to advise Leeds Borough about a new prison, warnings had to be given that the Liverpool magistrates would be likely to abuse any provisional agreement for extension for their prison, whilst justices at Bideford had frankly to be appraised of penal inadequacies.[111] Thirdly, there was much involvement with the centrally-administered Millbank prison (first occupied in 1816) and the new Juvenile prison opened at Parkhurst on the Isle of Wight in the late 1830s to ensure that the discipline at these two prisons approximated to the reformist aspirations of Crawford and Russell. Thus applicants for jobs at Parkhurst had to be interviewed to assess suitability, new cells at Millbank had to be certified as fit for separation, and health care at Millbank was criticised.[112] Fourthly, the shaping of new laws to strengthen the reformatory aspect of prison discipline required much detailed advice from Crawford and Russell who were mainly responsible for preparing the 1839 Prisons Act after it emerged at Millbank that separation might not be legal.[113] Fifthly, the inspectors were instruments in securing a more decisive intervention in local affairs by means of circulars sent from the Home Secretary to the local branches. Their new duties were placed before all the visiting justices in late-1835 and local magistrates were made aware of their duty to submit plans for extension of buildings to the Home Secretary in 1836, as well as a general emphasis given by the Home Office to the importance of the new inspectors engaged in this work.[114]

Crawford and Russell were working at a number of levels, also corresponding with experts on penal discipline who disagreed strongly with separation,[115] advising about colonial prisons,[116] and considering whether separation ought to be applied to military offenders.[117] It was not surprising that they on occasion fell behind with their reports for they worked without any clerical assistance.[118] The work sometimes produced difficulties for all the inspectors and in a sense these were increased because the government was unwilling to pursue the more decisive policies of state enforcement which had been desired by Frederic Hill in Scotland and Crawford and Russell.[119] In late-1839 all five complained that the law gave insufficient power to the Home Office.[120] They were often reduced to endeavouring to calculate the probable results of action when faced with wily magistrates who might wring permissions out of the Home Office on condition of future action and then, as in Suffolk, renege on the guaranteed action.[121] Frequently Crawford and Russell were in direct disagreement with magistrates over rule certification, for the two Home District Inspectors did not hesitate sweepingly to demand of astonished local justices total reconstruction of prisons (as at Wakefield)[122] nor continuously to confront the London Corporation over Newgate.[123] Doubtless the two Home District Inspectors felt that they had earned the good opinions of their superior Lord John Russell, who confessed himself 'much pleased with the zeal and intelligence you have shown in the execution of your duty'.[124]

Although the inspectors Bisset Hawkins for the South West and Captain Williams were more geographically bound to their areas (neither of them being separatists in any event), apparently bearing a less onerous burden of work than their two London-based colleagues or Frederic Hill (at this point engaged in planning the entire reconstruction of the Scottish prison system), it is clear that by 1840 in all areas of the country the new officials were busy seeking to initiate changes in prisons which were plainly strongly reformatory in purpose. Crawford and Russell, in particular, seemed inexhaustible, even supplementing their great annual reports to the Home Office with other perorations in favour of separation.[125] Early on, the architectural aspect of their certification and construction advisory work became so complicated that Joshua Jebb, a Captain of Royal Engineers, was seconded to the Home Office to advise about architecture. Clearly the relationship between Jebb and the two senior inspectors was a touchy one between 1837 and 1840, with Crawford and Russell requesting clarification of his role on a number of occasions[126] following Jebb's appointment in November of 1837 as 'a person conversant with architectural drawing and the arrangement of buildings'.[127] Later the relationship became even more awkward as Jebb rose in Home Office estimation being appointed Surveyor General of Prisons and Inspector General of Military Prisons in 1844 and Chairman of the Directors of Convict Prisons in 1850. Even at an early stage, Crawford and Russell felt that Jebb was unwarrantedly intruding in their functions,[128] steadily gaining influence both in the new state prisons at Parkhurst and later Pentonville[129] and more generally.

So it was that reformation, as part of a more uniform and

regulated prison system was promoted at a high political and administrative level. Nevertheless, it must be reiterated that two of the inspectors were not separatists in the purest sense of Crawford and Russell, and that many in both Houses of Parliament remained sceptical. Local counties and boroughs were often resistant to these new theories and evasive in the face of growing pressure from London. Still, there was by 1840 a marked difference in legal and administrative arrangements which now provided a more solid base for the promotion of reformatory practice in prisons. Despite the hostility evoked locally by such inspectors as Whitworth Russell, local autonomy in prison affairs was no longer as robust as before but had become subjected to firm pressure towards implementation of, among other things, stronger, more effective reformatory action within the prisons of the realm.

References

1. J. Howard, *An Account of the Principal Lazarettos*, 2nd edn, Cadell, 1791, p. 233.
2. Sir W. Blackstone, *Commentaries on the Laws of England*, vol. 4, 15th edn, Cadell, 1809, p. 371.
3. J. Fitzpatrick, *Thoughts on Penitentiaries*, H. Fitzpatrick, 1790, p. 7. See also 19 G.3. cap 74.
4. Society for the Improvement of Prison Discipline and the Reformation of Juvenile Offenders, *Third Report*, 1821, p. 15; *First Report*, 1818, pp. 7–8.
5. J. J. Gurney, *Notes on a Visit made to some of the Prisons in Scotland . . . in Company with Elizabeth Fry*, Constable, 1819, p. 103.
6. H. Roscoe, *The Life of William Roscoe by his son Henry Roscoe*, Cadell, 1833, p. 206.
7. J. E. Bicheno, *Observations on the Philosophy of Criminal Jurisprudence*, Hunter, 1819, p. 241.
8. J. Hanway, *Solitude in Imprisonment*, Bew, 1776, pp. 70–1, 81.
9. J. Neild, *The State of the Prisons*, Nichols, 1812, p. 57.
10. W. Smith, *The State of the Gaols in London*, Bew, 1776, p. 40.
11. S. Denne, *A Letter to Sir Robert Ladbroke*, Oliver, 1771, p. 15.
12. G. O. Paul, *Proceedings of the Grand Jury for the County of Gloucester*, 3rd edn, Walker, 1808, section entitled 'To the Gentlemen of the Grand Jury . . . at the Summer Assizes 1783', p. VII.
13. W. Roscoe, *Observations on Penal Jurisprudence and the Reformation of Criminals*, Cadell, 1819, p. 88; *A Memoir of the Life of Elizabeth Fry — by Two of her Daughters*, Gilpin, 1847, vol. 1, rules printed pp. 269–70.
14. T. F. Buxton, *An Enquiry into whether Crime and Misery are produced or prevented by our present system of prison discipline*, Arch, 1818, p. 101.

15. J. Howard, *An Account of the Principal Lazarettos*, 1791, p. 16.

16. S. Denne, *A Letter to Sir Robert Ladbroke*, p. 32.

17. See for example G. O. Paul, *Address to Her Majesty's Justices of the Peace for the County of Gloucester*, Walker, 1808.

18. H. Roscoe, *Life of William Roscoe*, p. 207.

19. J. Hanway, *Observations on the Dissoluteness Which Reigns among the Lower Classes of the People*, Rivington, 1772, p. 50.

20. 'Sermon of Dr. Haggit, at Durham', *The Times*, 11 May 1820, p. 2.

21. *Society for the Improvement of Prison Discipline, Fourth Report*, 1822, p. 16.

22. W. Kingsbury, *A Sermon Preached at Southampton*, Baker, 1805, p. 16.

23. G. O. Paul, *Proceedings of the Grand Jury*, section entitled 'To the Gentlemen of the Grand Jury . . . at the Summer Assizes 1783', p. 38.

24. H. Drummond, *A Letter to the Justices of the Peace for the County of Surrey,*, Hatchard, 1824, p. 38; G. Holford, *Thoughts on the Criminal Prisons of this Country*, Rivington, 1821, p. 69.

25. J. Brewster, *On the Religious Improvement of Prisons*, F. C. & J. Rivington, 1808, pp. 12, 18; W. Smith, *Mild Punishments Sound Policy*, 2nd edn, 1778, p. 117.

26. E. Fry, *Observations on the Visiting, Superintending and Governing of Female Prisons*, Arch, 1827, pp. 21, 22, 79.

27. J. I. Briscoe, *Letter on the Nature and Effects of the Treadwheel as an Instrument of Prison Labour and Punishment*, Hatchard, 1824, pp. 20, 174; J. C. Hippisley, *Prison Labour — Correspondence and Communications addressed to His Majesty's Principal Secretary of State*, Nicol, 1823, p. 19.

28. W. Roscoe, *Additional Observations on Penal Jurisprudence and the Reformation of Criminals*, Cadell, 1823, p. 7.

29. J. E. Bicheno, *Observations*, 1819, p. 157.

30. *A Memoir of the Life of Elizabeth Fry*, vol. 1, p. 204.

31. Rev. J. Clay, *Twenty Five Sermons preached to the Inmates of a Gaol*, Rivington, 1827, pp. 331, 133, 1.

32. Society for the Improvement of Prison Discipline, *Third Report*, 1821, p. 27; *Fourth Report*, 1822, p. 41.

33. G. O. Paul, *An Address to His Majesty's Justices of the Peace for the County of Gloucester*, Walker, 1809, Rule 28, Gloucester Penitentiary.

34. Thomas Wontner, *The Author of the Schoolmaster's Experience in Newgate — Old Bailey Experience*, Fraser, 1833, p. 284.

35. T. Le Breton, *Thoughts on the Defective State of Prisons*, Rivington, 1822, p. 17.

36. Sir Eardly Wilmot, *A Letter to the Magistrates of England on the Increase of Crime*, Hatchard, 1827, p. 14.

37. Prison Discipline Society, *First Report*, 1818, p. 18.

38. A. Citizen, *The Gaol of the City of Bristol compared with what a Gaol ought to be*, Longman, 1815, p. 20.

39. Thomas Wontner, *Schoolmaster's Experience*, p. 4.

40. *SC of the House of Commons on Criminal Commitments and Convictions*, PP, 1828, vol. VI, Evidence of Sir Thomas Baring, p. 25.

41. W. Brebner, *A Letter to the Lord Provost on the Expediency of a House of Refuge*, Smith, 1829, p. 4.

42. *SC of the House of Commons on Gaols and Houses of Correction*, PP, 1819,

vol. VII, pp. 371, 380.

43. W. Roscoe, *Observations on Penal Jurisprudence and the Reformation of Criminals*, part III, 1825, p. 71.

44. Prison Discipline Society, *Fifth Report*, 1823, p. 71.

45. Prison Discipline Society, *Seventh Report*, 1827, p. 118.

46. H. Roscoe, *Life of William Roscoe*, p. 195.

47. Despite this, a remarkable optimism often characterised the view of reformation of juveniles before their attitudes and behaviour became hardened. See W. Brebner, *Letter to the Lord Provost*.

48. *Edinburgh Review*, 1821–2, vol. XXXVI, p. 354.

49. *Edinburgh Review*, 1821–2, vol. XXXVI, p. 374.

50. 4 G IV cap. 64, Sec. XLIX.

51. Felony is originally a term derived from feudal law meaning an act on the part of a vassal which entitled his lord to deprive him of his land and goods. By transition it came to mean serious crimes and in Blackstone's time conviction for felony normally required in law the passing of the death sentence — increasingly commuted by 1800. Misdemeanours were offences not amounting to felony.

52. See for instance, *SC of the House of Commons on Criminal Commitments and Convictions*, PP, 1828, vol. VI.

53. *SC of the House of Commons on Criminal Commitments and Convictions*, PP, 1826–7, vol. VI, p. 43.

54. U. Henriques, 'The Rise and Decline of the Separate System of Prison Discipline', *Past and Present*, vol. 54, Feb. 1972, pp. 61–93.

55. *Report of William Crawford to Lord Duncannon on the American Prisons*, PP, 1834, vol. XLVI.

56. 5 & 6 W 4, cap. XXXVIII.

57. The classificatory silent system will be discussed later.

58. *Third RInsP*, Home District, PP, 1837–8, vol. XXX, p. 11.

59. Ibid., p. 2.

60. W. Crawford, *Report*, p. 12.

61. Ibid., p. 19.

62. *Third RInsP*, pp. 16, 17, 28.

63. Ibid., pp. 16, 17.

64. Ibid., pp. 5, 6, 8.

65. Ibid., p. 6.

66. See W. Greenleaf, *The British Political Tradition*, vol. 1, 'The Rise of Collectivism', Methuen, 1983, p. 233; O. MacDonagh, *Early Victorian Government*, Weidenfeld & Nicolson, 1977, pp. 8–13.

67. See C. Hill, *Frederic Hill, An Autobiography*, Bentley, 1893.

68. C. Buxton, *Memoirs of Sir Thomas Fowell Buxton*, Murray, 1848, pp. 98–9, 79.

69. U. Henriques, 'Rise and Decline'; G. Himmelfarb, *Victorian Minds*, Weidenfeld & Nicolson, 1968, pp. 32–81.

70. R. Smith, *The Evils of the Silent and Separate Systems Removed and the Systems combined and reconciled*, Norman, 1838.

71. P. Laurie, *Prison Discipline and Secondary Punishments*, Whittaker, 1837, p. 11.

72. Rev. D. Nihill, *Prison Discipline in its Relations to Society and Individuals*, Hatchard, 1839, pp. 85, 5, 76.

73. A. Such, *Remarks on Prison Discipline and the Model Prison*, Shaw, 1841, p. 29.

74. For an account of the American history of this system see W. Crawford, *Report*.

75. G. L. Chesterton, *Peace War and Adventure: An Autobiographical Memoir*, Longman, 1853, vol. 2, p. 235.

76. Ibid., p. 237.

77. G. L. Chesterton, *Revelations of Prison Life*, Hurst & Blackett, 1856, vol. 1, p. 7.

78. Ibid., vol. 2, p. 40; *SC of the House of Lords on Gaols and Houses of Correction*, PP, 1835, vol. XI, p. 94.

79. G. L. Chesterton, *Revelations*, vol. 1, pp. 8, 13.

80. Ibid., vol. 2, p. 15.

81. Ibid., vol. 2, pp. 14 – 15.

82. Ibid., vol. 2, p. 39.

83. Ibid., vol. 2, pp. 247 – 8.

84. Ibid., vol. 2, p. 42.

85. Ibid., vol. 2, p. 39.

86. Ibid., vol. 1, p. 44.

87. Ibid., vol. 1, p. 158.

88. Ibid., vol. 1, p. 165.

89. Ibid., vol. 2, p. 27.

90. Ibid., vol. 2, p. 26.

91. *SC on Prison Discipline*, PP, 1850, vol. XVII, p. 627.

92. Ibid., vol. 1, p. 158; also PP, 1850, vol. XVII, p. 632.

93. Ibid., vol. 1, p. 11.

94. *Third RInsP*, Northern and Eastern, PP, 1837 – 8, vol. XXXI (quoted in S. McConville, *A History of English Prison Administration*, vol. 1, 1750 – 1877, Routledge & Kegan Paul, 1981, p. 244).

95. G. L. Chesterton, *Revelations*, vol. 1, p. 13.

96. Ibid., vol. 2, pp. 247 – 8.

97. Ibid., vol. 1, p. 11.

98. Ibid., vol. 2, p. 53.

99. W. Wilberforce, *A Practical View*, 1818, pp. 81, 83, 91 – 2.

100. J. Buckle, *Prison Discipline — The Charge of the Recorder*, Ridgway, 1837, pp. 33 – 4.

101. *Parliamentary Debates, Third Series*, vol. 24, cols 607 – 9.

102. Ibid., vol. 41, col. 199.

103. Ibid., vol. 27, col. 155.

104. Ibid., vol. 35, cols 1155 – 6.

105. Ibid., vol. 47, col. 632.

106. Ibid., vol. 49, cols 137, 145.

107. Ibid., vol. 43, cols 760 – 71; vol. 45, cols 220 – 1.

108. 2 and 3 Vict. Cap. 56, Sections 3 & 4.

109. PRO HO-20-6, Chaplain Oakham Prison to Home Office, 30 Jan. 1838.

110. PRO HO-20-8, Whitworth Russell to Sheriffs of London, 13 Aug. 1839, 19 Aug. 1839.

111. PRO HO-20-6, Crawford and Russell to Home Office, 11 Jan. 1838, 3 Jan. 1838, 18 Feb. 1838, 16 Jun. 1837. HO-20-9, Crawford,

Russell and Jebb to Home Office, 22 Jan. 1840.

112. PRO HO-21-6, S. M. Phillips to Millbank Committee, 4 Feb. 1835. PRO HO-20-6, Crawford and Russell to Home Office, 3 Sep. 1838; HO-20-9, Russell and Crawford to Home Office, 23 Jan. 1840, 1 Jan. 1840; PRO HO-20-11 *passim*, Millbank Committee to Home Office on various matters.

113. PRO HO-20-7, Millbank Committee to Secretary of State, Home Office, 6 Apr. 1838.

114. PRO HO-21-7, Home Office Circular to all Visiting Justices 12 Oct. 1835, 7 Mar. 1836.

115. PRO HO-20-9, Maconochie to Crawford and Russell, date unreadable 1840.

116. PRO HO-20-9, Crawford and Russell to Home Secretary, 21 Jul. 1840.

117. PRO HO-21-7, Home Office to Crawford and Russell, 25 Jul. 1836.

118. PRO HO-20-9, Crawford and Russell to Home Secretary, 21 Jul. 1840.

119. PRO HO-20-6, Frederic Hill to Home Secretary, 13 Oct. 1838.

120. PRO HO-20-8, Inspectors to Home Office, 7 Sep. 1839.

121. PRO HO-20-8, Crawford and Russell to Undersecretary of State, 4 Feb. 1839.

122. PRO HO-20-9, Crawford, Russell and Jebb to Home Office, 30 Mar. 1840.

123. PRO HO-21-7, Lord John Russell to Lord Mayor of London, 14 Jun. 1836.

124. PRO HO-21-8, Home Office to Crawford and Russell, 31 Dec. 1836.

125. PRO HO-20-6, Russell and Crawford to Home Secretary, 1 Jan. 1838.

126. PRO HO-20-8, Crawford and Russell to Home Secretary, 18 Sep. 1839.

127. PRO HO-21-8, Undersecretary of State to Jebb, 28 Nov. 1837.

128. E. Stockdale, 'The Rise of Joshua Jebb 1837–1850', *British Journal of Criminology*, vol. 16, no. 2, April 1976, pp. 168–70.

129. PRO HO-21-2, Home Office to Earl of Scarborough, 29 May 1839; S. McConville, p. 177.

2

The Address to the Spirit
1840 – 1865

The Chaplain and the Prisoner

All major works concerned with nineteenth-century penal history
have detailed the fact that by 1865 the central state had a more
effective presence in local prison discipline. They have dealt
exhaustively with the emergence of the new convict prisons which
by 1865 had replaced transportation colonies as the site of punishment for more serious offenders.[1] By 1855, a state-appointed
Directorate of Convict Prisons administered an interlocking
system of specialist convict prisons at Millbank (transportation
depot), Pentonville (model separation), Portsmouth and Portland
(associated labour), Parkhurst (juveniles), Brixton (women) and
Dartmoor (invalids), whilst in Ireland a convict prison system had
been set up under its own directorate.

It is worth noting that transportation had been widely criticised
for its alleged vitiating effects and in particular it had been somewhat paradoxically argued that it offered a luxurious reward for
crime in sunny Australia as well as the possibility of cruelty to
offenders sent there.[2] It was further suggested that the novice in
crime would quickly be contaminated in colonies heavily settled by
transportees.[3] Consequently in the late-1830s changes were introduced in Australia but by 1850 the emphasis was upon the British
convict prison as the reformatory part of the sentence and
therefore removal to the colony in question would only be undertaken after twelve months' separation in one of the convict prisons
and a further two to two and a half years in associated labour at
one of the public works prisons.[4] The tendency was to release the
convict on a 'ticket of leave' when landed in the colonies on the
assumption that he had been reformed.

However, it was generally agreed that the local prisons also had by 1850 made great strides towards a full-blooded reformatory approach and that the separate system in particular was characteristic of many county and borough prisons. In these it was said that 'a great majority of convicted prisoners are open to . . . good influences and motives', and in which 'the best practicable arrangements should be made for the instruction of all prisoners in their religious and moral duties'.[5] The degree to which this was in fact the case will be examined in detail later but by 1850 it was asserted that some 11,000 purpose-built separate cells and some 55 separate cellular prisons had either been built or were near completion. As Joshua Jebb remarked, 'separation is the only basis on which the discipline of a prison can exist'.[6]

The search for a change of heart — not so much from mere calculative avoidance of crime because of its guaranteed pains, but mainly from the permanent sense of revulsion against sin and crime and a love of Christ — was the constant theme of the many chaplains and officials who adhered to separation and more general spiritual reformism as the basis of prison discipline, although there were often disagreements between them about the precise methods to be employed. In the zenith of the separate system up to the early-1850s there was evident within the prison system a determined attempt to pierce through the wordly, idle and luxurious propensity to self-indulgence and excitement which it was assumed had been environmentally learned by prisoners. Chaplains such as Joseph Kingsmill of Pentonville spent much of their time conversing with, admonishing and instructing prisoners in their individual cells, hoping that through them the grace of God would flow so that the heart would turn, and examples of success were recalled in order to encourage those who might flag in the great work. 'My dear parents . . . I earnestly pray to God who alone can help me that He will give me His aid in keeping my resolution for ever . . . I hope you will warn sister Mary's children not to follow in my steps; for if they do, their ruin is certain';[7] 'Dear Father . . . how many hours do I keep awake and fancy that I hear your voice speaking and telling me to keep from bad Company, or it would be the ruin of me! If I had done this it would have been different with me at the present, but it is too late now. I hope it is not too late to be forgiven for all my wickedness. I pray to God morning, noon and night to give me a new heart, instead of this wicked one that I have got' . . . 'our crimes were the cause of our meeting and must also be the cause of separation, and that to opposite sides of the world, in all probability, never to meet more on this side of the grave. Oh may we all, through rich and free grace, meet in heaven.'[8]

The bearers of the tidings which must so change the heart constantly emphasise the identity of criminals not merely as heirs to the human condition of sinfulness but as reclaimable children of God and therefore worthy. Thus the prisoner must be treated as one 'for whom the Son of God was content to die, as a prodigal son of Heaven, of whose wanderings angels are intently observant and for whose return they are waiting to rejoice'.[9] Therefore some chaplains were very particular in their endeavour to treat prisoners not as distinctly given to evil but as sharing a common human tendency to depravity. One of the most notable early-Victorian prison chaplains was John Clay, at first assistant chaplain and from 1823 to 1858 chaplain at Preston House of Correction. Clay deliberately eschewed involvement in religious controversies such as Maynooth or Protestant Defence and in later life seldom attended worship outside the prison chapel. His son wrote in his lengthy biography of him: 'about the same time that he began to preach extempore he dropped his former mode of addressing his congregation and, instead of the title prisoners, never afterwards used any other but fellow sinners'.[10] He made it a rule to spend at least six hours a day with prisoners and reminded those who saw themselves as moral superiors 'that the respectable citizens who frequented comfortable churches were not an especially privileged class in the sight of heaven . . . a doctrine which he held very firmly and would occasionally announce very emphatically'.[11]

Many of the spiritual reformists of the 1840s and 1850s were aware that the mere spoken word, however passionately delivered, was not sufficient in itself to effect the kind of penetration of heart and mind which was desired. For this purpose men like Kingsmill and Clay sought to win the trust of prisoners and to allow prisoners in their isolated cells to share their deepest anxiety and guilt so that not only might the past be purged by confession and admission of truth but comfort be given upon the sure basis of the particular fear and desperation of the individual. They would have agreed with the chaplain of Perth Prison that 'whenever the unhappy criminal ascertained that the curtain was drawn aside from his heart, not through idle curiosity, but with a friendly design, no attempt was made to replace it'.[12] Thus 'where tears, or mental uneasiness, or the desire to relieve the conscience by speaking was manifest, Mr. Clay would stay at once to offer help and sympathy, and to encourage the outpourings of confession'.[13] In all dealings with prisoners an attempt was made to appeal to the feelings by small acts of kindness: 'observed in a prisoner's cell, long confined with a bad leg, a bit of mignonette which I plucked from the little garden of a dear child. I had it in my bosom; but seeing the poor sufferer look wistfully at it I presented it to him. He seemed as much pleased as a man who had come in for an estate and evinced much gratitude, heartily blessing the little maid that plucked it'.[14] Chaplain Burt of Pentonville frequently emphasised what he called 'the centripetal and the centrifugal forces of the moral world . . . kindness and severity'[15] so that amidst the sorrows and pains of imprisonment in separation the kindness of the spiritual messenger would have a particular impact on the emotions. At Chester Castle Prison the Reverend Joseph remarked that 'none but good and kind words are calculated to find their way to the heart of the poor prisoner. Even the simple words "God bless you" I have often witnessed to be too much for the unhappy convict. They have reached his heart, they were strange words to him; they have often caused tears to flow from the eyes of the once most desperate character.'[16]

It is against this background of earnest conversations, prayers, admonitions and acts of kindness that it is possible to see the devices to prevent the undoing of the good work by the contamination inherent in association. Thus the long lines of cells and corridors, the masks which prisoners had to wear when they left their cells, and the stalled chapels which were built in many prisons such as Reading and Pentonville, served to allow the freest flow of the work of redemption. Prisoners, humbled and thrown in upon themselves by isolation, reduced to sorrowing repentance, might turn avidly to the comforting kindness and consoling truths of the minister of God. Continued over long periods of time, religious faith and Christian hope would become permanent and the heart be turned to charity and atonement. As the chaplain of Parkhurst put it: 'It is [in their cells] that I get into their spirit and worm out their individual trials and temptations, then that I can apply the Gospel remedy to each lad, that I can listen to their regrets on account of past conduct, and to their little tales of home scenes and recollections. It is there that I can calm the troubled mind and cool the fiery temper roused by an imagined injustice.'[17]

In the prison, therefore, 'the gospel with its precepts, its warnings, and its promises must be not only taught in the letter but applied in its spirit' so that 'a tribunal in the heart' would be erected by which the prisoner would judge all his own actions henceforth, not merely ceasing to do evil but learning to love good and follow in the footsteps of Christ. The central actor in this drama of spiritual resurrection, the prison chaplain, was thus enabled to take his true place as a 'messenger of peace, a mediator between repentance and heaven', exhibiting 'a wonderful power in kindness'.[18] In such an environment, Kingsmill described the result in an oft-quoted passage: 'all may be reasoned with and every single prisoner experience the influence of that which inspiration so beautifully calls the law of kindness'. Arguing that government of prisons by 'perpetual surveillance and perpetual punishment' at best merely created passive obedience, he also pointed to the likelihood that such a system would turn the offender away from the staff: 'distrust a prisoner and he will not trust you; oppress him, and he will kick against authority openly, or retiring within himself will spend his time in concocting plans for escape, for evasion, for arrogance. Treat him as a fellow man, though fallen and debased, and there is hope'.[19]

Separatists set much store by the discovery of the individual characteristics of each prisoner for, although the general characteristics of the system were applicable to all the 'frail and fallen', it was argued that unless the particular 'disposition and character' were known, the officials of the prison would not be able accurately to focus their efforts.[20] Thus Kingsmill undertook detailed surveys of cohorts of prisoners in order to distinguish clearly the aspects of history and character which he believed had given rise to crime. In the 1840s he examined five hundred of those received into Pentonville and concluded overall that their life histories clearly showed that 'total neglect or total inability to discharge the proper duties of parents, low neighbourhoods, vile lodging houses and the training which they get in the streets are quite enough to account for excess of crime'. Within such environments, he argued, unrestricted enjoyment of particular vices such as gambling and drunkenness led them into crime, either to finance the vice or because recognition of consequence or moral conscience were removed. Many were entirely lacking in the most basic religious and secular knowledge, being 'practically atheistic, having no Christ, having no hope and without God in the world'.[21] This assessment of individuals became an important part of the work of many chaplains, particularly those at the convict prisons. In 1860, for example, the chaplain of Millbank reported in detail on nearly 1,500 new prisoners whom he divided into five categories of potential reformability. In the same way, the Park-hurst chaplain estimated the criminality of the young prisoners there, recording information about each under such headings as 'former conditions and habits', 'period of criminality' and so forth.[22]

Undoubtedly the exemplar of these reformist chaplains was John Clay of Preston, although few possessed his dedication or skill. He took great pains to avoid intrusive religiosity in discussions with prisoners in their cells, preferring gentle ministration and patient understanding of past difficulties and future hopes. Like all prison chaplains he placed great emphasis on the capacity of the chapel service to move prisoners deeply and therefore he centred much of his cellular discussion on the link between the services and the individual prisoner's situation. All the same, 'he would never go into a cell and sit down and cross question a man about the state of his soul' because 'he shrank from spiritual intrusion', being 'convinced that no man had a right to pry unasked into the mysteries of another man's heart'. His aim was to listen courteously and intently and he resisted temptations to attempt instant conversions, preferring to lead the prisoner gently to the relationship of Christian grace to the situation of the individual. Out of the same respect for individual choice he frequently dissuaded prisoners from abjuring the Catholic church, advising them not to make so important a decision until they were released. At other times, so successful was he at engaging prisoners, he was overcome by 'agony so intense as to defy description' after listening to confessions and confidences of prisoners.[23]

Plainly Clay was outstanding and indeed was seen to be so by other chaplains such as Joseph Kingsmill. Yet he illustrates the aspirations of spiritual reformists of this period and although the great majority were more clumsy or dogmatic than he, he was imitated and quoted by chaplains and other reformists throughout Britain. More often, however, the chaplain's approach was that of 'sermonising' the individual prisoner and admonishing that the Christian moral code should govern action, usually suggesting consequences if this did not take place. Kingsmill illustrates this more distant exhortatory/instructional approach. To one man he 'recommended close self-examination' and admonished another that 'you will deserve a worse punishment . . . if you don't make that woman happy . . . when you have it in your power'. However, like Kingsmill, most chaplains emphasised that they had not 'come to reproach' the prisoner but 'to do him good and give him counsel if he desired it'. Naturally at times prisoners feared that the minister had come to judge them or disbelieved the claim to offer help, but chaplains carefully noted that others referred to these discussions as 'the turning point in my life'.[24]

Often they were amazed at the ignorance of many prisoners. Kingsmill noted that one man at Pentonville, when asked whether he had been born in Europe, Asia, America or Africa replied 'in none of these — it was in Somersetshire', whilst another, correctly answering that a spade was 'a shovel', did not know the meaning of the word 'wheat' and thought that a harrow was 'for boys to shoot with'.[25] On occasion they adopted a somewhat dogmatic or dismissive attitude when confronted with ignorance or stubbornness. Thus the chaplain of Kingston-upon-Hull Prison irritably pointed out errors in preference to engaging in patient discussion. So J.B. was 'a downright predestinarian' when he blamed God for his fate, whilst the chaplain at Cambridge County Prison found H.D. 'a very extraordinary fellow, half knave, half fool who professes to disbelieve that Jesus is the saviour of the world'. At other times chaplains rather lugubriously noted personal details without comment. So M.W. listened to the Hull chaplain 'with a strange undercurrent of feeling' as he 'denounced' certain undisclosed things to her, and W.P. 'had not much value for his wife when he first married; was compelled to marry by the parish as she was pregnant by him; likes her better now.'[26]

Clearly the writings and poems which they occasionally found made it clear to startled chaplains that some prisoners were concerned for other things than the Book of Job, as with a poem written by a female prisoner to her soldier boy friend.

> The time is fast approaching
> When you and I shall meet
> And we shall have our liberty
> And that is very sweet
> One kiss from your sweet lips
> Is my desire
> To cool my heart for it is on fire[27]

Furthermore, as Philip Priestley has recently made clear, these endeavours were often experienced as coercive or meaningless interventions, some of which could be opportunistically turned to advantage.[28] Thus prisoners were often corralled in military fashion into their individual chapel cubicles. Frequently chaplains would report those who misbehaved in the services for subsequent disciplinary punishment. Many prisoners used well known hymn verses for coded communication between each other. Certain prisoners did not understand the meaning of what had been learned by rote. Some chaplains seemed harsh or vindictive in their condemnations. Notwithstanding, as Priestley himself conceded, the evangelical vision lay at the heart of the establishment of these regimes and, however inevitable the failure of that vision and however idiosyncratic the practice, the aim of the approach continued to be to respect the individual as a child of God and to restore him both to his society and to the God whom he had offended.

Environmental Theory and Educational Influence

All reformists proceeded upon an analysis of the causes of crime which was entirely environmental and which emphasised the influence of the family and social environment upon the moral development of the individual. Alexander Thomson, the promoter of Scottish reformatory schools, particularly pointed to the influence of parents upon the child: 'a little child rarely regards as wrong what he sees his parents habitually do; and this at once explains what has been regarded as a modern discovery, that crime is to a considerable extent hereditary, that it runs in certain families . . . for it is formed by an accumulation of daily sinful example, acting upon the originally corrupted heart of man and thus aggravating its every evil propensity.'[29] There were also particular aspects of the wider environment which could be pointed up as especially dangerous to the young whose bad family training had left them vulnerable. To Kingsmill these were 'those dens of iniquity, the penny theatres, gin palaces and beer shops . . . cheap literature', whilst Joshua Jebb described a cycle of pauperisation in workhouse schools by which 'the mind of the pauper child binds him to the workhouse as a home . . . associates it in his mind with the state of life attached to him and his destiny'.[30]

They therefore commonly adhered to a notion of criminal drift, a process of deterioration beginning within a home where vice was either unchecked or encouraged and where Christian vital spirit was absent, and pointed to the existence both of neglect and unchecked appetite in the backgrounds of criminals. As the medical officer of Parkhurst put it: 'the inmates of this prison have most of them, previous to their admission, lived in extreme irregularity

51

and, young as they are, have been in the habit of drinking to excess when they have had the means to gratify their inclinations; but they have been badly clothed, wretchedly lodged and accustomed to the practice of almost every vice.'[31] The young offender then grew up to become the parent of the next generation of criminals ruined by self-indulgent habits and lack of religion. Kingsmill saw them as the victims of 'the ungodliness, the immoralities, the vices of the people . . . ensnared, corrupted, demoralised and sunk into misery and crime every year literally by the thousands.'[32] Another chaplain lamented that 'on the opposite side of our social system stands another class towards whom much of our sympathy is turned. It is the miserable outcast who has been taught nothing that is not bad — whose abode by day has been a filthy alley and his bed by night a railway arch or a lime kiln — beating and blasphemy are all he has ever had from a father except of training for crime.'[33] The drift involved a movement from minor occasional offences to great crimes which was explained by William Miles as being the result of older associates displaying the pleasures of easy acquisition by theft. What little honesty remained within the mind was gradually discredited as the joys of crime and ready money gathered strength, leading to the voraciousness of unchecked appetite for further pleasure, the eventual acceptance of crime as a natural part of life and finally the progression from small offences to great and multiple crimes, 'from which', in Kingsmill's words, 'they would at first have shrunk with horror'.[34]

Most, with Alexander Thomson, pointed to the parental failure which marked the beginning of the criminal career. They argued that particular features of the criminogenic family were the failure of parents to know or learn their duties, overcrowded dwellings in which sexual decency[35] was undermined, the addiction of parents and young to alcohol ('a canker corroding and consuming the very vitals of society[36] . . . their God strong drink . . . they are cast under the wheels of this car of Juggernaut which is rolled along on British ground')[37] and a lack of religious vital fervour within the home. The state of their homes meant 'it is impossible for children to be brought up as Christian children ought to be when huddled together, male and female, like pigs in a sty . . . it is difficult to say whether these dens of horror are most injurious to the bodies or the souls of those who frequent them.'[38]

Another feature of the reformist/environmentalist analysis of the causes of crime which was argued with great force was the evangelical view that such conditions thrived in a society whose social

ties had become loosened by a process of abandonment of the
lower orders by those who ought to have been their stewards.
Believing, as the chaplain of Parkhurst suggested, that a majority
of criminals came from the cities, many feared like Thomson that
there had developed in the great urban conglomeration a 'wide
separation . . . betwixt the various classes of society . . . and the
consequent want of mutual kindly sympathy'.[39] The result was
that moral and social obligations were no longer taught or
exemplified by social superiors to whom it had ceased to matter
whether men were drunken, immoral or destitute. Reformists,
particularly, called for a reversal of this process of abandonment.
'Neglect the poor and ignorant and they will go bad; neglect above
all their dwelling places and let them live, herd together and die
like dogs — as they live and die in every city throughout the
kingdom . . . and we need not wonder at the increase of crime . . .
all ranks and orders of the men in the social scale must co-operate,
must enlist their sympathies and their energies in the indispensable
work of reclaiming the fallen and preserving the inexperienced.'[40]
Indeed, a number of mid-century reformists and their friends
added a criticism of the free market economic philosophy which
underpinned political economic liberal theory, complaining that
this 'competition so unconcerned with the benign spirit of Christianity' exposed the poor to overcrowding, squalor, crime,
immorality and the tyrannical powers of 'capricious dismissal' by
greedy landlords. Urging a conservative interventionary reply to
competitive economics, John Minter Morgan pointed to the
anomalous coexistence of 'riches and poverty, knowledge and
ignorance, religion and infidelity' and demanded large-scale
residential provision in self-sufficient settlements where hundreds
of families could be housed and submitted to 'spiritual, intellectual
and physical education', plainly reminding the nostalgic that
science and industry 'had superseded the spinning wheel at the
cottage door' and that 'machinery has given a death blow to
existing society'.[41]

Morgan hinted at the dangers of civil strife and was echoed a
few years later by Thomas Beames who studied the lowest classes
of London. Beames reminded his contemporaries that a widening
'gulph' separated the 'higher and middle ranks from the working
classes'. He insisted that the latter were enfeebled by foul atmospheres, struck down by disease as a result of the miasmas in which
they lived. In such wretched localities drunkenness further
weakened the body and disordered the mind with an inevitable

increase in domestic conflict and family breakdown. Thus were produced 'human abortions' inhabiting a criminal society with its own teachers, customs, oaths of allegiance and systems of enforcement. Furthermore, uncontrolled economic expansion was making social conditions in the cities worse and deterioration would necessarily continue because of 'that laissez faire, that unreadiness to act' which is 'the bane of the English character'.[42]

By the mid-1850s this environmental analysis was widely argued. *The Times* in a leading article asserted that crime resulted from a lack of religious and moral education and that young offenders were 'begotten in vice, nursed in vice, weaned in vice, trained in vice, instructed to consider vice as their only means of avoiding starvation . . . this is no fault of theirs but the fault lies at the door of our fathers and our own doors if so little has been done to reduce the moral squalor of our great towns to a minimum.'[43] C. B. Adderley, writing slightly earlier, pointed out that many 'juvenile delinquents' were morally innocent because the administrative and constitutional apparatus established by the state and the more general social environment were most important in preventing or encouraging crime, since 'a man's character is mainly formed by the circumstances by which he is surrounded'. It was considered that young offenders in particular ought to be subjected to re-education because these had merely responded to the circumstances around them and lacked moral guilt, requiring correct moral learning, 'government tutelage', whereas adult criminals should be reformed by new prisons, 'our Pandora's box of penal resources'.[44]

Although Adderley's reasoning was influenced strongly by evangelical concepts, he was only one of an army of writers like John Morgan, Thomas Beames, Frederic Hill the prison inspector, Matthew Davenport Hill (Recorder of Birmingham), or Alexander Thomson who not only argued a strong environmentalist analysis of the causes of crime but also suggested wide-ranging changes in law. These ranged from control of property speculators to reduction of 'artificial offences'[45] caused by unnecessary laws, and better educational provision for the young. To spiritual reformists these discussions were particularly important because they provided clues to the best treatment for offenders within prisons which could bring about change to true Christianity and moral reformation.

These analyses of the causes of crime overall made it clear to the reformist that the prisoner had suffered severe moral and intellectual disabilities during his earlier life and it was therefore of primary importance that these deficiencies should be remedied alongside the attempt to address and awaken the spirit which had slumbered for so many years. Those who worked in prisons came to recognise that a major characteristic of the offender's environment was an acquired habit of idleness and a lack of knowledge of self-maintenance skills. Spiritual reformists accordingly added to their arsenal of religious instruction, reflection and repentance, an emphasis upon useful skills to enable the offender to work after release. John Field emphasised the importance of securing the motivation of the prisoner in this training at Reading Prison where occupational instruction was only offered if voluntarily requested. So in some separate system prisons tailoring and shoemaking were taught, not as compulsory parts of the regime, but offered as a relief from monotony. This voluntary aspect of labour was seen as especially important, for 'a succession of such acts will produce the habit and the pleasing association will render it permanent'.[46] Secondly, in accordance with the belief that 'the filth and confusion' which abounded 'in the homes of our criminal population . . . encouraged and increased habits of profligacy and vice',[47] a determined attempt was made to create 'that disposition and those practices which may produce opposite effects'[48] so that bodily and mental purity would interact to produce physical and attitudinal improvements. Thirdly, because godlessness had thrived for so long in the lives of the prisoners, it was essential that knowledge of God be learned not merely from the words and conversation with the chaplain but also from the Bible and from literature about Christianity; determined attempts were made in the 1840s and 1850s to teach prisoners to read and write. Prisoners in Reading were made to learn long portions of scripture by rote and were required to answer questions about moral behaviour and social structure, quoting extensive biblical references to support the answers given.[49]

The educational aspect of spiritual reformism was subject to continuous debate and analysis. It was agreed by all that ignorance of religious, moral and intellectual knowledge was one of the most common traits of criminals, that they had indeed learned to perceive the world in ways which were entirely contrary to true principles and facts. They had firstly to unlearn assumptions which had previously been taken for granted — for example that the most pleasurable actions are criminal — before they could proceed to be taught the truth. This unlearning of bad principles was presumed to begin in the early stages of separation when 'a feeling of intense remorse . . . preys upon him and the punishment is most severe',[50] but as the attitudes towards the past began to change it was anticipated that there would be a growing receptiveness towards new understanding which, like labour, would be a relief from bored misery. Thus the teacher, like the chaplain or trade instructor, would be a welcome part of the prisoner's life and this voluntary feature of their relationship would be an essential basis for the implanting of new principles and ideas. The prisoner, alone in his cell with his teacher, undisturbed by any interruption, would respectfully and gratefully ingest and learn the new knowledge imparted.[51]

As indicated, one method of religious education practised at Reading and other prisons was learning the Gospels by rote. 'I found this criminal entirely ignorant of the contents of the Bible . . . he shewed much penitence, and the earnest attentions with which during almost every hour of the day he was studying the sacred scriptures attracted special notice. He was but three months in prison yet learnt the four Gospels and several chapters of the Old Testament'.[52] However, the learner was also required to apply this learning to his present and past life. In conversation with the chaplain and in written essays, he was required to discuss various questions to do with morality and religion, supporting his views with scriptural texts. 'In what sense is God our father? Why should I obey the fourth commandment? Give reasons why we should always speak the truth. Give reasons why we should not frequent the public house'.[53] In addition, prisoners were to analyse the effect upon themselves of their instruction: 'I know that when I came I was most ignorant, and a very wicked man; I knew nothing about what was good . . . I bless God for what I have learnt . . . I often think what a blessing it will be for my poor children that I have been brought here'[54] . . . 'the first cause of my troubles was bad company and the love of money and because I would not hearken unto my parents' good advice, but followed the inclinations of my own wicked heart . . . I have been a lover of the pleasures of this world more than of God, have indulged my body, but neglected and starved my soul' . . . 'Leaving my master's house at night without his knowledge for the purpose of gratifying my sinful propensities which at last caused me to be dismissed from my place without a character. I then fell to drinking and gambling until I was almost starved, having neither food nor clothing. So drink has brought me here, and here I hope to leave it' . . . 'there can be, I think, but one answer, however large a number may be asked this question: the absence of the fear and love of God'.[55]

However, spiritual reformists quickly realised that there were two problems in their educational work. They discovered that, although there could be no doubt that gospel truths, however taught, were incontrovertible as a base for such work, there was a good deal of debate about the desirability of other material. Some suspected that increased knowledge enhanced the cunning invent-iveness of the criminal and it was thus universally accepted that the aim of all prison education must be explicitly and self-evidently improving. They must therefore learn to read so as to master scripture, to cultivate a habit of reflection and observation in order to counter the tendency to precipitate action, to learn to love reading to enable them to use leisure time profitably rather than in 'low and grovelling pursuits', to learn how to discover by personal investigation and study the true principles of a complex universe — understanding of which must, it was presumed, inevitably lead to a greater love of its creator and to 'the formation of habits of industry, sobriety and order'.[56] The chaplain of Perth demanded that the knowledge learned should be part of the growth of a virtuous attitude so that a man would say at the end of a lesson or discussion: 'Yes. You are correct, I did not view the matter in that light', adding that secular education without a moral and religious base merely made a thief 'an educated thief' whilst sound moral and religious education was on the other hand 'the most powerful and indispensable engine in carrying into effect the great objects of prison discipline'.[57] At Millbank the teachers were carefully supervised by a principal master who observed their teaching and suggested improvements, not merely of method but of the subject matter taught, and to whom each master had daily to report in detail. At Parkhurst, whether learning literacy or numeracy or religious texts, great care was taken to exclude any undesirable material, for example cheap novels, so that all knowledge taught led to desired principles. As Kingsmill put it, 'education without motive and sound Christian principles is as the moving power to machinery which has no regulator, or as widespread sails to a ship which has neither chart nor compass to steer by. Mere education changes the character of crime'. At Pentonville he intended that all education should give 'the impression . . . that independent, hard working honesty is infinitely better than riches without right or advancement without fitness'. As a later prison chaplain remarked, instruction in 'Euclid, Algebra, Latin or French . . . Virgil or Homer' meant that the prisoner would be suitably occupied and not using his time to dwell 'on past schemes of fraud with glee and weave new ones'.[58]

The second problem which naturally arose with the spread of religious instruction and general education in prisons was that of method. By 1850 almost all the larger prisons had their libraries of religious and moral texts upon which chaplains and teachers might base their work. Prisoners were introduced to the prison library which was full of tracts and books carefully selected to drive home to them the fact that numerous traps for the hard-hearted and godless man lay waiting in open society and that immediate preparations must be made for the last awful trumpet blast. So at Lincoln County Gaol might be found 'The Pious Christian's Daily Preparation', 'Pious Country Parishioner Instructed', 'Green's Four Last Things — Death, Judgement, Heaven and Hell', 'Syneg's Answers To All Excuses and Pretences For Not Coming To The Holy Communion' and at Brixton were 'The Evil Consequences of Attending The Race Course', 'A Peep Into The Gin Shop', 'The Roll Call or How Will You Answer it?', 'The Dying Criminal', 'Missionary Records of China', 'Alleyne's Alarm To The Unconverted'.[59] Such as these were considered valuable texts upon which to base the reformatory endeavour and the use of them as well as of more secular but nevertheless moral works (such as lives of well known British statesmen and heroes) was common both in the classroom and in individual discussion. However, as the practice of both religious and other education increased, it began to be realised that learning was more than just listening and reading and that it was by no means sure that mere statement of truth was sufficient as an educational method. Some prisoners, for example imbeciles, were exceedingly difficult to teach[60] whilst the attention of others might wander. Consequently experiments were made with visual aids in some prisons to render the lessons more interesting. For example, the chaplain of Portland believed that 'a few models of steam engines, an air pump, a small collection of geological specimens and chemicals together with simple illustrative appliances . . . would do much to promote a thirst for reformation amongst those who without such incentives may continue to the end of their days haters of books, lovers of degrading vice and consequently enemies to the best interests of society'.[61] Another teacher remarked 'I have the model of a ship and sails and I get my young fellows more or less up in the practical workings of a ship and give them a knowledge of the technical terms of the rigging, and so on, and this cultivates in them a taste for the sea and, if they emigrate, they emigrate in this way that some of them pay part of their passage and work out the remainder', a method also used at the Bridewell House of Occupation where a sailing ship was built and used to train young men in seamanship so that they 'get a liking for it'.[62]

The aim of all the education — whether studying the workings of a ship, applying to one's own life the moral lessons to be learned from the lives of great men who from humble beginnings had made good (such as George Stephenson), learning the Gospels and writing essays about them, mastering arithmetic or reading manuals of technical instruction — was to strengthen the capacity of the individual to lead a virtuous and godly life. Thus it was particularly important that the prisoner be in a calm and receptive state, for 'the schoolmasters may exhibit their maps, books, globes and appliances for imparting secular knowledge yet comparatively little will be learned by pupils whose minds are fretted with real or imaginary grievances'.[63] The separate system or the rigorous discipline of the convict prisons were deemed especially suitable for such quiet peacefulness. The contents of the educational programmes were often ambitious, yet each had its moral and utility emphasis, whether on man's 'dependence on his creator', 'courtesy and conduct towards our fellows', 'conscientiousness regarding the rights of others', 'procrastination, its evils', 'the National Debt', 'reflection upon the starry firmament' or 'the pleasure of learning, the necessity of life assurance, emigration, some account of the gorilla, circulation of the blood'.[64] As one of the leading prison teachers and exponents of assessment of individual educational need James Organ, said, 'I speak to them upon social questions such as taxes, strikes, combination, illegal societies, industry and honesty, what they have to gain by the commission of crime and what they have to lose . . . air, water, plants, Canada and her resources, the ocean, temperance and self control, Australia past and present, Life — its battles and how to fight them'. In each of his lectures he painstakingly pointed his listeners' minds to the moral lessons to be learned. 'In every one of God's works there are a thousand things which we are not able to explain . . . the wicked and vicious man is never happy, no matter what may be his riches or power in the world', adding after a disquisition on the properties of water and oceans that in the midst of all this mystery above the roar of the sea may be heard the voice of God declaring 'I am the

Lord and none else'.[65] Amongst all this activity, ideas about good educational practice were developed: that instruction be characterised by 'singleness of subject and simplicity of language',[66] that curricula be carefully planned and co-ordinated to include 'practice of simple rules of arithmetic, reading lesson heard and examined, meanings, spelling . . . catechism analysed and memories refreshed . . . sacred music, psalmody'.[67] As one sceptic sarcastically remarked of Parkhurst, 'they study converse, read and so on for an hour or more . . . there stands the lecturer in the midst of his retorts, his batteries, his receivers . . . music, geography, geology, and generally speaking all the elements of science'.[68]

To the spiritual reformists, religious and moral education of offenders was of huge importance because through this, prisoners could be made aware of the infinite power of God and the extraordinary justice and complexity of His created world. Thus Clay argued that lack of education made it inevitable that prisoners would seek to satisfy their sensual natures, deprived of 'the thousand delights born and growing with the progressive development of mind. What can they know of the just or the true, the fit or the beautiful? Does hope that comes to all come to them? for them is there any pleasure of memory? Any gladness of anticipation?'[69] Or as Field put it, the simple man with reliable truthful knowledge no longer need 'lie prostrate and afloat on the current of incidents liable to be carried whithersoever the impulse of appetite may direct'[70] but would be able 'to judge between truth and error, good and evil'.[71] He would learn of God, understand the inevitable misery of drink and vice, be numerate and literate so that such learning might be fully studied and understood and would see the essentials of God's world in all its extraordinary perfect unity and complexity of regulation. Once the process had begun the sense of it all could not fail to shine through the pages of the books and the words of the teacher, and the intellectual rational part of man would check and subdue the love of sensual pleasure. Habits of thought, reflection and observation would be created and the capacity and desire for investigation and study be made permanent.

It was clear to all reformists of this period that the experience of human relationships among most prisoners had been very seriously defective and it was believed that many prisoners had not had the experience of firm and virtuous familial care. The natural tendency of all human nature towards evil had consequently remained unchecked and, because prisoners, had not experienced the redirection of their natures in religious and moral families towards God and virtue, their tendencies had merely been further strengthened by experience of vice and pleasure in society which had itself been followed by crime and prison. Imprisonment was intended to create an experience in which moral example and benevolent human relationship would rectify this environmental deficiency, prison staff providing what ought to have occurred at a much earlier stage of life. In the first place, therefore, prison warders must 'strive to acquire a moral influence over the prisoners by performing their duties conscientiously but without harshness. They should especially try to raise the prisoner's mind to a proper feeling of moral obligation by the example of their own uniform regard to truth and integrity even in the smallest matters'.[72] In the daily experience of such officers the prisoner would understand that a man 'in humble life' could attain such 'moral character . . . fidelity . . . trust . . . zeal and strict attention to his superior's commands'[73] and he would be won over to esteem such firm yet gentle custodians. Prisoners were never to be struck or abused but always treated with human dignity (although never familiarly) and warders were charged to take 'an intelligent interest in the prisoners' employments and a readiness to help them through their difficulties, rather leading than driving them . . . [being] examples of strict integrity and truthfulness in word and act and thus [inducing] the prisoners to aim at a higher standard of moral conduct than that with which previous associations have familiarised them.'[74] As the chaplain of Dartmoor pointed out, warders were with prisoners for very long periods and therefore their influence 'for good or evil . . . can scarcely be overrated'.[75]

In particular, it was believed that a prisoner would often be more deeply influenced if a sincere and dedicated warder attached himself to the man early in the sentence when 'a criminal has often had no-one to give him counsel or sympathy, no virtuous parent or kind relative to feel for him or guide him aright; and that there is, consequently . . . a void which is perhaps filled by a kind prison officer. This may account for the almost filial affection often shown, particularly by the younger prisoners towards a good governor, chaplain or matron' as well as towards prison warders offering 'a fatherly counsel and judicious bearing'. Prisoners would be deeply affected by the trust and faith placed in them and if, by a sudden impulse or rush of temper they failed their officer, would at once say to themselves, as at Brixton female penitentiary, 'Oh, what would Miss Martin say, just when she has given me

my badge?'[76] Small acts of kindness, which implied a rejection of
social condemnation of the individual and an active hopefulness
towards those who had lost hope in themselves, were seen as being
of especial importance. At first, prisoners might be perplexed by
such kindness but would begin to take notice as the firm moral
example and compassionate care for the individual persisted
amongst staff. The latter carefully 'noted the look of surprise, the
joyful surprise at . . . believing that anyone could possess an
interest in her . . . [for] a chance phrase, the right word falling at
the right time on the heart that has been touched by a kindness
often lead to a new train of thought in the prisoner'.[77]

The aim of spiritual reformists was to create an environment in
which the old would be put off for ever, the new embraced with
joy, 'a repentance not repented of, as transient short lived resolution, but sustained resolve', the awakening and nourishing of the
slumbering conscience subdued by years of adverse influences
which 'play upon the soul like a galvanic battery of vice'.[78] Many
prisoners subjected to such a regime would become saved in Christ
by the grace of God, whilst others not so favoured would
experience an entirely different moral world and would discover
'what could be done as free persons if only reason were allowed to
rule instead of passion'.[79] They would learn new truths, both
about this world and the next, experience firm, rational and kindly
authority over them, have their own wills enlisted in the great
work of their reform and, at length, emerge from the prison
committed to a new religion or at the very least a new moral life.
Within their hearts would be awakened faith, charity and hope,
and their reformation would in its turn illuminate the lives of
spouses and children. The prisoner could thereby carry the torch
of moral truth and Christian spirituality back from the prison
house to his own people who, in their turn, might begin the long
march back from vice and death.

Problems and Preoccupations within Separation

Soon after 1840, separatists and more general spiritual reformists
began to encounter difficulties with these attempts 'to destroy the
habits of sin . . . to create those of virtue' and to awaken 'feelings
. . . in the heart and mind which appreciate the virtuous practices
of life'.[80] In the first place there developed an uncertainty about
the capacity of separation alone to create permanent change in

the offender. A particular fear was that, although there would be
formed moral and spiritual resolve, this would not have been
tested in separation and thus when exposed to the difficulties and
temptations of life on release the apparent conversion and
reformation would speedily be shown up as artificial. Joshua Jebb
worried that when released from the cocoon of separation the
progress made would be dissipated[81] and the Bishop of Melbourne
insisted that temptation sorely tried prisoners released from
separation to conditional freedom as transportees.[82] By 1850 some
of the strongest advocates of separation were concerned that the
dramatic impact of separation led to false conclusions about
successful reform among both prisoners and staff alike. Kingsmill
himself pointed out that men were often very deeply moved by a
'zealous and affectionate' ministry and indeed felt that over time
the minister's 'sentiments become the prisoners' and his mind
their will'.[83] Prisoners easily mistook their love of the minister for
a true conversion and this error would be fully revealed when
temptation subsequently overcame them after release. Indeed, by
the end of the 1850s, Kingsmill was urging considerable hesitancy
in respect of apparent conversion of prisoners whose situation 'is
one of affliction and the absence of active temptation to their
besetting sins . . . they are in a subdued, softened state of mind'.[84]

To this problem of artificiality of impact was added the problem
of accurate individual assessment. It was admitted that large
numbers became remorseful, tearful and responsive to the work of
staff whilst subjected to separation. However, this made it difficult
to gain an accurate picture of the kind of man the prisoner was
before sentence, a matter which was of great importance to those
who wished to plan the precise direction of their work. Consequently the Governor of Pentonville emphasised the need to discover the 'stability of character prior to sentence' and for staff to
discover information from all sources about 'his past life, the
nature and frequency of his convictions, the quality of his crimes,
the circumstances which originated and influenced his criminal
course, the restraints which family ties and social relations are
likely . . . to impose'.[85] By investigation and discussion among
staff the nature of the offender and his background would be discovered and the work of reformation more accurately directed.

Another problem reported by all spiritual reformists, whether
separatist or not, was that certain categories or groups of prisoners
were most difficult to affect at all. In particular, women with a long
history of crime, prostitution and prison sentences who were

eventually subjected to penal servitude, were seen as a problematic group whose conduct was frequently 'uninfluenced by the word of God'.[86] Repeatedly, startled chaplains and scripture readers described these women convicts as very aggressive, abusive and uncontrollable in their conduct, having a tendency to 'violent and sudden outbursts of feeling together with the destruction of prison property'.[87] Others seen as especially unresponsive were usually identified by reference to number of criminal convictions, previous sentences in associated prisons where maximum contamination was presumed to have occurred and their associations; all agreed with G. L. Chesterton that young London thieves were exceedingly difficult to reclaim because they seemed to take huge joy in it: 'Lord, how I do love thieving! If I had thousands I'd still be a thief'.[88] Some identified aged and invalid prisoners, 'merely stranded wrecks of human beings, almost hopeless' as very difficult to affect or influence.[89] By contrast, the young man who had fallen into temptation and acted contrary to his previous conduct, or the man in middle age who had fallen into vice, were seen as hopeful. In a sense it seems that reformists felt more hope for those who shared some at least of their own social and moral assumptions at the outset than those whose environmental experience had been wholly different. At times, when confronted by dedicated young thieves, even the firmest chaplain might be discouraged: 'they are so headstrong, so insolent when checked, so addicted to lying and deceit, that none but those who have experience can form any idea of the great difficulties we have in meeting the various turnings of their evil tempers'.[90]

A major problem for separatists in this period was the belief held by many that the long periods of isolation created insanity. Largely on account of this worry, periods of separation at Pentonville were, much to Chaplain Burt's displeasure, reduced from an original eighteen months before proceeding to the associated labour convict prison at Portland to nine. The medical debate about this need not detain us in the study of reformism, but it is worth noting that some reformists such as Kingsmill were concerned by the 1850s that the system might paradoxically produce both over- and under-stimulation of the mind. He worried that there could be 'a gradual and perhaps imperceptible decline of the physical and mental energies of the mind of persons subjected to the trial', 'a prostration of spirits', but also that 'the prisoner should have the horrors', subjected to long periods of sorrowful aloneness followed by intense 'exhaustion of exciteability by overaction' as a result of the intervention of chaplain and staff. In particular there were fears that 'the educated and sensitive mind' could be unbalanced by the remorse that removal of external stimulation induced 'a state of inertia or torpor of mind' in men of low intellect, and that lack of exercise led to deterioration of the body with consequent 'morbid influences acting on the mind' together with 'the exhaustion of nervous power induced by the solitary vice'.[91] Undoubtedly, as Ignatieff has pointed out, some men and women were overwhelmed by this system of discipline with its awesome silence, long isolation broken only by the homilies and discourses of chaplain and staff. 'Sometimes there were screams. Men came apart in the loneliness and the silence. One prisoner kept dreaming that his sister was . . . outside the wall. One midnight he leapt from his hammock, ran to the window, clutched the bars with his fists and began crying her name. Another man saw burning lights in his cell and began screaming out in fear. Another saw snakes coiled round the bars of his window . . . one man became convinced that the hand that pushed the food through the trap door was trying to poison him'.[92]

It was partly as a result of misgivings about the possible destruction of the mind as well as the fear that the reformation of the offender ought to be tested by controlled association that the separate system did not become the sole theory of prisoner reformation throughout Britain between 1840 and 1865. As we shall see later, separation and spiritual reformism were attacked on other grounds also. Although prisons such as Pentonville Convict Prison or Winchester or Reading County Prisons practised separation in its purest form, most prisons imported elements of the system which were added to other more traditional ways of working. However, the impact of spiritual reformism in a more general sense was immense during this period as chaplains in the large prisons dedicated themselves to the conversion of prisoners, being regarded by society at large as most important officials promising substantial benefits in the name of God. Although some like Chaplain J. T. Burt stood out for pure separation to the very end and castigating all association as destructive of the reform achieved, 'blasted under the withering blight of such companionship',[93] the majority by 1860 were content to pursue their work, no less dedicated, amidst systems which were only in part derived from the pure separation proposed by Crawford and Russell. None the less, the aim remained the same: 'to sow the same seed in every prisoner's heart: in some it produces no fruit — in many it springs up and produces a harvest of good so far as regards this world — and in a few it brings forth unto life eternal'.[94] The chaplain of the associated labour convict prison at Portland was able to remark: 'some of our charges are earnest and genuine soldiers of Christ, evincing deep and true repentance by their altered lives . . . [it is] indescribably touching to see this body of prisoners on their knees and to hear them with one voice saying we do earnestly repent and are heartily sorry for these our misdoings',[95] whilst Kingsmill pointed out that in the convict prison system as a whole, although some were truly converted, others were 'presumed to be in some measure affected in the general features of their character and to have advanced in fact a stage or two in moral civilisation'.[96]

Lastly, the great majority of these prison chaplains knew well that they would frequently be subjected to trickery by prisoners wishing for one reason or another to mislead them as to the genuineness of their conversion. This was a problem entirely different from the emotional conviction held by a prisoner that he had become converted. Partly in order to test genuineness and partly because they felt that reformation would not occur swiftly, many argued, with Field and the Berkshire magistracy, that sentences ought to be increased in order to make reformation more probable. The chaplain of Parkhurst suggested that the discipline there 'is too short for reformation';[97] William Merry, chairman of the visiting committee of Reading prison, criticised sentencers who 'say of a prisoner brought before them "Poor Fellow, it is the first offence, we will give him a short imprisonment"'.[98] In general, spiritual reformists insisted that genuine conversion was not achieved within a short time but was rather a lengthy and arduous business in which the subduing of the self-indulgent, pleasure-seeking appetites might well take several months before the new structure of morality and religion could even begin to be erected. Chaplains were also of course aware of the need to beware of 'that religious trickery which shows itself chiefly in pious phrases, a whining voice and a demure countenance'.[99] Thus whilst in the early 1840s there was often a most marked optimism concerning reformatory success, by 1860 more caution was evident with a recognition that many factors could operate to give a false indication of a prisoner's state of mind.

It was not in Britain alone that spiritual reformism flourished; in Belgium, France and elsewhere considerable efforts were made to import the pure separate system from America. However, in Britain between 1840 and 1860 such reformism gave a particular direction to the practice of prisoner reformation. Moreover, although the actual extent of the practice has to be considered separately, there can be little doubt that, however tailored to meet local conditions, the prison chaplain was accepted by 1850 as a profoundly important official in the prison system. Crawford and Russell would doubtless have disapproved of much of the adulteration of pure theory which occurred but they would have recognised at once the aspiration to centre the reformatory endeavour upon knowing 'the inner man, his thoughts, grievances and causes of complaint . . . his fears . . . his present hopes and intentions; without such information our efforts in criminal reformation must turn out to be but partially successful if not wholly ineffectual'.[100]

The aim then was the profoundest penetration of spirit and mind, the insistence upon the God-given value of the individual and the necessity for his social inclusion. The chaplain of Parkhurst lamented: 'what is to become of them if no-one will pity and help them?'[101] Chaplain Sherwin, a later chaplain at Pentonville, mourned that 'the miserable criminal . . . is in danger in present times of being so loathed as to be abhorred of men not pitied'.[102] They were thus aware of the great gulf fixed between the convict and his society and yet pursued the spirit of the prisoner, believing that through the grace of God 'a wonderful metamorphosis' could be perceived among their flock, examples of 'visages brightened by . . . renovation, beaming with hope, looking up to God . . . reconciled . . . by the son of His love',[103] a process of the deepest stirring of heart and soul. Mayhew and Binny wrote wonderingly of their experience of a chapel service at Pentonville when the chaplain spoke of the death of a convict's daughter:

'Some buried their faces in their handkerchiefs . . . others sobbed aloud . . . so that we could hear their gasps and sighs telling of the homes they had made wretched by their shame . . . when we heard the convict multitude . . . cry aloud to their Almighty and most merciful Father that they had erred and strayed from his ways like lost sheep . . . we are not ashamed to confess that the tears filled our eyes and choked the most devout Amen we ever uttered in our life.'[104]

It was only in such pain, lamentation and intimacy with God's earthly agents that the lost prisoner could begin to reach out for the hand of God and turn from the insidious evils of passion, vice and crime seeking to ensnare and deliver him to the infernal realms of darkness ruled by the power of Lucifer.

References

1. For example, S. & B. Webb, *English Prisons under Local Government*, Cass, 1963. S. McConville, *English Prison Administration*.

2. *Report from the SC on Transportation*, PP, 1837–8, vol. XXII, p. VIII. R. Whateley, *Thoughts on Secondary Punishments*, Fellowes, 1832, pp. 70–1, 91.

3. *Parliamentary Debates*, Third Series, vol. 54, col. 276.

4. *Report on the Discipline and Construction of Portland Prison*, Lt. Col. Jebb, PP, 1850, vol. XXIX, pp. 11–12.

5. *Report from the SC on Prison Discipline*, PP, 1850, vol. XVII, p. IV, V, VI.

6. Ibid., Minutes of evidence, p. 14; see also S. McConville, *English Prison Administration*, p. 254, note 116.

7. J. Kingsmill, *Chapters on Prisons and Prisoners*, Longman, 2nd edn, 1852, p. 235.

8. Ibid., pp. 304, 373.

9. J. Burt, *Results of the System of Separate Confinement*, Longman, 1852, p. 260.

10. Rev. W. L. Clay, *The Prison Chaplain — A Memoir of the Rev. John Clay by his Son*, Macmillan, 1861, p. 205.

11. Ibid., p. 232.

12. *Report of the General Board of Directors*, PP, 1842, vol. XXII, p. 51.

13. Rev. W. L. Clay, *Memoir*, p. 207.

14. Kingsmill, *Prisons and Prisoners*, p. 225.

15. Burt, *Results*, p. 253.

16. H. S. Joseph, *Memoirs of Convicted Prisoners*, Wertheim, 1853, p. 119.

17. *RDCP 1852*, PP, 1852–3, vol. LI, pp. 68–9.

18. J. Field, *The Advantages of the Separate System of Imprisonment*, Longman, 1846, pp. 271, 272, 276.

19. *5th RCGPP*, PP, 1847, vol. XXX, pp. 36, 38; J. Kingsmill, *Prisons and Prisoners*, pp. 117–18.

20. J. Field, *Advantages of Separate System*, pp. 185, 192.

21. *6th RCGPP*, PP, 1847–8, vol. XXXIV, pp. 27, 28.

22. *RDCP 1859*, PP, 1860, vol. XXXV, Report of Millbank Chaplain; *Reports Relating to Parkhurst Prison*, PP, 1844, vol. XXVIII, p. 35.

23. W. L. Clay, *Memoir*, pp. 205, 207, 206.

24. J. Kingsmill, *Prisons and Prisoners*, 1854, 3rd edn, pp. 217, 261, 253, 232.

25. Ibid., p. 228.

26. *Fifth RInsP*, Northern and Eastern District, PP, 1840, vol. XXV, pp. 60, 74.

27. Ibid., p. 64.

28. P. Priestley, *Victorian Prison Lives*, Methuen, 1985, pp. 91–119.

29. A. Thomson, *Punishment and Prevention*, Nisbet, 1857, p. 168.

30. *RDMCP* by J. Jebb, PP, 1854, vol. XXXIII, pp. 39–40, 81.

31. *RDCP 1850*, PP, 1851, vol. XXVIII, Parkhurst Report, p. 9.

32. *RDCP 1857*, PP, 1857–8, vol. XXIX, pp. 25–6.

33. *RDCP 1860*, PP, 1861, vol. XXX, p. 148.

34. *5th RCGPP*, PP, 1847, vol. XXX, p. 33.

35. A. Thomson, *Punishment and Prevention*.

36. Ibid., p. 120.
37. *RDCP 1859*, PP, 1860, vol. XXXV, p. 205.
38. A. Thomson, *Social Evils: their Causes and Cure*, quoted PP, 1852–3, vol. LI, p. 85.
39. *RDCP 1852*, PP, 1852–3, vol. LI, p. 63; A. Thomson, *Punishment and Prevention*, p. 84.
40. A Prison Matron, *Memoirs of Jane Cameron*, Hurst and Blackett, 1864, vol. 1, p. 22. *RDCP 1856*, PP, 1857, Session 2, vol. XXIII, p. 307.
41. J. M. Morgan, *Religion and Crime*, Longman, 1841, pp. 13, 19, 4, 33, 2, 45.
42. T. Beames, *The Rookeries of London*, Bosworth, 1850, pp. 113, 5, 21, 36, 84, 121, 140.
43. Quoted PP, 1854–5, vol. XXV, p. 116. No date given.
44. C. B. Adderley, *Transportation Not Necessary*, Parker, 1851, pp. 30, 26, 62, 70.
45. F. Hill, *Crime: its amount, causes and remedies*, Murray, 1853, p. 34.
46. J. Field, *Advantages of Separate System*, p. 152.
47. Ibid., p. 158.
48. Ibid., pp. 158–9.
49. *Report from the SC on Prison Discipline*, PP, 1850, vol. XVII, Minutes of Evidence, p. 240.
50. Ibid., p. 240.
51. A. Thomson, *Punishment and Prevention*, p. 49.
52. J. Field, *Report Read at the Berkshire Quarter Sessions by the Chaplain of the County Gaol and House of Correction*, E. Welch, 1845, pp. 46–7.
53. Ibid., pp. 47, 48, 49.
54. Ibid., p. 55.
55. J. Kingsmill, *Prisons and Prisoners*, 2nd edn, pp. 305, 307, 325.
56. *RDCP 1858*, PP, 1859, Session 2, vol. XIII, Part 1, p. 84; *RDCP 1861*, PP, 1862, vol. XXV, p. 181.
57. *Report of the General Board of Directors of Scottish Prisons, 3rd Report*, PP, 1842, vol. XXII, p. 53; Ibid., *5th Report*, PP, 1854, vol. XXVII, p. 63.
58. J. Kingsmill, *Prisons and Prisoners*, 2nd edn, pp. 42–3; *RDCP 1872*, PP, 1873, vol. XXXIV, p. 165.
59. *RDCP 1853*, PP, 1854, vol. XXXIII, p. 139; *3rd RInsP*, North and East, PP, 1837–8, vol. XXXI, pp. 42–3; *4th RInsP*, Home District, PP, 1839, vol. XXI, pp. 395–6.
60. *RDCP 1853*, PP, 1854, vol. XXXIII, p. 98.
61. *RDCP 1856*, PP, 1857, Session 2, vol. XXIII, p. 165.
62. *Minutes of Evidence Penal Servitude Acts Commission*, PP, 1863, vol. XXI, p. 378; *SC on Prison Discipline*, PP, 1850, vol. XVII, p. 375.
63. *RDCP 1858*, PP, 1859, Session 2, vol. XIII, part 1, p. 259; *RDCP 1856*, PP, 1857, Session 2, vol. XXIII, p. 161.
64. C. P. Measor, *Irish Fallacies and English Facts*, Ridgway, 1863, p. 33. *RDCP 1861*, PP, 1862, vol. XXV, p. 181.
65. *Minutes of Evidence taken before the Penal Servitude Acts Commission*, PP, 1863, vol. XXI, p. 372; James P. Organ, *Lectures on Educational, Social and Moral Subjects*, Kelly, 1858.
66. W. L. Clay, *Memoir*, p. 201.

67. *Reports Relating to Parkhurst Prison*, PP, 1846, vol. XX, pp. 19–20.
68. W. Hepworth Dixon, *The London Prisons*, Jackson & Walford, 1850, pp. 188–90.
69. W. L. Clay, *Memoir*, p. 508.
70. J. Field, *Advantages of Separate System*, pp. 243–4.
71. Ibid., p. 249.
72. *RDMCP 1853*, Lt. Col. Jebb, PP, 1854, vol. XXXIII, pp. 16–17.
73. *RDMCP 1851*, PP, 1852–3, vol. LI, pp. 52–3.
74. *RDCP 1852*, PP, 1852–3, vol. LI, p. 57.
75. *RDCP 1856*, PP, 1857, Session 2, vol. XXIII, p. 259.
76. F. Hill, *Crime*, p. 307; *RDCP 1857*, PP, 1857–8, vol. XXIX, pp. 216, 257.
77. A Prison Matron, pp. 101, 114.
78. M. Carpenter, *Our Convicts*, Longman, 1864, vol. I, p. 110; J. T. Burt, *Results*, p. 49.
79. *RDMCP 1853*, Lt. Col. Jebb, PP, 1854, vol. XXXIII, p. 47.
80. *Report on the Discipline and Construction of Portland Prison*, Lt. Col. Jebb, PP, 1850, vol. XXIX, p. 121.
81. *RDMCP*, Lt. Col. Jebb, PP, 1851, vol. XXVIII, p. 52.
82. Ibid., p. 54.
83. *RDCP 1850*, PP, 1851, vol. XXVIII, p. 24.
84. *RDCP 1856*, PP, 1857, Session 2, vol. XXIII, p. 23.
85. *5th RCGPP*, PP, 1847, vol. XXX, p. 18.
86. *RDCP 1856*, PP, 1857, Session 2, vol. XXIII, p. 68.
87. *RDCP 1853*, PP, 1854, vol. XXXIII, p. 88.
88. Quoted Henriques, *Rise and Decline*, p. 74.
89. *RDCP 1858*, PP, 1859, Session 2, vol. XIII, part 1, p. 260.
90. *RDMCP 1853*, Lt. Col. Jebb, PP, 1854, vol. XXXIII, p. 70.
91. *RDMCP 1852*, PP, 1852–3, vol. LI, p. 94, 101; *RDMCP 1851*, PP, 1852–3, vol. LI, p. 119.
92. M. Ignatieff, *A Just Measure of Pain*, p. 9.
93. J. T. Burt, *Results*, p. 63.
94. A. Thomson, *Punishment and Prevention*, p. 52.
95. *RDCP 1853*, PP, 1854, vol. XXXIII, pp. 137–8.
96. *RDCP 1858*, PP, 1859, Session 2, vol. XIII, part 1, p. 28.
97. *RDCP 1856*, PP, 1857, Session 2, vol. XXIII, p. 93.
98. *Report from the SC on Prison Discipline*, PP, 1850, vol. XVII, Minutes of Evidence, pp. 222–3.
99. *RDCP 1852*, PP, 1852–3, vol. LI, p. 68.
100. James Organ, quoted in C. P. Measor, *Irish Fallacies*, p. 19.
101. *RDCP 1863*, PP, 1864, vol. XXVI, p. 98.
102. Ibid. for 1862, PP, 1863, vol. XXIV, p. 19.
103. Ibid. for 1860, PP, 1861, vol. XXX, p. 15.
104. Henry Mayhew and John Binny, *The Criminal Prisons of London and Scenes of Prison Life*, Ch. Griffin and Co., 1862, pp. 165, 167.

3

Pains, Pleasures and Stages in Reformatory Treatment 1840–1865

Convict Prisons and Progressive Stages

The associationist psychological approach — the repetitive infliction of severity to discourage undesirable conduct and attitude and regulated reward for exhibition of desired traits — was a particularly important basis of reformatory aspirations within the convict prison system between 1840 and 1865. The regimes developed within these prisons were therefore in part a natural outcome of well over half a century of theorising about the association between crime, sensation and habit among prisoners, but such an approach was given a particular emphasis in convict prisons because these initially served as stages in the wider sentence of transportation.

Pentonville has already been described as a first stage of transportation, 'the portal to the penal colony'[1] a new colonial world free of 'early association'.[2] However, the period of separation which was to precede transportation in the early 1840s was not merely viewed as a chance of spiritual renovation. It was also emphasised that future conditions to a large extent depended upon conduct at Pentonville.[3] An exemplary performance there might allow full freedom when landed in Australia, whilst those who showed 'great industry or extra work'[4] would earn sums of money (gratuity) to be sent to the officials of the transport colony for use by the prisoner on discharge from the total institutional part of his sentence. As the convict prison burgeoned in the late-1840s/ early-1850s this individualist adjustment of conditions of sentence on the basis of performance became characteristic. It depended on the assumption that if prisoners perceived that their self-interest lay in behaving in ways desired by their custodians they would permanently learn such conduct and attitudes.

Portland Prison was established in 1848 to enable a period of associated labour to be enforced in England after the period of spiritual reformation and prior to the voyage to the transport colony. Both the period at Pentonville and that in associated labour varied according to 'conduct and character' and some were allowed to proceed to the relevant colony directly from Penton-ville. The majority, however, proceeded to the public works prison where conduct of an 'exemplary manner' and an encouraging 'demeanour and willing industry' might enable others to be sent out to Australia to conditional freedom after only half the period normally served in associated labour (normally at least two years on a seven-year sentence, $3\frac{1}{2}$ on a fifteen).[5] Thus at Portland conduct was carefully recorded and within the public works part of the sentence stages were introduced, three different classes graded according to severity and privilege, and the prisoner promoted and demoted on the basis of his 'actual conduct, industry and observed character'.[6]

Between 1840 and 1863 the convict system grew into a network of different prisons (together with cells rented from the county magistrates) under the rule of Joshua Jebb, the Chairman of the Directorate. The link with transportation gradually weakened as that system entered its last years, during which it gave way to penal servitude. Sentences of less than fourteen years' transporta-tion were abolished in 1853 and replaced by a new prison sentence of penal servitude, whilst in 1857 transportation was theoretically finally abolished although the law in question included provision for those sentenced to penal servitude to be removed to colonies which had previously held transportees if the government so directed.[7] Although about 6,000 prisoners were taken to the vast empty colony of Western Australia between 1855 and 1862, no convicts were conveyed there after 1867 as this system of disposal came to an end, the convict station at Gibraltar being closed in 1875. This long decline of transportation resulted in the convict prisons of England having to contain prisoners for longer periods than when the system was at its zenith. By the 1850s and early-1860s they were becoming prisons which no longer acted as ante-chambers to the new world but were places where sentences of penal servitude were served in full. Thus the exact conditions in which such sentences were served needed to be very precisely defined, and the idea of different stages of the sentence was present in the management of all convicts, whether transportees or penal servitude men. At Parkhurst Juvenile Prison three classes were introduced, each with their particular severities and privileges: 'when the usual dinner on Sunday is over, prisoners in the third class . . . are marched out of the dining halls, the others remain and receive each a ration of pudding in addition to their ordinary diets'.[8] At Portland and Chatham Convict Prisons differential wages were introduced to create motivation within three classes and throughout the entire system attention was paid to definition of the exact conditions to be attached to each stage — whether severity of labour, earnings, receiving and sending letters, visits, diet (beer on Sunday, roast meat instead of boiled)[9] on the basis that prisoners would begin at the most severe stage and gradually work through the system to the final stage which was early release from the prison before expiry of the full term of years ordered by law.

The remission of the period which convicts were to serve in the total institution before release had, as indicated, been part of transportation for many years, but between 1840 and 1863 it became a major part of the management of convict prisons. When the new sentence of penal servitude was introduced in 1853 it had not been intended that it should include provision for early release. The government, true to the principles of transportation, did in fact release in England several thousand convicts sentenced to transportation prior to 1853 but unable to be sent abroad as a result of the closure of Tasmania to transportees. It had argued in respect of these that 'the power of revoking that license without assigning any cause whatever at the pure pleasure of the crown would hang in terrorem over these unfortunate persons and would hold out the very strongest inducements to them to conduct themselves properly and to abstain from any violation of the law.'[10] Concerning penal servitude, however, the government initially insisted that there would be no system of early release on licence, save in exceptional cases such as grievous illness or saving a warder's life.[11] This changed so that after 1857, early release on licence was generally applied to penal servitude, as it had been to transportation, such licences being awarded not for special merit but merely on the grounds that the prisoner's 'conduct in prison should be such as not to deprive them of that indulgence'.[12] A scale of remission was introduced which varied from one-sixth on a three-year sentence to one-third on a fifteen-year term. Detailed regulations were laid down as to the way in which prisoners who had 'by misconduct or idleness' forfeited their licence opportunity

73

might yet regain it by good behaviour in prison. Similarly, the release licence was revocable if licensees committed further offences, associated with other criminals, led 'an idle and dissolute life' or had 'no visible means of obtaining an honest livelihood'; nor would a licence be granted unless a man had been free of adverse prison reports for six months.[13] Between 1853 and 1862 nearly 13,000 convicts were released on licence in England, Wales and Scotland, of whom nearly a thousand were women. At this stage no supervising agent was appointed to oversee their conduct, although in the late-1850s part of the gratuities owed to prisoners on release was often withheld until a favourable report had been received from the local clergyman or the London Prisoners' Aid Society following some months of liberty.

By the early-1860s over 2,000 prisoners were being released on licence from convict prisons each year, having been subjected to a system which began with a period of pure separation, proceeded to associated labour in conditions which varied according to class, and eventually resulted in release on licence awarded in the absence of adverse discipline reports. Clearly much of the reasoning behind this system was that it made the government of large numbers of convicts easier because they would be less likely to infringe the rules of the prison if they perceived that it was in their interests not to do so. Thus in the early-1860s it was possible to employ large working groups in building the new criminal lunatic asylum at Broadmoor with the confidence that 'they could not be induced to run away' as by doing so they would forfeit their chance of a licence.[14] In addition, the stages of associated labour appealed to those who desired rigorous severity in order to deter, and indeed the work carried out by convicts in labour gangs was often exceedingly harsh. At Portsmouth, 'a party of from ten, twelve to fourteen on the average drag a loaded cart, the weight of which is from one and a half to two and a quarter tons, a distance of from ten to sixteen miles backwards and forwards during the day'.[15] Furthermore, the work undertaken might be justified as a penal measure on the grounds that the convicts were making reparation to the offended society in that the projects undertaken were of great value to the state, whether reclamation of parts of Dartmoor, construction of dockyards at Chatham or quarrying and sea defence at Portland.

However, this system was firmly promoted on its reformist merits. In the first place, the stages system was intended to 'produce in the minds of the prisoners a practical and habitual conviction of the effect which their own good conduct and industry will have on their welfare and future prospects'.[16] Over a period of time there would be instilled in the mind of the prisoner 'an invigorating hope and a salutary dread',[17] together with the knowledge that every act within the prison was noted and would play its part in promotion or demotion within the class system and eventual date of release. The prisoners would quickly discover that they could win better conditions by their own efforts. From the very outset of the associated labour stages prisoners were invited to make a rational decision to 'contend against their propensities' towards self-indulgence, defiance or disobedience as they realised that the immediate pain of self-denial was later followed by a greater pleasure.[18] Work would come to be associated with the idea of self-interest and the eventual pleasure of early release, obedience with the idea of improved conditions as a result of the staff report, and gradually the convict would understand that such behaviour brought an ultimate reward far greater than that resulting from idleness or resistance: 'under the present system his motives to good conduct not only continue but grow stronger till the last moment of his remaining within the prison'.[19]

In addition to the appeal to rationality was the view that the repetitive long-term impact of years of exercise of reason within the system would create a habit 'of self control and submission to authority' which 'alone is calculated to give strength and stability to good resolutions and to create the desire to give satisfaction to their employers'.[20] By habituating the convict to new responses to temptations and surrounding circumstances and new spheres of activity, permanent influence would result: 'by months and months of patient labour the habit of work is gradually made a part of his nature'.[21] The decision to engage in action to bring reward, repeated daily, would ultimately over the years in prison become permanent, no longer requiring the painful self-mastery necessary earlier but continuing without noticeable exercise of the will. 'If in the course of that discipline he has found his conditions, generally speaking, correspond with his own diligence in industry, there is the greater probability that the species of blind logic thus taught to his sensations will direct him out in the world'.[22] Inherent in this reasoning was the idea that by achieving such action, other similar actions became easier. Jebb quoted with approval the remark of Bishop Butler that 'by accustoming ourselves to any course of action we get an aptness to go on, a facility, a readiness and often a pleasure in it' and drew particular attention to Butler's view that, in proportion as certain actions are undertaken successfully, aversion to them grows weaker as the difficulties attendant upon them reduce in the mind. Eventually, as men accustom themselves to such actions 'the least glimpse of them is sufficient to make us go on in a course of action to which we have become accustomed . . . and thus a new character in several respects may be formed and many habitudes of life not given by nature but which nature directs us to acquire'.[23]

The artificial environment of the convict prison was thus intended to place men in such a situation that their reason dictated their course of action; greater rigour was avoided, privilege obtained, and as a result of their undertaking, over years, desired actions, there ensued a permanent automatic diligence, obedience and respectfulness. The regime would have two further results. First, the body would become inured to hard physical labour and then be suited to continuance of such work on release; secondly, the mind would understand that what had seemed essential parts of life before sentence were in fact not so. So, for example, the belief among prisoners that copious draughts of spirits were a necessary precondition to undertaking successfully heavy labour would be rapidly disproved, and in many ways men would perceive that previous assumptions which had become articles of faith were based on false knowledge. In other words, new habits resulting from new perceptions of self-interest would become fixed and would destroy the old false knowledge and habit as the prisoner moved through the system.

In addition, stage reformists included in their overall concept the notions of naturalness and maturation. Although they accepted that the separation which preceded the associated labour was an important part of the total discipline, and although most of them accepted the importance of spiritual reformism, generally it seemed to them that the second staged phase of convict prison discipline was essential to mature reformation. Without it the unnatural chastened and repentant state of mind created by the separate system experience would be insufficient to achieve sustained change of attitude and behaviour. Jebb, again using Butler as a supporting authority, emphasised this: '[Bishop Butler] remarks that nature does not qualify us wholly, much less at once, for a mature state of life, and that maturity of understanding and bodily strength are only arrived at gradually by the continued exercise of our powers from infancy . . . it seems that men would be strangely headstrong and self-willed were it not for some acquired moderation and self government, some aptitude and readiness in restraining themselves. Thus the beginning of our days is adapted to be and is a state of education in the theory and practice of mature life.'[24] Jebb and other stage reformists argued most strongly that associated labour and staged privileges were most important means of bringing about full moral development after the initial impact of separation. Men would be faced with a half-way house between separation — in which stage they could not experience the natural temptations inherent in human society — and full freedom — which might overwhelm after mere separation because there had been no supervised trial of the resilience of a prisoner. So the associated labour convict prison served to prepare men 'whilst under control for the temptations which awaited them when released from penal discipline', quite apart from its superior propensity to inure them 'to useful labour and . . . persevering industry'.[25] The stage system put them under more real and natural temptation than separation and invited them to translate the rarefied principles and ideas learned at Pentonville into practical application. Given no alternative they obviously made the correct responses in separation, but in association the prisoners had to exercise power of will, would experience the temptations, trials and tribulations of human society in controlled conditions which artificially served to try to bring the prisoner's behaviour into line with the desires of society and to bring the prisoner, awakened by separation, to mature realism.

The stage system, therefore, was closer to the world as it really was and as it had been set up by God, and it would both test reformation and habituate the prisoner to responses which he must make if he were to avoid crime outside the prison in a much deeper and more testing way than was possible under separation. In separation man was treated as though he were in a social vacuum in which 'it is sought to destroy the habits of sin' by the means of spiritual reform. In the subsequent stage the public works prison would create a deeper and more permanent understanding of and facility in 'the virtuous practices of life' because social pressures and demands had to be mastered before a man could proceed through the stages and ultimately to an early release.[26] As he daily encountered such things his responses would be subtly shaped by the environment to habituate him to the desired outcomes. Because 'the restraints are necessarily fewer, the temptations are much greater. The association of the prisoners . . . although under inspection and control is assimilated to that of ordinary life . . . it

is impossible, I think, that any person can visit the works of Portland prison . . . without being much struck with their willing and
cheerful industry . . . the once idle and dissolute may be seen
diligently quarrying or with alacrity following pursuits requiring
skilled labour' and, as these actions and attitudes continued year
after year, the prisoner would ultimately be permanently
changed.[27]

This system of rewards and penalties was clearly deeply rooted
in associationist psychological assumptions, but within the convict
prison system as a whole there was no necessary conflict between
such an approach and spiritual reformism. In all the convict
prisons there were of course chaplains who carried out the basic
spiritual reformist operations detailed earlier and who were important officials within them; indeed, there was much common
ground between the two reformatory theories. Both held that God
had created the world in such a way that vice and crime, whilst
appearing attractive, ultimately reaped a terrible harvest of
suffering. The depraved nature of man in evangelical terms had to
be mastered in order for true human happiness to be achieved, and
both taught that this mastery was won by a process, involving both
mind and feelings, of learning true principles and their application. However, the method of learning clearly varied, depending
on the relative emphasis placed upon the chaplain as a vehicle of
God's grace on the one hand and, on the other, upon learning true
self-interest by planned experience as a corrective to acquired
habits of vice and crime in a deficient family and social environment. In fact, the two systems appeared to work so well together
that many of those chaplains such as Kingsmill and Clay, who in
the 1840s had deeply deplored any return to association amongst
prisoners, came to believe strongly in the value of it: thus the combination of Portland and Pentonville 'sends out the convict capable
of exertion in the field of humble industry and furnishes the best
means of reformation under the zealous and affectionate ministry
of the Gospel'.[28]

Stage reformism within English convict prisons represented a
complete application of associationist psychological theory to the
problem of reforming convicts. It sought permanent relearning of
behaviour and attitude and it required careful scrutiny of
individual behaviour in order to permit promotion or demotion on
the basis of reports about obedience and industry. It identified
certain groups as easier to reform than others. At Dartmoor, the
age of the convict group being high, it was felt that 'senility, bodily

infirmity and mental weakness' made this reformatory system much more difficult to operate successfully than was the case with the young, who 'may be trained while young and pliant',[29] having less implanted false knowledge and habit. In addition, the individual response would be automatically identified by reference to their progress within the regime and noted by the authorities as 'satisfactory', 'considerably improved', 'slightly improved', 'unsatisfactory', 'incorrigible'.[30] As Jebb remarked, the moral example of the officers, whose reports were so important to the progress of the prisoner, was plainly essential to the maintenance of 'a cheerful submission to authority, respect towards the officers and a confidence in them and a gratitude to the government for the considerate and just manner in which all their claims are attended to'. In consequence, if prisoners were not justly judged the entire system broke down, for the rewards and penalties would be inappropriately distributed and basic principles flouted. 'Everything depends upon just and considerate treatment';[31] in such a system, resentments caused by tyranny or injustice would be most damaging to successful reformation.

Stage reformism was also characterised by a concern that the environment to which the prisoner would go after release should be much improved in comparison to the previous faulty one. At the end of the institutional period it was felt that two kinds of reformation were likely. On the one hand there were those who had been 'reformed in a much higher sense, who having received during three or four years religious instruction, spent their Sundays in peace and quiet and attended prayers twice a day have through the blessing of God greatly profited by these means', having undoubtedly been primarily influenced by the spiritual impact of the system. On the other hand, those whose habituation to new attitudes and conduct had finally made these too strong to efface had clearly been reformed by a regime which inculcated 'habits of order and industry, forethought and forbearance, cheerfully and steadily persevered in for years'.[32] In both cases it was seen as important that the environment of the prisoner after release did not at once undermine the confidence of men who had not experienced complete freedom for many years. It was partly for this reason that the Directors of Convict Prisons were so unwilling to give up transportation to Western Australia, for the environment there was seen as especially conducive to newly reformed offenders. The society was a simple rural one, from which all the horrors of the urban slum were absent, and in addition there was work available. It was asserted that 'due principally to the absence of temptation and the certainty of being punished with promptitude' transportees avoided the commission of crime and many of them became established and respected members of society.[33] The colony formed an excellent final stage for rubbing off any rough edges which might have survived the reformatory discipline of the convict prison. However, this vision of newly reformed man receiving his fullest opportunities in a vast and pure new colonial world was greatly disappointed by the decline and eventual demise of transportation. For this reason much of the enthusiasm for aftercare in the late-1850s was centred on facilitating the emigration of ex-convicts through the prisoners' aid societies of London and Birmingham with which the Directors of Convict Prisons maintained a close relationship. For example, by the end of 1862, nearly nine hundred of those who were friendless and yet had shown clear signs of reformation were assisted to emigrate,[34] and Jebb himself argued strongly that convicts released without some benevolent and concerned authority were placed under severe strain because 'every man's hand would be against him'. Jebb maintained that aftercare societies were 'a connecting link between the prisoner and society' which gave the prisoner familiar security and supervision in a cold new world from which he had been so long absent[35] and were necessary because the colonies were apparently no longer available.

Lastly, the rigorous hard labour and spartan simplicity of the convict prison was promoted on the ground that it reformed the physique of the offender. This was seen as especially important because it was believed that the physical condition of criminals had been weakened by the insanitary conditions in which they lived and the intemperate course of their lives. Matthew Davenport Hill, echoing Thomas Beames, insisted that the health of the poorer classes was gradually being destroyed by their environment and the vices to which this gave birth.[36] He spoke of 'heavy and poisonous' atmospheres.[37] foul sanitation and crowded lodging houses as creating a 'deluge of misery and vice'.[38] This was especially relevant, for contemporary physicians believed strongly that there was an interaction between mind and body; in a lethargic, declining body whose 'vital powers' were being allowed to wither, food was not properly assimilated. As 'the vital action of the body'[39] declined, the mind became depraved, vapid and filled with a sullen desire for excitement.

Dr W. Guy, the medical superintendent of Millbank, was one of those who argued that a prison regime requiring fresh air, hard labour and a 'due and scientific combination of nitrogenous food such as milk and cheese with other kinds of food' must produce a higher 'tone of vitality' among prisoners, a striking physical improvement so that the mind housed within the body would become sharper, more vigorous, more alive as the body improved and regained its full health.[40] The psychologist Sir Benjamin Brodie referred to 'the vast influence which the condition of the body has on the temper and even on the moral character'. He went on to point to the mental and moral effects of physical self indulgence: 'there is many a person in whom a muddled intellect and a peevish temper may be traced to a too great indulgence of the appetite — to eating more than the stomach can digest; to drinking a bottle or even half a pint of wine daily, and leading otherwise a lazy and luxurious life'.[41] The severe discipline, labour and controlled diet of the associated labour convict prison were thus seen as most important to physical reconstitution, and indeed the separation stage was at times criticised because it lacked the invigorating, exhausting activity of labour on public works.

Alexander Maconochie and the Marks System

The associationist theory of rewards, punishments and habituation as a basis of reformation was also at the heart of the work of Alexander Maconochie, a Royal Naval captain who from 1840 to 1845 had superintended transportees at the Norfolk Island penal establishment in Australia. He developed a system which he claimed would enlist the energies of prisoners more decisively than he believed to be the case either in spiritual reformist systems or stage reformism. Furthermore, this innovation would be suitable for the use in those county and borough prisons which had not adopted either system. In the first place, he offered a radical criticism of separation, arguing that mere instruction — whether spiritual, moral or intellectual — inevitably had little effect because it was detached from the impact of reality upon the individual. Men, he maintained, were primarily social beings learning from social experience: 'No example of ascetic discipline has proved morally beneficial. All the hermits and other persons have lost by separation. In fact I think God Almighty sent us into this world with social tastes and powers and if we allow these to rust they must become comparatively speaking impaired.'[42] Separation in particular might reduce men to sorrow and remorse but had no power to create permanent change. The instruction offered by spiritual reformists was thus detached from social experience, mere words, and, in any event, the prisoner had no freedom of movement or choices to make. As he put it in an early exposition of his system, 'a man issues from confinement like a child and like a child is swayed, coaxed . . . the mere feeling of helplessness which continued solitary imprisonment must produce is enervating'. Instead, he urged that since criminal behaviour was the result of surrounding social circumstances, if these could be changed such 'exhibitions of character' would be altered. He sought to discover a system of discipline which would invariably lead the convict to direct his energies towards goals desired by the prison yet without involving 'degradation'. That merely created vindictiveness; instead there should be 'an enlarged interest, or feeling of benevolence . . . It is a mistake . . . to seek reform by making vice painful, instead of making virtue pleasing and advantageous'. In associationist terms, once the behaviour–reward link was established, the repetition of the desired behaviour would lead eventually to 'many evil passions and propensities . . . for ever laid aside'.[43]

Maconochie went on to analyse the problems of convict prison stage reformism. In his view this failed to 'imitate the state of society in free life as closely as possible'.[44] He insisted that it did not sufficiently enlist a man's dedication and energy towards making choices about securing more desirable experience, and hence the formation of new ideas about conduct and attitude was impaired. To Maconochie, this failure resulted from the tendency of all prisons to use time sentences which must expire at a given point laid down by the court. Even in convict prisons which, with tickets of leave, came closest to his proposed model, Maconochie emphasised that the convict, knowing that he would be fed, clothed and eventually released early if he was obedient, submitted inertly to the process. He disbelieved Jebb's view that tickets of leave and class promotion created positive effort and dedication within the prisoner, and claimed that the convict learned merely from them how to obtain advantage with the minimum possible effort (in other words, negatively, to avoid bad reports). In county and borough prisons, moreover, 'the time sentence . . . is . . . whiled away in any manner the most easy or the most gratifying by indolence, idleness, self indulgence, prurient thought, word or act, pretended sickness or the like'.[45] For convict and local prisons alike, the lesson taught was that the minimum effort, or indeed actual effortlessness, secured comfort, ease and pleasure, with the result that the defective overall perceptions of the criminal, which it ought to be the aim of the system to alter, were actually reinforced. Prisoners must therefore be placed in a situation where they could learn to make virtuous choices which inevitably reaped pleasure and reward, to commit their efforts to those choices, and the entire prison must be based upon this: 'my endeavour would be to make the whole lives of the prisoners a religious lesson by bringing good motives to bear upon the performance of their duty'.[46] The task of the reformer was therefore not to instruct people in truths of existence but to oblige them to experience those truths so that they made the necessary association between experience and sensation to form the desired idea, comprehending that their own effort was an essential prerequisite for pleasure-giving action.

The proposal, then, was that time sentences be abandoned, being inherently flawed in that they were a denial of reality. In life neither the minimum of effort nor an entire lack of industry secures reward or comfort. In place of them, Maconochie suggested that prisoners be sentenced to earn a defined number of marks, to be meticulously awarded by staff, in a prison from which release would be substantially delayed unless they were earned. In addition, all comforts and all but the very lowest diet would have to be earned by marks gained by performance of all the tasks required, 'personal demeanour, kind of employment, diligence, chaplain's report, schoolmaster's report'[47] etc. The prisoner would have to take decisions about use of his earned marks which he would also forfeit for misdemeanour. In consequence, the entire energies of the prisoner would be harnessed to success in all the tasks required of him, because his predicament and release date would wholly depend upon his own efforts. The prisoners would learn that 'exertion and good conduct'[48] were inevitably associated with reward and pleasure and they would go out with 'habits and . . . intentions and views founded upon those . . . full of ambition and a desire to rise:'[49] 'an inseparable connection in the mind of the prisoner between industry and self denial and advantage to himself' would thus have been established.[50]

Maconochie argued that this system exactly enforced those rules of conduct and habits of mind which were required for individual advancement within society which could not result without energy and effort being devoted by the individual to his own progress.[51] He maintained that adversity was only overcome permanently when the will of the individual was wholeheartedly engaged in his own improvement.[52] This could most successfully be achieved when the feelings and mind were impressed with an indelible association between experience and pleasure as a result of effort in a virtuous direction and the idea that such effort should be repeated until eventually the convict would emerge from this artificial replication of reality adjusted to an entirely different view of the sources of pleasure and pain. Furthermore, the prisoners themselves could be given responsibility for ensuring maximum effort on the part of each other by allowing marks to be earned or forfeited by groups of individuals, thus again ensuring an imitation of 'the nature of social relations'.[53]

Maconochie claimed that even the most stubborn and defiant prisoner would surrender to the marks system and allow the process of change to begin, because there was no choice but to commit energy and effort to ameliorating his situation and winning freedom. In the work and the instruction (which he did not wholly exclude but attention to which was marked, like all else) new 'knowledge and skill'[54] would be learned which would be of practical value after release. But the most important reformatory basis was the associationist psychological redirection of attitude and behaviour and for the success of this it did not much matter to Maconochie whether the prisoners were young and new to crime or well experienced in conventional prisons. Regarding old criminal contacts, 'they will be raised for the most part above danger from contact with any of their old confederates. They will have learnt to despise their seductions'.[55] As M. D. Hill explained, the desire to act well overall would be 'implanted in the mind of the prisoner' who would thereafter 'yearn after good instead of evil and by so training his habits as that he should be able to give effect to his new aspirations' he would acquire 'some faculty of action or endurance not possessed before'.[56] In the initial early struggles with himself, in the steady steps towards mastery of his old inclinations, the subsequent persistent effort to win marks, swift obedience to staff recording and assessing his individual progress, and in energetic effort and expectation of reward by endeavour, the prisoner would be permanently influenced by new experiences which 'expensive and effeminate'[57] separation could not give. As Charles Pearson, one of Maconochie's chief supporters and a Member of Parliament, put it: 'I propose that he shall be fed the zero diet of the gaol, water and coarse bread . . . all mankind are influenced by two motives; the one is a desire to provide for their present wants and the other is to secure future independence. I want to implant these motives in the prisoner so that after release he will still carry the force of those motives along with him.'[58] To Maconochie and Pearson this plan merely established in artificial form the unchangeable discipline, 'founded upon the word of God as given to mankind both in the Old and New Testaments',[59] that he who exerted himself would be rewarded and delivered and that prolonged experience of this would permanently change ideas of conduct.

Certain aspects of the marks system, as will later be shown, were in fact put into effect in a number of English prisons but they were also adapted for use by the Irish convict prison system in an attempt to overcome the inert progress through the various stages of convict prison described by Maconochie. In Ireland in the late-1850s and early-1860s, to the familiar pattern of separation, associated rigorous labour and classes, was added a system of intermediate imprisonment as well as active supervision of convicts released on tickets of leave.[60] At each stage marks were awarded for positive effort. Sir Walter Crofton, Director of the Irish Convict Prisons stated, 'Each man realises his progress . . . You see recorded very carefully a man's shortcomings and in what point he has failed. It is a record of character which I think is very useful . . . [marks] are of the utmost value . . . they are the means of acting upon the man as an individual and of realising to him his own position and his own means of progress. I know of no other way in which you can equally produce that effect upon him.'[61] At the two intermediate prisons at Lusk and Smithfield the reorientation of the convicts was tested by allowing them considerable freedom to work in nearby villages or towns (with officers present). They were able to spend earnings on such luxuries as tobacco as 'a test of the character of these people and it is a very good test . . . there has been a great deal of self denial exercised to my knowledge by a large number of the men'.[62] The emphasis was upon behaviour which gained marks rather than avoidance of bad reports as in English convict prisons, and the officers were required to mark all aspects of behaviour from month to month in order to pass individuals from one stage to the next. Supporters held that it was in this requirement for positive action by the use of marks that it was most sharply distinguished from the English convict prisons, although of course this was hotly disputed by Jebb and other members of that service.

There were in fact a number of substantial differences between the two systems (for example, in Ireland a penal, not spiritual reformist, initial phase of separation and intermediate prisons), but the two sharpest differences were the use of marks and the supervision of licensees in Ireland. In Dublin the lecturer of the convicts cited earlier, J. Organ, sought to persuade those convicts who were believed to have been reformed to emigrate, and he arranged this for them, but for others he carefully organised employment and subsequently made fortnightly visits to the men and their employers. 'I always lay the facts clearly before the employers because if I were not straightforward with them and I was once detected I should never be able to show my face again . . . no man has relapsed into crime whose relapse has not been foretold by me'.[63] Organ patiently developed relationships with potential employers and vigilantly watched the progress of convicts on tickets of leave: sometimes 'I do not like the way in which this man is going on. He may have too smooth appearance for a hard working man or he may be lounging about or I may find him at home when he should be out working or out when he should be in'.[64] Furthermore, until such time as the ticket of leave expired, the man might be recalled for failing to adhere to the licence conditions so the emphasis upon positive effort rather than inert avoidance continued to the very end. The results were said to be spectacular and indeed 'I have never seen greater anxiety or eagerness displayed to improve themselves by men of the non criminal class than among the men of Smithfield and Lusk[65] . . . [they] feel throughout their detention that their advancement depends on themselves through the active exercise of qualities opposed to those which have led to their imprisonment'.[66]

This system was of course substantially different from Maconochie's plan (it was, for example, a time sentence system) but it nevertheless attracted its panegyrists such as Mary Carpenter[67] and others. They drew attention to the fact that, amidst many other advantages, marks enabled the staff to gain a rapid and intimate knowledge of the individual and they could shape their efforts accordingly. In addition, the greater freedom in association offered in the intermediate stage was 'an almost self acting operation of well devised moral machinery'[68] in which staff would be able to assess the behaviour of men under the greatest temptation and thus gain a true appreciation of readiness for release. Because the interest of the prisoner was identical to that of the staff, a remarkable degree of trust was said to exist between staff and prisoners at Lusk and Smithfield, where the normal equipment of truncheons and chains was absent. In this adaptation of the marks system, as in its pure theory, the emphasis was upon effort and rationality. As the London prison explorer Hepworth Dixon remarked '[Maconochie has] succeeded in taming the hitherto tameless, making the savage gentle and calling out human feelings from bosoms long dead to the amenities of life.'[69]

One of the most influential supporters of marks and 'progessive stages of imprisonment' as a basis of reformation was Matthew Davenport Hill, cited earlier, who consistently emphasised the tendency of such systems to stimulate effort and commitment to improvement among prisoners. To Hill it was self-evident that rewards won as a result of labour undertaken, an opportunity to improve diet by expending marks earned, yet a strong inducement to self-denial by alternative use of such marks to win an earlier freedom would steadily build anew the character of the prisoner. He compared personal reformation with the art of learning to swim and he emphasised that the inevitability of recoil of consequence of behaviour upon the prisoner whilst in prison would compel him to develop a long-term capacity to sustain effort in newly acquired competence so that at last, as with all men learning new tasks and abilities, after the initial plunge and struggle an ability 'for keeping our heads above the surface' is learned. Because stages and marks were closer to the realities of life he eventually came to believe that separation was akin to instructing a prisoner in swimming whilst he was on dry land.[70]

In these kinds of system the staff were crucial to successful operation and it was assumed that they would be rational, benevolent, humane men whose virtuous and dedicated commitment to the prisoners would lead naturally to obedience, trust and conciliation. Such staff must record effort justly, explain the reasoning behind the system, engage in rational, patient and detailed discussion and work closely with the prisoner. The latter 'is thus trained to see that, in exerting himself to do his best, he is directly promoting his own interest, and instead of acting in antagonism to the authorities he learns to work with them knowing that by so doing he is working for himself'.[71] Matthew Hill expressed this aspiration in his report of the remarks of a German prison governor to him after that official had constructed a prison regime carefully based on rewards and punishments. 'I tell [the prisoner] that I am his friend and not his enemy . . . I explain to him the rules of the house and tell him that they are all calculated for the improvement of the prisoners, that if he will be my friend I shall be his, and that suffering and misery will overtake him here only in consequence of his own fault. The rudest natures . . . can scarcely resist such an appeal. The big tears often roll down cheeks that were never met with weeping before and I soon make them feel that my words are not speeches but the expression of actual things . . . should the new convict . . . begin to behave ill to his fellow convicts they soon check him and set him right . . . they say to him, Herr Obermaier is our friend and we shall not allow you to act contrary to the rules of the house'.[72]

References

1. *1st RCGPP*, PP, 1843, vol. XXIX, p. 5.
2. Ibid., p. 5.
3. Ibid.
4. *RDMCP* by Lt. Col. Jebb for 1851, PP, 1852–3, vol. LI, p. 18.
5. *Report on the Discipline and Construction of Portland Prison*, Lt. Col. Jebb, PP, 1850, vol. XXIX, pp. 11, 12, 27.
6. Ibid., p. 28.
7. *16 & 17 Vict. Cap 99; 20 & 21 Vict., Cap 3.*
8. *RDMCP 1851*, Lt. Col. Jebb, PP, 1852–3, vol. LI, p. 39.
9. *Minutes of Evidence Penal Servitude Acts Commission*, PP, 1863, vol. XXI, p. 93.
10. *First Report from the SC on Transportation*, PP, 1856, vol. XVII, p. 4.
11. Ibid., p. 23.
12. *Report of the Penal Servitude Acts Commissioners*, PP, 1863, vol. XXI, p. 12.
13. Ibid., p. 15.
14. Ibid., Minutes of Evidence, p. 59.
15. *RDMCP*, Lt. Col. Jebb, PP, 1854, vol. XXXIII, p. 50.
16. *General Report on the Convict Prisons 1860–61*, Maj. Gen. Sir Joshua Jebb, PP, 1862, vol. XXV, p. 9.
17. *RDMCP*, Lt. Col. Jebb, PP, 1854, vol. XXXIII, p. 15.
18. *RDMCP 1851*, PP, 1852–3, vol. LI, p. 47.
19. *Report on the Discipline of the Convict Prisons and Operation of the Act, 16 & 17 Vict., Cap 99*, Lt. Col. Jebb, PP, 1854–5, vol. XXV, p. 7.
20. *RDMCP 1851*, PP, 1852–3, vol. LI, p. 47.
21. Alexander Thomson, *Punishment and Prevention*, p. 68.
22. M. D. Hill, *Suggestions for the Repression of Crime*, Parker, 1857, pp. 490–1.
23. *General Report on the Convict Prisons*, Maj. Gen. Sir Joshua Jebb, PP, 1862, vol. XXV, pp. 106–7. Jebb is quoting Bishop Butler, *Analogy of Religion, Natural and Revealed*.
24. Ibid., p. 106.
25. *RDMCP 1850*, Lt. Col. Jebb, PP, 1851, vol. XXVIII, p. 49.
26. *Report on the Discipline and Construction of Portland Prison*, Lt. Col. Jebb, PP, 1850, vol. XXIX, pp. 120–1.

27. *RDCP 1850*, PP, 1851, vol. XXVIII, p. 28; *RDCP 1851*, PP, 1852, vol. XXIV, p. 161; *RDCP 1853*, PP, 1854, vol. XXXIII, p. 140.

28. *RDCP 1854*, PP, 1854–5, vol. XXV, p. 22, Pentonville Report.

29. *RDCP 1857*, PP, 1857–8, vol. XXIX, p. 213.

30. *RDMCP 1850*, Lt. Col. Jebb, PP, 1851, vol. XXVIII, pp. 13–14.

31. *First Report from the SC on Transportation*, PP, 1856, vol. XVII, pp. 112–13.

32. *Report on the Discipline of the Convict Prisons and Operation of the Act, 16 & 17 Vict., Cap 99*, PP, 1854–5, vol. XXV, p. 27.

33. *Minutes of Evidence taken before the Penal Servitude Acts Commission*, PP, vol. XXI, p. 187.

34. Ibid., Evidence of William Ranken.

35. *Report on the Discipline of the Convict Prisons and Operation of the Act, 16 & 17 Vict., Cap 99*, PP, 1854–5, vol. XXV, p. 29.

36. M. D. Hill, *Suggestions*, pp. 301–2.

37. Ibid., p. 311.

38. Ibid., pp. 311, 328.

39. *Report from the SC of the House of Lords on the Present State of Discipline in Gaols and Houses of Correction*, PP, 1863, vol. IX, pp. 85, 82.

40. Ibid., p. 351.

41. Sir Benjamin Brodie, *Psychological Enquiries — In a Series of Essays*, Longman, 2nd edn, 1855, vol. 1, pp. 75, 76.

42. *Report from the SC on Prison Discipline*, PP, 1850, vol. XVII, p. 427.

43. Captain A. Maconochie, *The Mark System of Prison Discipline*, Harrison, 1855, p. 17; Captain A. Maconochie, *Thoughts on Convict Management*, Macdougall, 1838, pp. 67, 64, 93, 100, 22.

44. *Report from the SC of the House of Lords appointed to inquire into the execution of the Criminal Law*, PP, 1847, vol. VII, p. 103.

45. Captain Maconochie, *The Mark System*, p. 4.

46. *Commons SC on Prisons*, PP, 1850, vol. XVII, p. 423.

47. Captain A. Maconochie, *Prison Discipline*, Harrison, 1856, p. 1.

48. *SC of the House of Commons on Prisons*, PP, 1850, vol. XVII, p. 415.

49. Ibid., p. 421.

50. Ibid., p. 459.

51. Ibid., pp. 458–9.

52. Ibid., p. 448.

53. Ibid., p. 461.

54. Captain Maconochie, *The Mark System*, 1855, p. 18.

55. Ibid., p. 22.

56. M. D. Hill, *Suggestions*, pp. 251, 284, 541.

57. C. Pearson, *What is to be done with our Criminals?*, Hall & Virtue, 1857, p. 16.

58. *Report from the SC on Prison Discipline*, PP, 1850, vol. XVII, p. 531.

59. C. Pearson, *What is to be done?*, p. 22.

60. See *Minutes of Evidence taken before the Penal Servitude Acts Commission*, PP, 1863, vol. XXI, Evidence of Sir Walter Crofton, pp. 252–302.

61. Ibid., 1863, vol. XXI, pp. 261, 260.

62. Ibid., pp. 270, 271.

63. Ibid., pp. 377, 375.

64. Ibid., p. 375.

65. Ibid., p. 387.

66. Sir W. Crofton, *Convict Systems and Transportation*, Ridgway, 1863, p. 7.

67. Mary Carpenter, *Our Convicts*, Longman, 1864, vol. 2, pp. 174–81.

68. Four Visiting Justices of the West Riding Prison at Wakefield, *Observations on the Treatment of Convicts in Ireland*, Simpkin, 2nd edn, 1863, p. 27.

69. W. Hepworth Dixon, *The London Prisons*, p. 12.

70. M. D. Hill, *Suggestions*, pp. 539, 541.

71. Four Visiting Justices of the West Riding, *Observations*, p. 67.

72. M. D. Hill, *Suggestions*, p. 580.

4
Variations and Problems in Reformatory Practice 1840–1865

Groundwork

A glance at the voluminous literature produced in the mid-nineteenth century about reformation of prisoners, tempts one to conclude that the prisons must have in the main been brought to such reformatory excellence that they did indeed endeavour to suppress vigorously dissident attitudes, immorality and crime by the means outlined.[1] That impression is further encouraged by the belief held by, amongst others, Bishop Blomfield that the new efficient social institutions of Victorian Britain had led to the disappearance of 'the spirit of insubordination and tumult . . . from amongst us'.[2] Although it was well known that substantial problems could arise in new prisons, whether with personnel or technology (such as bursting of central heating pipes,[3] blocking of lavatories in separate cells, severe cold owing to unglazed cells), in general it appeared to many that there had been a substantial movement towards the reformatory models either of separation or silence. All 'whistling, singing or loud or disturbing noise of any sort'[4] were banished therein, as were all earthly pleasure and lightness of conduct: be ye sure your sins will find you out — the eyes of the Lord are in every place, model prisons as places of mournful, severe, ordered reformation.

Despite the comparative ease with which one can analyse and describe penal reformatory theories and illustrate their practice, a deeper understanding is necessary of the actual changes in British prisons between 1840 and 1865. At once it becomes apparent that this exploration will produce a more varied picture. For one thing, experience of penal and more general social administration in the

91

late-twentieth century suggests that practice at local level often differs substantially from the intentions of theorists, legislators and propagators of new approaches, and that as policy and theory work their way down to local level they are often profoundly influenced by local interest groups, local priorities and particular problems which exist in county or city. Certainly modern experience warns us to be ready for substantial adjustments to the pure approaches of theorists and the prescripts of the state.

If this is true of modern Britain, which possesses sophisticated bureaucratic structures, means of very fast transport, instant communication of information, it is likely to have been even more so during the years 1840 to 1865 and a cursory glance at the local institutions of social policy confirms this expectation. For example, although a central body was set up in London in 1834 to supervise the administration of the Poor Law by the new Boards of Guardians, local politics, problems and interests revised much of the actual shape of Poor Law administration where regimes in workhouses and infirmaries perhaps bore only a slender resemblance either to the aspirations of the investigating Royal Commissioners of 1832 to 1834 or the London supervising authority created to implement their report. Of reformatory prison discipline it must be said at once that local idiosyncracy was a notable feature.

The degree to which these theories were generally applied has been the subject of recent dispute amongst authorities on Victorian prisons, some of whom have tended to see reformatory aspirations as mere frothy rhetoric applied perhaps in Pentonville and Reading but little further, whilst others have argued a much more general application. Thus Michel Foucault and Michael Ignatieff in his earlier work invited us to accept that the disciplinary system of regulated order within Western European prisons (heavily dependent upon reformatory theory) was firmly in place by 1850; indeed Foucault — in the manner we have come to expect of him — decided that the date of the 'completion of the carceral system' was the official opening of Mettray Reformatory on 22 January 1842.[5] Ignatieff gave the clear impression that during the years 1780–1850 there occurred the steady growth of the penitentiary model which, by the latter date, glowered balefully across the realm. On the other hand, as Ignatieff himself later acknowledged,[6] (conceding perhaps too much of his original position in the process) there has been some recent research by scholars into local changes in mid-nineteenth-century prisons and these have implied that local policy was highly idiosyncratic and, in the case of one very important county (Lancashire) there was limited emphasis upon reformation.[7] We will return to these writers later, but on a more general level assertions and counter-assertions abound. Thus Sean McConville asserted that after 1850, following a decade of separatist zeal, 'the reformatory objective in penal policy underwent an almost total eclipse', earlier remarking that even before 1850 'the eclipse of the separate system' had occurred.[8] Yet only a short time before, another authority on Victorian prisons, Heather Tomlinson, remarked that by 1850 over fifty local prisons had been reconstructed or altered to institute the separate system — 'Pentonville and her grim brood were hatched' — maintaining that the larger prisons between 1835 and 1877 were based upon the desire 'to reform and better their charges' with separation being an 'established principle of both local and convict prison discipline'.[9] Indeed, somewhat tangentially, she compared mid-century prisons favourably with hotels and pointed to their central heating, running water and bathing facilities as especially noteworthy.[10]

There are some points which must be made before embarking upon the daunting task of assessing reformatory practice throughout British prisons. These relate to the general changes in most prisons during the years in question. First, by 1850 the convict prison sector with its five walled institutions, rented cells and five surviving hulks was holding some 6,000 convicts; by 1865 in eleven walled institutions and no hulks it was holding nearly 7,000.[11] In English and Welsh local prisons on the date of a return in 1844, just under 16,000 were held, at the beginning of 1857 just over 17,000, and at the beginning of 1867 17,500.[12] However, although numbers held in prisons between 1840 and 1865 did not greatly alter, some important changes in the shape of prisons did occur. In the convict sector, prison hulks were gradually phased out in favour of walled establishments so that percentage numbers of convicts held in them prior to transportation declined from 69 per cent in 1840 to around 33 per cent in 1847 down to the destruction of the last hulk in Britain in 1857.[13] The new convict establishments at Chatham and Portsmouth, for example, were built to hold convicts who had earlier been placed on hulks and who were, as explained earlier, in any event now serving the new sentence of penal servitude.

With regard to local prisons, a striking feature of the period was their reduction in number. It is in fact very difficult to be precise about numbers of prisons in the early-nineteenth century, although Sean McConville reports estimates for England and Wales which hover around the 300 mark between 1812 and 1833.[14] Some ten years later the figure for England and Wales had fallen to 217 (which includes the three convict prisons)[15] and by 1856 the number had further reduced to 121 English local prisons, 14 Welsh and 41 Irish.[16] This decline in numbers continued until the Prison Commission within a year of its taking office decisively reduced the 113 prisons which it had inherited in England and Wales to 68.[17]

The overall daily local prison average population remained fairly constant between 1840 and 1865 at between 16,000 and 18,000 in England and Wales, and this figure included debtors (around 11 per cent on the 1844 return date,[18] 10 per cent of all commitments to local prisons in 1857, 8 per cent of all in 1867[19]) as well as prisoners held on remand or committed to a higher court (24.6 per cent of all commitments to local prisons in 1857, 19.3 per cent in 1867).[20] Furthermore, it must be noted that a large number of actual sentences to imprisonment were for very short periods by modern standards — 30.7 per cent of prison sentences passed by magistrates' courts in 1857 were for 14 days or under, 34.3 per cent between 14 days and one month; 42.4 per cent and 30.4 per cent respectively for 1867.[21] This fact will become important as discussion of reformatory practice gets under way.

Local Application of Reformatory Practice

It is clear that there was not a symmetrical set of reformatory approaches in all the county and borough prisons. In England complaints of reformatory inefficiency regarding borough prisons remained persistent. The Inspector of Prisons for the South West (and later the entire South) John Perry lamented in 1850 that 'the only remedy . . . is to abolish these small prisons and send the borough prisoners to the county prison',[22] pointing out that in a number of them, such as Penzance, Bradninch, Rye, Falmouth and Faversham, prisoners were crowded together under inadequate discipline.[23] A colleague, the Inspector for the North, Herbert Voules, bluntly declared 'I should like to level many of them to the ground and rebuild them. It is impossible with some of the present buildings to have any good system of discipline carried out.'[24] Admittedly, inspectors such as Whitworth Russell and William Crawford (whose first report was almost entirely dedicated to a bitter condemnation of London's Newgate) or John Perry held strong preconceptions about borough prisons and conducted protracted campaigns against them, often vilifying what reformatory approaches they did apply.[25] Nevertheless, many of the larger city prisons were built or rebuilt and administered plainly according to reformatory theory, as at Manchester, Leeds, Holloway (for London) or Liverpool.[26] At these institutions spiritual engagement, separate cells, occupational training and education were developed, although it is clear that in many of the smaller borough prisons reformatory practice was often a good deal less in keeping with the wishes of the theorists. In many areas boroughs chose to close their prisons and agreed with the county magistrates to lodge prisoners in their prisons — a tendency which contributed strongly to the reduced numbers of prisons.

As one turns to the largest sector of the system, the English county Gaols and Houses of Correction, the reformatory presence is much plainer throughout. Yet, here again there was unevenness, and official prejudice must also be taken into account. Crawford and Russell were antagonistic to Coldbath Fields because it was a silent system county prison, and they were followed twenty years later in this by Perry.[27] Between and within English counties, almost all of which maintained a number of prisons, a good deal of variation in reformatory progress and practice could be seen. In most there was a growing tendency for active chaplains to seek to engage prisoners on an individual basis, increasingly separate cellular architecture, new prison schools and schoolmasters. In others these elements were less obvious and in a few there seemed little change since pre-separation days. For example at Springfield Gaol and House of Correction (for Essex),[28] Chester and Norwich Castle prisons,[29] Shrewsbury,[30] Stafford,[31] Exeter,[32] Bodmin,[33] Devizes, and Wandsworth and Horsemonger Lane (for Surrey) county prisons,[34] considerable development of a spiritual reformist/cellular-isolation regime had occurred by 1860, even if practice in these prisons was not entirely in keeping with pure theory (associated labour or exercise being retained, for example). In other areas the magistrates implemented the silent system, as at Dorchester County Prison[35] or in parts of Wakefield in the early part of the period.[36] Middlesex House of Correction for women at Westminster, or Maidstone County Gaol and House of Correction,[37] or Oakham County Prison in Rutland[38] were examples of prisons where it seemed that there had been no such alterations, retaining the traditional association and lack of reformatory discipline which had prevailed in the earlier years of the nineteenth century; inspectors persistently lamented this failure to change.

It is clear that most counties in England were influenced by the reformatory endeavour in their prison arrangements but also obvious that they tended to adapt in accordance with their own wishes or needs. By 1860 the county prisons of England as a whole had undoubtedly moved significantly towards reformism; typical of these institutions were active chaplains, prison schools, ranges of separate cells, rigorous prevention of communication, purpose-built chapels and cubicled treadmills. Only in a few prisons were prisoners entirely confined to cells or Crawford and Russell's notion of voluntary labour practised. If one looks at such counties as Cambridgeshire, Lincolnshire, Lancashire, Cheshire or Norfolk,[39] despite the unevenness or diversity which is plain, emphasis upon these features of reformism is clear. By 1860 even the recalcitrant Corporation of London (which had for decades steadfastly resisted prison reformists) had undertaken the reconstruction of that great baneful example of unreformed prisons, Newgate, to enable separate cellular confinement to be enforced.[40] Again one must beware of exaggeration, for even in large county institutions inspectors found much to criticise — the lack of a schoolmaster at Salisbury County Prison in the 1850s or bad architectural construction at Salford New Bailey in 1859.[41]

Turning now to Wales, there were persistent criticisms of Welsh county prisons, right up to 1860, that they remained in a state more typical of an earlier era of prison discipline and substantially lacked reformatory approaches. In Cardiganshire County Prison 'all the prisoners are associated and are under no supervision . . . while at the treadmill', tobacco was permitted in Caernarvonshire County Prison, unsupervised association led to plans for escape at Montgomery, with undisciplined corruption at Dolgelly.[42] Further south, however, 1860 saw both Cardiff and Swansea county prisons converted to separation.[43] In general, the Home Office officials seemed to feel that there were many central and northern Welsh magistrates who were unwilling to accept English versions of reformatory discipline or the expense of these and preferred to maintain their original ways of conducting prisons.

This was much less the case in Scotland. In 1839, responding to the reports of Frederic Hill (the Inspector for that county) and to severe earlier criticism of Scottish prisons, radical changes had been wrought in the administration of prisons, which had been vested almost entirely in the Royal Burghs prior to 1839. The centralising Board of Directors of Scottish Prisons, set up in 1839, has been discussed in a recent article[44] and there is no doubt that, quite apart from the general central penitentiary at Perth, reformatory theory had become an important part of Scottish prisons. Nevertheless — once again in contrast to pure separatist theory — these also emphasised severe cellular hard labour as part of separation. The Board of Directors greatly reduced the number of prisons in Scotland and, through the new county prison boards responsible to the central board, pressed for separation, religious instruction and education firmly across Scotland. The aim was that 'for each county in Scotland' there should be one main prison 'on the separate system'[45] and within ten years the number of prisons had been halved from 170 to a mere 85 — in Aberdeenshire a major modernisation programme was undertaken at Aberdeen County Prison and seven small ones were closed in 1847; in Perthshire there were four closures and two new replacement prisons in the same year; in Forfarshire entire reconstruction of Dundee County Prison took place;[46] in Ayrshire 1854 saw Ayr and Kilmarnock prisons rebuilt and smaller ones closed; a great separate system prison was opened in Glasgow, while in Caithness a reconstituted prison at Wick now catered for the entire county.[47] Even here inert resistance to central influence might be prolonged. The local county board at Perth — whose prison stood near to the penitentiary — and that at Edinburgh were slow to engage in reconstruction, whilst in the outlying Shetlands and the Orkney Isles the prisons of Lerwick and Kirkwall were seen as inadequate.[48] Here then, despite the firm deliberate promotion of uniform separation, inequalities in standards survived, although by 1860 separation was plainly the basis of almost all the larger prisons which modelled themselves on Perth Penitentiary. As John Kincaid, the prison inspector, remarked: 'while undergoing separate confinement they are more respectful in their manner and contented with their treatment, make more progress in their education and are more industrious in their work . . . the separate system has a tendency to lead them to serious reflection on their past misconduct'.[49]

Lastly, quite apart from the Irish convict sector, there was evident a movement towards separation and moral and religious instruction in Irish county and town prisons, as well as unevenness in its application. In 1860, of the 42 town and county prisons, complete separation was enforced in 9, while in a further 18 substantial elements had been introduced, together with the familiar energetic and influential chaplain, libraries, education and cell visiting. In the remainder, traditional association and absence of such reformatory discipline prevailed.[50]

It is clear that there was substantial variation in reformatory practice in the prisons of this period and indeed the mosaic quality of them was emphasised by Hepworth Dixon in his description of the five different regime types which were either practised or advocated for prisons in 1850.[51] Furthermore, within a single prison there were different regimes for various classes of prisoners, so that short-term offenders (such as vagrants) were subjected to deterrent non-reformatory treadmill labour without education and with dormitory accommodation, whilst longer-term offenders were subjected to the familiar regime of cellular isolation (at least by night), instruction, trade instruction and cellular visits of chaplain and governor.

As far as the convict prisons were concerned, before the demise of transportation there was a very strong reformatory emphasis at Pentonville, Portland and Parkhurst, as well as in the rented cells of such county prisons as Wakefield and Bath where pure separation was practised. Even Millbank — by 1850 used as a depot for transportees who were subsequently selected for allocation within the system according to perceived likelihood of reformation, age and physical condition — retained a good deal of its earlier reformatory practice. It had been compelled by pressure of numbers to adopt a mixed system of 600 in separation and the rest in silent association but Millbank prisoners continued to spend two half-days a week in schools run by nine schoolmasters and two schoolmistresses employed by the prison. They also attended daily religious services with two chaplains and a religious instructor, and learned various occupations such as tailoring, weaving and shoe-making (if in separation) under sixteen trade instructors.[52] Obviously, reformatory practice was at its most perfect in Pentonville where in the early days each prisoner was assessed on the basis of his 'proficiency' and subjected to one of three educational regimes in which he would receive two days' instruction per week. The 'third or most ignorant class' received 'scripture lessons, reading, explanation of words and sentences, arithmetic and geography', whilst the 'first class or the best informed' received 'scripture, Faith and Duty of a Christian, Geography, English grammar, mensuration and the higher branches of Arithmetic, Exercises in the British and Foreign School Book No. 4 containing lessons in history, elements of natural philosophy and subjects of general use and interest'. Although by 1850 the educational work at Pentonville had been reduced it remained the pre-eminent reformatory prison of England with two chaplains spending six hours every Sunday visiting prisoners in cells, very detailed occupational training, an extensive library and, at the heart of it all, the great cubicled chapel.[53] It ought to be reiterated, however, regarding the convict prison sector that before 1850 many were sent to the hulks prior to transportation rather than to Pentonville or Portland from Millbank. Despite the introduction of increased religious instruction and education on these in the 1840s, reformists of all persuasions considered them to lack reformatory facilities.

In the local prisons greater inequalities were evident and a number of recent studies have highlighted this. Lancashire, for example, was examined by Margaret De Lacy, who suggested that in fact 'prisons never quite became those machines for grinding men good that the reformers have claimed and the critics have charged',[54] and pointed to lack of separate cells, defective trade training, association and indiscipline among prisoners as contradicting the notions of Victorian prisons as regimented reformatory devices. However, much of her evidence is selected from the very early years of Victoria's reign. Plainly, about this early era she is right and a cursory glance at the reports of, say, Captain Williams, Inspector for the North and East, confirms this picture for the whole of his area.[55] Nevertheless Lancashire by the mid-1850s saw substantial movement towards separation in Manchester, Liverpool, Kirkdale and Preston, following reconstruction and reform. And again the reports of Herbert Voules, Inspector for the North and East confirm this as typical of his area.[56]

The fact is that the orderly, disciplinary, reformatory regimes did not become characteristic of the larger prisons before 1850 and that the seed sown by Russell and Crawford took a good ten years to harvest. Voules' report for 1852 provides a wealth of information about reformatory progress in his area which most strongly contradicts the view that all this talk of making rogues honest was mere rhetoric. At Knutsford House of Correction the women's wing was being extended, daily religious services were held, there was daily teaching by a salaried schoolmaster, all were interviewed by the chaplain on admission, discharge and application. At Salford House of Correction a schoolmaster taught daily for eight hours, those placed in separate confinement were visited by the chaplain, while over twenty industrial occupations were taught in the manufactory. On the other hand there remained the familiar treadmill and oakum picking and it is clear that for short-sentence prisoners the emphasis was upon severe deterrent shock and that the reformatory aspects were reserved for those serving longer sentences which would, according to reformatory theory, permit the personal changes to be achieved.[57] At Preston, those placed under separation (the longer-term prisoners) received the full range of cellular visits, the use of the Mimpriss educational system to teach the Gospel, four hours' schooling per week, a large library and an extensive manufactory wherein seven trades were taught. This regime was reserved for all serving over two months, the remainder being subjected to the silent system; at Wakefield the full reformatory system was aimed only at all serving over three months.[58]

Although in the early years of the Victorian era fragmentary elements of the later systems may be found in local prisons, it was not until 1850 and later, in amended form, that the subjection of longer-sentence prisoners to a reformatory regime of instruction, cellular isolation (at least by night), instruction in numeracy and literacy, religious exercises and occupational training became characteristic of many of the local county prisons in England and Scotland. Some of the large borough prisons became models of reformatory discipline: purpose-built separate-system prisons were exemplified by Liverpool, Leeds and Bristol, of which latter prison the governor remarked in 1863 that the prisoners never 'see each other', are subjected to a regime of a cubicled chapel and school rooms, daily services, schoolmasters and mistresses and thrice-weekly separate instruction in cells.[59]

The practice of educational instruction varied like all aspects of reformatory discipline. In the larger prisons by the early-1860s almost always there had been appointed a lecturer or teacher who had obtained the certificate awarded after pupil teacher apprenticeship training or as a result of attendance at a teacher training college. In the largest prisons there was often more than one teacher, whilst in the smaller prisons a chaplain, governor or warder undertook the instruction. This instruction tended to be offered to the longer-serving prisoners, although again this varied. In some institutions only the younger were taught, in others adults; sometimes teaching was done in individual cells, sometimes in chapels, sometimes in purpose-built cubicled school rooms so that each prisoner could see and hear the teacher but not his fellows. John Perry reckoned in 1863 that an hour of instruction a day for prisoners selected for education was by no means rare.[60] Whilst in local prisons education was more rudimentary than, say, at Chatham Convict Prison in the early-1860s, with its four teachers and half a day's schooling per week for all 1100 convicts,[61] the prison schoolmaster was by 1865 an established feature of the English county prisons; indeed, by 1850 the use of more highly educated prisoners as monitors had been phased out. Lastly, it ought to be noted that educational provision was almost always under the direction of the chaplain, whose duty was to ensure that schoolmasters and mistresses were teaching according to correct principles and were applying themselves energetically to their task.

One problematic aspect of reformation was the desire to train prisoners in a useful trade. In classic separate system theory this needed to be done in the cell so as to instil a love of labour because of the relief from boredom which would be felt, and in such prisons as Pentonville or Reading this was characteristic of trade training. However it is clear, as Janet Saunders has recently observed, that there were four main approaches to prison labour outside the convict sector in British prisons: the use of the non-productive hard labour machine (treadmill and crank),[62] the use of the hard labour machine to produce (treadmill to grind corn), lighter work concerned with production and involving the learning of a trade (shoemaking), and labour concerned with maintaining the prison or other prisons or nearby institutions (cleaning, laundering).

It seems to have been the case that for short-sentence prisoners the hard labour machine, which did not of course involve learning a trade, was popular, being easy to organise and to install and possessing a notable deterrent aspect. Prisoners serving longer sentences, however, were commonly engaged in occupational training; as with education, Victorian prison officials did not consider it worthwhile to waste their time endeavouring to teach the large numbers of men and women serving less than a few weeks a trade, also believing that the primary purpose of the short sentence was deterrent. At Leeds Borough Prison six trades were taught, whilst hard labour machines were seen as very suitable for short-term vagrants; at Beverley House of Correction there was a manufactory where mat-making, bookbinding, shoemaking and cloth work were undertaken but where also a treadmill was used. At Norwich Castle the treadmill again coexisted with such trades as carpentry, coopering and painting, whilst at Salford some 25 occupations were practised, though nearly a quarter (presumably recalcitrant and short-sentence prisoners) were set to the treadmill, crank or oakum picking.[63]

Clearly in some prisons it was considered that those with an order to hard labour ought to be placed on machines whilst in others the desire to make profit encouraged the establishment of large manufactories in which goods were produced — for example mat-making on looms.[64] In addition it was only very rarely indeed (Reading) that the original separatist dream of isolated prisoners begging for useful occupational instruction and employment in their cell became the basis of a prison's approach. Very often prisons tended to select those with special skills or with longer sentences and seek to use or to train them. Industrial labour was thus selectively made available — for example at Stafford County Prison, Wakefield, Norwich — partly on the basis of length of sentence. At Petworth the treadmill was reserved for recalcitrant or reconvicted men, a large number of occupations (mop- and mat-making, weaving, needlework) required of the rest.[65]

Occupational training, therefore, was by 1865 a feature of most of the larger prisons of England but it was usually selectively offered, undertaken in manufactories rather than cells and the amount of this activity had clearly increased since 1837. Nevertheless, it must also be remembered that large numbers of prisoners worked at maintaining the prisons and that in manufactories the emphasis was often on profit rather than reformation.[66] Indeed, bearing in mind the large proportion of short sentences, it is difficult to see occupational training as a particularly successful part of the reformatory presence in British prisons between 1840 and 1865, or to escape the conclusion that in many prisons (such as Coldbath Fields) the heavy dependence on the harsh work of oakum picking occurred not merely because such labour seemed suitably deterrent but because it was much easier to organise and required no complicated instruction. Yet some governors were enthusiastic about their prison manufactories and it would be wrong to dismiss this aspect of reformation as of negligible importance.

By 1856, of the 121 prisons 40 claimed implementation of separation and a further 43 claimed to operate substantial parts of the system.[67] Clearly the avoidance of contamination so essential to separation was, in practice, most hard to achieve; De Lacy pointed out that pressure of numbers in Lancashire led to shared cells (anathema to Crawford and Russell) and to the overcrowding which occurred at Preston and other prisons.[68] What seems to have happened in Britain generally was that for longer-term prisoners a reformatory approach was offered, involving not the full isolation required by Russell and Crawford but substantial measures of religious instruction, education, nocturnal separation as well as occupational training, whereas for the large numbers of short-sentence prisoners such attempts were not made. They were instead subjected to mechanical labour, dormitory accommodation (as at Coldbath Fields) and silence on the basis that this at least would prevent contamination and that for the most hopeful of them some reformatory effect might be experienced in line with George Chesterton's original elaboration of the reformatory aspects of the silent system.

The Making of Local Policy

It must be said at the outset that our knowledge of the way in which counties and boroughs responded to the reformatory aspirations of central government is rudimentary. It is often remarked by historians that more local research into detail of their field is needed and in the case of local formation of Victorian penal policy this is undoubtedly very necessary. However, even at this early stage it is possible to make some judgements which will doubtless be tested by the research students of the next decade but which do seem at present justified by the knowledge which we have.

In the first place there can be little doubt that the Inspectors of Prisons had considerable effect upon local magistrates. As mentioned earlier, all of them were engaged in detailed negotiation with the localities and in making recommendations and criticisms in the reports which they published annually. During the zenith of the inspectorate in the 1840s, when there were five of them, every prison in the country was more frequently visited and inspected than later, and there is no doubt that these examinations were detailed. Admittedly, with the later reduction of inspectors to two, the amount of inspection was reduced, yet right up to 1865 large numbers of prisons were examined each year and their regimes discussed in lengthy reports subsequently published by Parliament.

These inspectors, and Jebb in his capacity as Surveyor General of Prisons, appeared frequently in local policy discussion. In 1839, for example, the Chairman of Bedfordshire Quarter Sessions met

Whitworth Russell and Joshua Jebb for discussion about the erection of a new prison. Russell complained three years later that no action had been taken (the prison was in fact opened in 1849), whilst at Exeter Bisset Hawkins and his successor John Perry were engaged in negotiations with Exeter City Council about the borough prison, witnessing considerable conflict after Hawkins' conciliatory approach was replaced by the more zealous separatist stance of Perry.[69] Some of the inspectors seemed able to win over local aristocrats and industrialists by careful diplomacy (as did Frederic Hill in Scotland by his painstaking cultivation of important local figures), whilst others, such as Russell and Perry, often found that their intractable manner made many foes.

It is obvious that the inspectors and Jebb were viewed, whether apprehensively or otherwise, as substantial forces in penal policy making and they frequently attended local meetings in order to clarify, discuss or recommend changes which were under discussion. Thus in the 1840s Joshua Jebb attended Warwickshire Quarter Sessions to press the justices to erect a new prison,[70] and at around the same time he angered Russell and Crawford by dealing directly with the Buckinghamshire magistrates regarding a new prison at Aylesbury without consulting them.[71] Whatever the tensions between inspectors, they were by 1850 heavily involved in negotiation about local policy as well as in certifying new plans and cells as suitable, an aspect of their work which remained of importance right up to 1865 despite the reduction in their numbers.[72]

The new penal discourses arrived in counties and boroughs, which were of course complex social and political entities in which decisions made were often the result of prolonged manoeuvre and intrigue by interested parties. A recent penetrating study by Janet Saunders[73] regarding the institutional policy of the county of Warwick showed that its administration was late in adopting the separate system for not until 1861 was a new separation county prison erected at Warwick to hold the county prisoners. Separation had been the subject of much controversy among county justices and initially the landed aristocrats had supported its introduction because of the paternalist/charitable influencing aspects of it, whilst industrialists had opposed it. Separation was also opposed by magistrates from North Warwickshire because they had recently rebuilt Coventry Prison and they feared that the influence and importance of Coventry would suffer.[74] Although only a small core of magistrates was concerned with the matter, there was often an 'intense personal involvement with the total institution';[75] eventually the South Warwickshire magistrates, led by a local pro-separatist peer, were successful in their pressure to gain Quarter Sessions' support for a new prison. Here, then, conflict had been prolonged (with Peter Laurie and G. L. Chesterton from London seeking to influence events against separation). Local concerns about Coventry and rates increases had also played a part, whilst the pro-separatists had been forced to make concessions about the purity of the separation to be introduced.

In the borough of Exeter, by contrast, a most complicated situation developed as a result of the municipal reforms of the mid-1830s. Here a Conservative magistracy was confronted with a new Liberal council whose members were sympathetic to the new reformatory thrust of the inspectors. A dispute therefore ensued in the late-1830s about which body possessed the legal right to make rules for the borough prison: the borough Quarter Sessions or the council. Eventually, legal opinions had to be sought. The collapse of the Liberal council in 1840 was followed by over 70 years of Conservative government in Exeter and, in the end, after the Recorder of Exeter had begun a campaign for separation but the money had not been voted by the council to build a new prison, John Perry entered into prolonged conflict with the city. At last, a contract was signed with the new Devon County justices to place their prisoners in the new separate system prison to the north of the city.[76]

Local politics, interests, inertia and rates bills therefore played a great part in local prison policy, quite apart from the ideological appeal of the disciplinary systems. Janet Saunders suggested that magistrates with strong London contacts tended to possess a more cosmopolitan view of prison discipline (favouring separation)[77] but it ought not to be forgotten that the campaign headquarters for the silent system was Middlesex. Throughout the 1840s and 1850s, conflict between leading protagonists of each system was often conducted in a mood of bitter personal animosity and written polemic, with strong moves to influence the prisons of England and Wales emanating from both sides in London.

Catholicism and Reformation

One aspect of local reformatory practice which must finally be considered was that concerning the application of spiritual reformist approaches to the many prisoners who were not members of the established church, and indeed the presence of Catholics in particular was a most controversial aspect of reformation in British prisons. In some prisons it was the case that the number of Catholics at times rose above that of Protestants (Liverpool Borough, for example), and in other parts of the country numbers remained consistently large — for example at Coldbath Fields often around one-fifth were Catholics.[78] From the earliest years, the Convict Prison Directorate was faced with the need to establish a plain policy about ministry to these, and the subject created much discussion and occasionally considerable dispute with regard to local prisons.

In the mid-1850s Joshua Jebb received complaints that in convict prisons Catholic priests were being denied the right to full exercise of their ministry — for example the provision of Catholic books, Catholic services, the right to see Catholics who were lukewarm in their faith.[79] Jebb's view was that firstly there should be a uniform policy with regard to Catholic ministry throughout the convict prisons, but secondly he was concerned that arrangements made should not disrupt institutional routine.[80] He had, however, to contend with a number of his own chaplains, such as Joseph Kingsmill, who were distrustful of Catholic priests on the grounds that these might proselytise other prisoners. None the less, by 1870 to all convict prisons containing Catholics was attached a visiting Catholic minister, salaried according to the average annual number of Catholics within the prison, as well as a Catholic chapel constructed in these prisons. In such prisons the numbers of Catholics could be great — in Portsmouth there were over 500 in 1870 and in Millbank over 400.[81] In Ireland, of course, this was even more the case, and there Walter Crofton considered that 'perfect equality' ought to exist between Catholics and Protestants and that religious instruction by Catholic priests should be a vital part of reformation.[82]

Some of these ministers were well known for their knowledge of prison discipline and their prison ministry. Father Vincent Zanetti for example was at Millbank daily during his long appointment there, holding four services each Sunday as well as daily services and visiting Catholic prisoners in their cells.[83] Catholic voluntary bodies were also engaged in maintenance of 'refuges' designed as part of the Irish Intermediate Convict Prison system (the Golden Bridge refuge in Dublin for women, for example, run by nuns).[84] Plainly in convict prisons as a whole, despite an apparently clear policy, there were in daily practice instances of obstruction and discrimination. But equally clearly, provided that Catholic ministers avoided 'polemical teaching'[85] and despite some resistance over the issue of the right to visit lukewarm Catholic prisoners, by 1870 the policy was established that Catholic prisoners should receive full ministry.

In the local prisons arrangements were less standardised. For example at Coldbath Fields in the mid-1860s there was a prolonged dispute which eventually involved both Archbishop Manning and the Home Secretary about denial of access to Catholic priests and proselytisation of Catholic prisoners by scripture readers, one of whom was said to have referred to 'Irish False Gods'.[86] It was also said that scripture readers read out Protestant tracts to the prisoners whilst they were at work, that Catholics were subjected to 'quasi-compulsory attendance' at Protestant services,[87] were forced to read Protestant literature and were denied a fair amount of relief on release.[88] These allegations were strenuously denied by the county Justices, who pointed out that prisoners often lied about their religion in order to obtain advantages. None the less, although they agreed to place Douai Bibles in Catholic prisoners' cells and to remove the Church of England prayer book, it is plain that there had been bitter disputes locally, and indeed the Catholic minister appointed to visit Westminster House of Correction for women in Middlesex had been dismissed for allegedly handing out religious literature to prisoners.[89]

In other areas it was said that better relationships existed. At Liverpool, for example, great care was taken to inform the Catholic minister of the religious persuasion of all prisoners and Inspector Voules believed that 'perfect harmony' existed there.[90] By 1870 there were four characteristic arrangements of the Roman Catholic ministry to prisons. In the larger prisons with many Catholics, the minister was appointed and salaried on the same basis as the Church of England chaplain. In prisons with smaller numbers the minister was salaried but not allowed to hold services, only to visit in cells. In others he was unpaid but allowed to conduct worship and visit in cells, and finally there were prisons where he might only see any prisoner who expressed the firm desire for this.[91] Obviously there were problems in all four arrangements for Catholic ministers. Some alleged discrimination against their flock, such as the denial of more popular types of employment; some felt that their unpaid status derogated their function in the eyes of staff; some encountered reluctance to admit Catholic scripture readers; some were restricted in the educational instruction which they could give.[92] On occasion, as at Westminster, a number of Catholic priests published damaging allegations in the press whilst others complained that Catholic prisoners were abused by members of staff or were forced to read such works as 'The History of the Spanish Inquisition'. In several prisons attempts were made to place Roman Catholic officers in charge of Catholic prisoners.[93]

Despite the problematic nature of Protestant–Catholic relationships it does seem clear that by 1865 Catholic ministers had gained a firmer place in British prisons, although they continued to encounter suspicion and denial of facilities. It is also true that Jewish and non-conformist prisoners were, on occasion, permitted to see their denominational minister. Thus at Wandsworth a salaried Rabbi was in attendance,[94] whilst in 1840 a Wesleyan minister was invited to see a prisoner in Nottingham County Prison by the Protestant chaplain.[95] In the main, however, it was expected that non-conformist prisoners would attend Protestant worship and receive the reformatory approaches of the established chaplain.[96]

Here then was a complicated aspect of reformatory treatment which attracted a good deal of attention, whether from those who distrusted Catholicism, those who greatly valued its reformatory possibilities or those who saw the controversy as a good deal of nonsense about rogues who could not have cared less.[97] Furthermore, some prisoners took into account the likely consequences to them of a Catholic declaration, whilst others believed that they would be punished if they refused to go to the Protestant chapel.[98] Understandably, it was on occasion difficult for Catholic ministers to make contact with imprisoned members of their faith. Nevertheless, by 1865 Catholic priests were engaged in the reformation of prisoners and saw this as an important aspect of ministry, determinedly facing opposition in their bid to retain their presence in prisons.

References

1. For prison inspectors' exploration of the attitudes of Chartist prisoners, see S. P. Frouxides, 'The English Prison Inspectorate 1835–77', Ph.D. thesis, University of London, 1983. See also PRO HO-20-10, Bundle marked confidential.

2. Quoted R. Soloway, *Prelates and People, 1783 – 1852*, RKP, 1869, p. 432.

3. H. Tomlinson, *Prison Palaces*, p. 65.

4. *2nd Report General Board of Directors of Scottish Prisons*, PP, 1841, Session 1, vol. XI, p. 65.

5. M. Foucault, *Discipline and Punish*, p. 293.

6. M. Ignatieff, *State, Civil Society and Total Institutions*.

7. J. F. Saunders, 'Institutionalised Offenders: A Study of the Victorian Institution and its Inmates with Special Reference to late Nineteenth Century Warwickshire', Ph.D. thesis, Warwick University, 1983; M. E. De Lacy, 'Grinding Men Good?'.

8. S. McConville, *English Prison Administration*, pp. 347, 294.

9. H. M. Tomlinson, 'Prison Palaces — A Reappraisal of Early Victorian Prisons', *Bulletin of the Institute of Historical Research*, 1978, vol. LI, pp. 63, 65, 70.

10. Ibid., p. 66.

11. S. McConville, *English Prison Administration*, p. 430.

12. Ibid., p. 336; for 1844, see *Ninth RInsP*, Home District, PP, 1844, vol. XXIX, p. 218. The actual figure given is 17,650 but 1,828 must be deducted for Millbank, Pentonville and Parkhurst.

13. S. McConville, *English Prison Administration*, pp. 198, 393.

14. Ibid., p. 223.

15. *Ninth RInsP*, Home District, PP, 1844, vol. XXIX, pp. 3 – 19.

16. *A Return of the Prisons in England and Ireland; distinguishing those in which the System of Separate confinement is fully carried out*, PP, 1856, vol. XLIX; *A Return of the Number of Children Under 15 years of Age . . . in Prison Schools*, PP, 1856, vol. XLIX.

17. L. J. Blom-Cooper, 'The Centralization of Government Control of National Prison Services With Special Reference to the Prison Act 1877', in *Prisons Past and Future*, ed. J. C. Freeman, Heinemann, 1978, p. 70.

18. *Ninth RInsP*, Home District, PP, 1844, vol. XXIX, p. 218.

19. S. McConville, *English Prison Administration*, p. 335.

20. Ibid., p. 335.

21. Ibid., p. 333.

22. *Report from the SC on Prison Discipline*, PP, 1850, vol. XVII, p. 66.

23. *Report from the SC House of Lords on the Present State of Discipline in Gaols and Houses of Correction*, PP, 1863, vol. IX, Minutes of Evidence, p. 13; *Twenty Fourth RInsP*, Southern District, PP, 1859, Session 1, vol. XI, p. 6.

24. *SC House of Lords on the Present State of Discipline*, PP, 1863, vol. IX, p. 184.

25. *First RInsP*, Home District, PP, 1836, vol. XXXV; see also W. J. Forsythe, *A System of Discipline — Exeter Borough Prison 1819 – 63*, Exeter University Press, Exeter, 1983, pp. 48 – 98.

26. *17th RInsP*, Northern and Eastern District, PP, 1852 – 3, vol. LII, Individual Reports on Manchester, pp. 38 – 45, Leeds, pp. 94 – 102, borough gaols; for Holloway: *23rd RInsP*, Southern District, PP, 1857 – 8, vol. XXIX, pp. 79 – 84; for Liverpool: *24th RInsP*, Northern District, PP, 1859, Session 1, vol. XI, pp. 41 – 2; *23rd RInsP*, Northern District, PP, 1857 – 8, vol. XXIX, pp. 47 – 9.

27. *2nd RInsP*, Home District, PP, 1837, vol. XXXII, pp. 73 – 98; *23rd*

RInsP, Southern District, PP, 1857–8, vol. XXIX, p. 57.

28. *24th RInsP*, Southern, PP, 1859, Session 1, vol. XI, pp. 17–20 (Springfield).

29. *17th RInsP*, N & E, PP, 1852–3, vol. LII, pp. 16–17 (Chester), 64–8 (Norwich).

30. *26th RInsP*, Midland, PP, 1861, vol. XXIX, pp. 102–6 (Shrewsbury).

31. *17th RInsP*, Southern, PP, 1852, vol. XXIV, pp. 66–72 (Stafford).

32. *14th RInsP*, S & W, PP, 1849, vol. XXVI, p. 37 (Exeter).

33. *24th RInsP*, Southern, PP, 1859, Session 1, vol. XI, pp. 7, 13 (Bodmin).

34. *23rd RInsP*, Southern, PP, 1857–8, vol. XXIX, pp. 133–7 (Devizes), pp. 112–16 (Wandsworth), pp. 106–12 (Horsemonger Lane).

35. *23rd RInsP*, Southern, PP, 1857–8, vol. XXIX, pp. 25–9 (Dorchester).

36. *17th RInsP*, N & E, PP, 1852–3, vol. LII, pp. 104–6 (Wakefield). Note however that Wakefield applied the full separate system to almost all its prisoners by 1863. See House of Lords Select Committee, PP, 1863, vol. IX, p. 255.

37. *23rd RInsP*, Southern, PP, 1857–8, vol. XXIX, pp. 63–76 (Westminster), pp. 48–52 (Maidstone).

38. *17th RInsP*, N & E, PP, 1852–3, vol. LII, p. 86; *20th RInsP*, N & E, PP, 1857, Session 1, vol. VII, pp. 48–9 (Oakham).

39. *17th RInsP*, N& E, PP, 1852–3, vol. LII, pp. 7–15, 50–61, 21–50, 16–18, 62–78. *19th RInsP*, N & E, PP, 1856, vol. XXXIII, pp. 7–13, 35–47, 21–34, 14–17, 48–54.

40. *25th RInsP*, Southern, PP, 1860, vol. XXXV, p. 7; *23rd RInsP*, Southern, PP, 1857–8, vol. XXIX, pp. 76–9.

41. *23rd RInsP*, Southern, PP, 1857–8, vol. XXIX, p. 132; *24th RInsP*, Northern, PP, 1859, Session 1, vol. XI, p. 43.

42. *24th RInsP*, Midland, PP, 1860, vol. XXXV, pp. 137, 141, 148, 145.

43. *24th RInsP*, Southern, PP, 1859, Session 1, vol. XI, pp. 22–5.

44. W. J. Forsythe, 'New Prisons for Old Gaols: Scottish Penal Reform 1835–42', *The Howard Journal*, vol. XX, no. 3, 1981, pp. 138–49.

45. *Fifth Report of the General Board of Directors of Prisons of Scotland*, PP, 1844, vol. XXVIII, p. 13.

46. W. J. Forsythe, 'New Prisons for Old Gaols', pp. 146–7.

47. *15th Report of the General Board of Directors of Scottish Prisons*, PP, 1854, vol. XXXII, p. 25; *14th Report*, PP, 1852–3, vol. LIII, p. 18; *21st RInsP*, Scotland, PP, 1856, vol. XXXIII, p. 39.

48. *14th Report of the General Board of Directors of Scottish Prisons*, PP, 1852–3, vol. LIII, p. 19 (Edinburgh); *17th Report*, PP, 1856, vol. XXXV, p. 18 (Perth); *14th Report*, pp. 22, 25 (Orkney and Shetland).

49. *24th RInsP*, Northern and Scottish District, PP, 1859, Session 1, vol. XI, p. 35.

50. *38th Report of the Inspectors General on the General State of the Prisons of Ireland*, PP, 1860, vol. XXXVI, p. XXVI.

51. Hepworth Dixon, *The London Prisons*, p. 10. These were 'The City System', such as used at Giltspur Street and Newgate, which were prisons of promiscuous association, the Separate System, the Silent System, the

Mark System and the 'Mixed System', which contained elements of separation and association in silence mixed.

52. *SC of the House of Commons on Prison Discipline*, PP, 1850, vol. XVII, pp. 167–9.

53. *2nd RCGPP*, PP, 1844, vol. XXVIII, pp. 11–12; *SC of the House of Commons on Prison Discipline*, PP, 1850, vol. XVII, p. 136.

54. M. E. De Lacy, 'Grinding Men Good?', pp. 182–216.

55. *5th RInsP*, N & E, PP, 1840, vol. XXV.

56. *17th RInsP*, N & E, PP, 1852–3, vol. LII.

57. Ibid., pp. 17–18, 35–7.

58. Ibid., pp. 46–9; *SC of the House of Lords on the Present State of Discipline*, PP, 1863, vol. IX, p. 258.

59. Ibid., p. 328, pp. 328–34.

60. Ibid., pp. 134–5.

61. *Report of the Penal Servitude Commission*, Minutes of Evidence, PP, 1863, vol. XXI, p. 467.

62. J. F. Saunders, 'Institutionalised Offenders', pp. 119–20. Regarding the crank:

> Crank labour [at Coldbath Fields] consists in making ten thousand revolutions of a machine . . . it is a narrow iron drum placed on legs with a long handle on one side which when turned causes a series of cups or scoops in the interior to revolve. At the lower part of the interior of the machine is a thick layer of sand, which the cups, as they come round scoop up and carry to the top of the wheel where they throw it out and empty themselves after the manner of a dredging machine. A dial plate fixed in front of the iron drum shows how many revolutions the machine has made. It is usual to shut up in a cell the man sent to crank labour so that the exercise is rendered doubly disagreeable by the solitude . . . a man can make if he works with ordinary speed about twenty revolutions a minute and this at 1200 the hour will make his task of 10,000 turns last 8 hours and 20 minutes.

H. Mayhew and J. Binny, *The Criminal Prisons of London and Scenes of Prison Life*, Ch. Griffin & Co., London, 1862, p. 308.

63. *17th RInsP*, N & E, PP, 1852–3, vol. LII, pp. 97–8, 89–90, 68.

64. J. F. Saunders, 'Institutionalised Offenders', pp. 121–2.

65. *SC of the House of Lords on the Present State of Discipline*, PP, 1863, vol. IX, pp. 144–5, 292, 376, 388–90.

66. J. F. Saunders, 'Institutionalised Offenders', p. 126.

67. *A Return of the Prisons*, PP, 1856, vol. XLIX.

68. M. E. De Lacy, 'Grinding Men Good?', pp. 210–11.

69. E. Stockdale, *A Study of Bedford Prison*, Phillimore, 1977, pp. 162–3; W. J. Forsythe, *A System of Discipline*, pp. 53–9, 79–93.

70. J. F. Saunders, 'Institutionalised Offenders', p. 91.

71. S. P. Frouxides, *English Prison Inspectorate*, pp. 361–2.

72. W. J. Forsythe, 'Prisons and Panopticons', *Social Policy and Administration*, vol. 18, no. 1, p. 76.

73. J. F. Saunders, 'Institutionalised Offenders'.

74. Ibid., pp. 98–9.

75. Ibid., p. 87.

76. W. J. Forsythe, *A System of Discipline*, pp. 48–94.

77. J. F. Saunders, 'Institutionalised Offenders', p. 107.

78. *Report from the SC of the House of Commons on Prisons and Prison Ministers' Acts*, PP, 1870, vol. VIII, pp. 149, 42.

79. *Correspondence on The Subject of The Religious Instruction of Roman Catholic Prisoners in Pentonville and Brixton Prisons*, PP, 1854–5, vol. XLIII, pp. 1–3.

80. Ibid., p. 3.

81. *SC on Prison Ministers*, PP, 1870, vol. VIII, pp. 196–7, 198.

82. Ibid., p. 202.

83. Ibid., p. 190.

84. W. L. Clay, *Our Convict Systems*, MacMillan & Co., 1862, pp. 41–2.

85. *Correspondence . . . Pentonville and Brixton Prisons*, PP, 1854–5, vol. XLIII, p. 4.

86. *Correspondence on The Subject of the Religious Instruction of Roman Catholic Prisoners in Prisons in the County of Middlesex*, PP, 1866, vol. LVIII, pp. 1–3.

87. Ibid., p. 2.

88. Ibid., pp. 4–6.

89. Ibid., pp. 7–9, 18–23.

90. *Correspondence . . . Middlesex*, PP, 1866, vol. LVIII, pp. 14–15.

91. *SC on Prison Ministers*, PP, 1870, vol. VIII.

92. Ibid., pp. 5, 14, 18, 42.

93. Ibid., pp. 12, 44, 88, 16.

94. *Return Showing as to Certain Boroughs and County Gaols named on 15th April 1866 Showing the Number Belonging to each Religious Denomination, whether any appointment has been made of any ministers of religion other than those of the Established Church*, PP, 1866, vol. LVIII, p. 25.

95. *Fifth RInsP*, N & E, PP, 1840, vol. XXV, p. 3.

96. *Report from the SC on Prisons and Prison Ministers' Acts*, PP, 1870, vol. VIII, p. 150.

97. *SC on Prison Ministers*, PP, 1870, vol. VIII, Evidence of Francis Glossop, pp. 49–58.

98. *Correspondence . . . Middlesex*, PP, 1866, vol. LVIII, pp. 4–9.

5

Staff, Prisoners and Reformation
1840 – 1865

The Dissemination of Reformatory Practice

Between 1840 and 1865 the tendency to close smaller prisons and
transfer their prisoners to larger county institutions[1] accelerated
the replacement of the somewhat dynastic paternalist basis of
prison management which had been prevalent earlier in the
century by a more pyramidal formal hierarchic organisation of
staff. In the convict prisons, with their elaborate ranking of
officers, detailed definitions of duty and determined penalisation
of defaulting officers, this tendency was more pronounced, but
nevertheless at this time a different style of administration of
county and large borough prisons developed. 'Governors' of
gentlemanly background (often military) replaced 'gaolers' and
their families, whilst larger bodies of 'warders' took over from the
old 'turnkeys' of the earlier-nineteenth century. These changes
have been exhaustively discussed by penal historians and need not
be discussed further here.[2] However it is most important to gain
some understanding of the way that all levels of staff regarded and
operated reformatory ideas, as well as how they discovered information about them.

A major problem here is that, although governors and chaplains
of this period were often urgent publicisers, prison warders have
left few accounts of their views and experiences. Thus it is necessary to attempt, from very little evidence, to piece together an
impression of the reformatory work of by far the biggest body of
prison staff. At all levels staff ratios were high[3] compared to
present British prisons, and warders and matrons in particular
were forced to work very long hours, often 14 hours a day or

more.[4] It was clearly felt necessary to bring influence to bear on warders so that they would understand and exemplify the reformatory aspiration. In the convict service, for example, well before Du Cane and the later-nineteenth century, sustained efforts were made to insist upon promotions on merit rather than influence.[5] Pressures were brought to bear to ensure that 'the warders must not be allowed to be going drinking and behaving like Blackguards, from alehouse to alehouse, any more than sergeants of a reg.'[6] This ideal of the dutiful, firm, understanding and upright warder as a type of reliable non-commissioned officer was prevalent in the convict service, which in any case increasingly recruited from the army. In order to create such attitudes a number of approaches were made. First, at convict prisons warders often had to live in or very close to the prison in purpose-built housing so as to be clearly differentiated as an organised body, subject to continuous institutional regulation, expectation and surveillance. Single officers were often required to live within the prison itself, so as to be unremittingly under the discipline of the governor.

Such a situation, as intended, provided an opportunity to influence warders. In its early days, warders at Pentonville had to attend chapel twice daily and were discouraged by chaplains from visiting local public houses.[7] By the mid-1850s in many convict prisons there were libraries and recreation rooms for warders, whilst at Portland the chaplain gave them bi-weekly lectures and at Dartmoor the Deputy Governor did the same.[8] Chaplains promoted Sunday schools for children of officers and savings banks for their families, together with regular attendance at Sabbath worship.[9] The theoretical base of such endeavours was plainly similar to that of the approach to offenders themselves: education, religion and proper moral pursuits were essential to the creation of an attitude of attachment to the prison and fidelity to the state.[10] The chaplain of Portland proudly pointed out in 1861 that warders were clean, devoted to their children, affectionate and very attentive to the duties of the Sabbath,[11] whilst at Millbank in its earlier days warders apparently sought to win the good opinion of superiors by talking in 'scriptural language' and going about 'ostentatiously carrying large bibles'.[12]

Reports about, say, enthusiastic choirs of prison warders and wardresses[13] cannot stand in the place of a detailed investigation of the attitude to reformation among them. Indeed, it has to be admitted that this important aspect can only be touched upon in this work and remains largely an unanswered question. Clearly, superiors were concerned to keep close watch on the action of warders — for example the 'Tell Tale' clocks at Pentonville[14] — but equally clearly the formation of staff attitude and conduct within a prison is the result of many influences which are beyond the control of prison superiors. Despite dismissal for misconduct occurring regularly[15] in the convict service and in the local prisons, as did promotion on grounds of merit, it is not unreasonable to expect that many officers were influenced by the same kinds of pressures as those described later in the century and discussed in a subsequent chapter of this work. Doubtless many regarded reformatory endeavours as the preoccupation of their gentlemanly superiors which had little effect on the nature of the criminal. They may well have differentiated between prisoners on the basis of either their perceived high influence over other prisoners or their threat (perhaps negotiating with the former and appeasing the latter), or may have brought their own expectations and customs from military life and applied a collective regimenting approach to prisoners.

There is one further observation which may be made, and that is to do with turnover of staff. In a recent study of the mid-Victorian police, Carolyn Steedman discovered that there was a high staff turnover among constables and that often men joined the police as an available occupation in times of employment difficulty, swiftly returning to their customary work when times improved.[16] It seems reasonable to expect, given the complaints later in the century about the hardness of conditions of warders' service (short holidays, heavy fines for misconduct, poor pay),[17] that there would have been a problem of high turnover in the prison system also. Certainly later in the 1870s this appears to have been the case in prisons[18] and it is also the fact that, although not as well organised as later, complaints about conditions of service were made from early on in the convict prison sector. The impression then remains that, although some warders were doubtless models of reformatory rectitude, it was difficult for the proponents of reformatory aspirations to secure the total reformatory commitment that had been anticipated earlier.

During this period there was no training for prison staff of any grade, instead they learned by what McConville dubbed 'doing and watching'.[19] None the less, there were clearly well-used ways in which information about reformatory practice passed amongst staff of the higher grades and their supervising committees of magistrates. These need to be viewed as a tiny part of the more general professionalising of many areas of public life during the mid-nineteenth century. In prisons, for example, this took the form of attempts to abolish appointment by patronage or the reduction of use of prisoners in staff roles (e.g. as monitorial teachers). It ought also to be reiterated that such circulation of reformatory knowledge would scarcely influence those governors and others who inherently distrusted reformatory approaches.

The many governors such as Edward Shepherd of Wakefield, J. A. Gardner of Bristol, George Pinson of Norwich or Charles Keene of Leeds, as well as large numbers of chaplains and justices who were acutely interested in reformatory practice, were accustomed to gather knowledge in various ways. As indicated, discussion with inspectors and the growing number of circulars from London were important vehicles of new practice, but it is also the case that reports of Royal Commissions and of Parliamentary Committees of Inquiry were studied closely. Frequently chaplains, governors and justices gave evidence to these bodies and thus had a personal interest in their outcome and, for example, the 1850 inquiry into prison discipline received evidence about reformation from many prison officials.[20] Before this body Edward Shepherd discussed his views in great detail and with careful thought, admitting a lack of statistical knowledge in some answers or pointing up problems in reforming juveniles in others.[21] On occasion these inquiries acted to discourage prison officials from rigorous reformatory practice and Inspector Voules reported that some were alarmed by the report which revealed cruelty at Birmingham Prison, fearing that they would themselves, if over-severe, face 'another Birmingham inquiry'.[22]

There was also mobility within the prison system which encouraged circulation of knowledge about practice by officials. In the convict service this was obviously the case and amongst the governor grades there was frequent movement from one prison to another on promotion, with the most successful reaching the status of convict prison director. This occurred further down the hierarchy too: for example William Linton, who was interested in industrial training as governor of Petworth, had begun as a warder at Pentonville for four and a half years and subsequently worked in prisons in Buckinghamshire, Gloucestershire and Nottingham in varying capacities.[23]

More important than this were the ways in which information was deliberately sought out by officials. In the 1840s and 1850s there was no voluntary organisation which disseminated knowledge about reformation of prisoners as had been the case earlier with the Prison Discipline Society and was again to be the case after the late-1850s with the Association for the Promotion of Social Science or the International Penitentiary Conferences of the 1870s and 1880s. First, there was correspondence between reformists. John Becher, a Nottinghamshire visiting justice, wrote to Wakefield Prison during the mid-1830s when he was considering introducing the silent system at Southwell House of Correction to discover how they operated it there in the days before Wakefield became a separate system prison, and the chaplain of Leicester County Prison wrote to other chaplains to discover the advantages of installing cubicles in the chapel there.[24] Secondly, there was a good deal of visiting of institutions by magistrates and governors in order to evaluate reformatory systems for possible introduction in their own area. Lord Cholmondley, the Chairman of Winchester Visiting Justices, travelled to Leicester Prison to inspect their system; George Pinson, governor of Norwich Castle, examined the separate system as practised at Leeds, Wakefield and Pentonville,[25] and a committee of Bedfordshire Justices went to Pentonville and Hertfordshire County Prison before embarking upon the building of a new prison.[26] Thirdly, they carefully studied the more important reports and books about prison discipline. Thus the chaplain of Lewes County House of Correction carefully read the annual reports of John Clay printed in the annual returns to the Home Secretary required by the 1823 Gaol Act, as well as those of the senior chaplain at Parkhurst, published by order of parliament.[27] Joseph Kingsmill, having read Alexander Maconochie's books on the marks system, pointed up the aspects of that system which he disliked.[28] Also easily available were journals which gave extensive coverage to reviews of books about prison discipline.[29] Lastly, it is clear that there were bonds of friendship between reformists within which knowledge naturally circulated — William Osborne, Chaplain of Bath, was for example a friend of John Field, Chaplain of Reading.[30]

In these prisons, therefore, knowledge about practice was passed on in a number of ways and practice imported from one prison to another. It does seem clear that this was mostly true of the larger county prisons and that many of the smaller borough institutions remained less receptive to new practice. None the less Pentonville was far from being the only prison to receive visits of observation by interested officials,[31] and it seems likely that usually a local authority deciding to make a substantial change in its prison regime would send emissaries to another area which practised the new idea in order to see how it worked in practice.

The Experience of Prisoners

It is by no means easy to excavate the actual experiences of prisoners during this period, for the vast bulk of the documentation was prepared either by highly placed officials or by outside experts, both of which groups tended to reshape accounts of prisoners according to their own preconceptions. Yet there is no doubt that on occasion prisoners within these reformatory systems experienced tyranny, terror and cruelty. One problem was that some prisoners were unable to grasp what was being attempted or were reduced to despair either by their unhappy lives or the treatment they received, apparently unamenable to the reformatory endeavours of their custodians. Hepworth Dixon illustrated the severity which could be visited upon such a prisoner in Millbank. ' "He is touched, poor fellow", said the warden [sic], "in his intellect." But his madness was very mild. He wished to fraternise with the other prisoners; declared that all mankind are brethren; sang hymns when told to be silent and when reprimanded . . . declared that he was the governor . . . they put him into darkness to enlighten his understanding; and alone to teach him how unbrotherly men are. Poor wretch. He was frightened with his solitude and howled fearfully. I shall never forget his wail as we passed the door of his horrid dungeon . . . on hearing steps he evidently thought they were coming to release him . . . he did not cease to shout and implore most lamentably for freedom . . . when the fall of the heavy bolts told him that we were gone he gave a shriek of horror, agony and despair which rang through the pentagon and can never be forgotten.'[32] In the hands of a cruel or a tyrannical governor or officer these systems could become instruments of dreadful suffering when rationality did not suggest instant obedience to the prisoner or physical ability was absent. In 1848 the Leicestershire magistrates introduced aspects of the marks system into the county prison and by 1853 prisoners who could not complete the 1,800 revolutions of the crank machine[33] to obtain breakfast, 4,500 for dinner and 5,400 for supper were showing plain signs of 'weakness and exhaustion'[34] having been forced to undergo several days at a time without food.

Undoubtedly a more obvious example of the effect of ruthless determination to subjugate prisoners at all costs was at Birmingham Prison, opened in 1849 and built for operation of the separate system. However, shortly before opening the prison, the magistrates invited Maconochie to be governor in order to apply his marks system. Early in 1850 a deputy governor, Lieutenant Austin, was appointed and the two officers clashed, with the result that Maconochie was dismissed and his deputy promoted to his place. With the prisoners now isolated in separate cells and subjected to crank labour, a remorseless tyranny came into being. The new governor was convinced that the prisoners were seeking to defy or trick him and determined to break their wills. Young offenders, who rapidly became terrified of the regime and acted in desperation, particularly annoyed Austin. Edward Andrews, aged 15, described by the chaplain as 'a very neglected . . . desolate child . . . mild, quiet, docile' was described by Austin as 'sullen . . . dogged'[35] and forced to labour repeatedly on the crank machine, being set tasks which he failed to complete. After repeated punishments and use of 'punishment jackets' in which boys were often kept strapped for hours, 'an engine of positive torture', the chaplain found the boy 'wailing most piteously and speaking of his misery and his wretchedness'.[36] Frequent use of the jacket followed and often cold water was thrown over him whilst he was in the jacket. Eventually he was found hanging in his cell, 'punished illegally and cruelly . . . driven thereby to the commission of suicide'.[37] Events such as these made plain the high dependence of reformist systems upon the quality of staff recruited for their implementation. Far-off transport settlements often lacked any to oppose tyrannical officers or to protect prisoners from the worst excesses of cruelty: 'several of them have been savagely flogged . . . I can hear in my cabin every cut of the sounding lash and the shrieks of the mangled wretches . . . the three torn carcasses have been carried down half dead to the several hospital rooms following sixty lashes with the cat o' nine tails'.[38]

On the other side there is some evidence of prisoner experience of reformatory prisons, for during the 1850s an attempt was made by the Directors of Convict Prisons to obtain some understanding of impact upon prisoners in order to secure good public opinion and they examined large numbers of letters sent by prisoners after release. It does not appear that any inducements or rewards were offered for writing these letters, which display a simplicity suggestive of both truthfulness and thoughtfulness. In these, discussion of spiritual progress was common, as indeed a different self-analysis is prominent among many prisoners subject to intensive therapeutic regimes in our own day. An ex-Portland man wrote to the chaplain: 'Touching my temptations I cannot say much yet, though they are far more strong and numerous than I anticipated and I doubt not that my greatest will be among my own family. However I know that the grace of Christ is sufficient, that His strength is made perfect in weakness and that with the temptation He will make a way to escape . . . one of the worst things I experience is my want of moral courage'. Three months later this man wrote to the chaplain's assistant 'Prayer is sometimes a dull and lifeless duty and my mind is crowded with vain thoughts. I have not forgotten the three rules you gave me, yet I do not find the same pleasure in reading the bible that I did. I daily experience the effects of an evil heart and of those evil propensities which for a while lay hid . . . I shall feel thankful for a letter from you'. Another prisoner wished 'to return you many thanks for the kindness I received while under your care . . . I am enabled to partake of the sacrament of the Lord's supper once a month'.[39] Most of these letters make reference to the particular spiritual state of the writer and to the great temptations faced on release. 'My difficulties and temptations are much greater than when I was at Portland . . . I still hope I am a child of God although an erring one'; 'it is indeed hard at first to acknowledge the events which seem most harsh and uncongenial to us to come from the hand of a loving father in Christ Jesus our Lord. Let me hear from you soon'; 'Do not think by what I have stated that I am what you would call a Christian man, fearing God and following him in all his ways. No, I speak truthfully and candidly, I am only a mortal man trying to dwell by the help of God'; 'How hard it is to believe it without a single doubt, but still I seem to believe it, but my evil heart will not let me follow it out. I have prayed for a new heart and a right spirit, but alas, they are both strangers to me. Ah, Sir, I have found the world full of temptation and vice. I find it more difficult in serving God now than when I was with you. But why is this so? I have every advantage necessary for such a course, but the truth is, Sir, the fault lies in myself.'[40]

The writers also wanted to express their thanks to the staff for what had been done on their behalf whilst in prison. 'Allow me to express how thankful I am to you for your kindness to me while in Dartmoor'; 'pray give my kind love to Mr. Aborn the schoolmaster [at Dartmoor]'; 'I assure you that I greatly feel the kind interest you have taken in my welfare and return you my grateful and heartfelt thanks'; 'My heart is very much drawn to Portland because the happiest days I ever spent on earth was there'; 'When I left Portland Prison it was with great joy that I returned to the world at large. But I soon had something to sadden my countenance. There always was and ever will be badly disposed men in the world to lead me to evil. There have been many traps laid for me but, Thank God, for the present time I have overcome them all. I am doing better in every respect than ever I did before for which I am thankful.'[41]

Similarly, these correspondents with chaplains and governors were anxious to give an account of their particular difficulties and general progress since release and to show that they had been able to meet and resist temptations. ' "Oh, come and have one glass" cried the others. I continued to refuse and said to them "If I had never visited that house I should never have been at Portland" '; 'I know it will give you pleasure to hear that I abstain from all intoxicating drinks. I mix with none but those who follow Christ'; 'I cannot attempt to describe my feelings in being again under my own roof with my dear wife and children . . . I believe my confinement will be a blessing to me all the days of my life, for I believe God, in mercy to my soul, has over ruled it for good.'

There was frequent reference to newly learned moral lessons, to attendance at worship and to the comfort derived from religion and a new status as a law-abiding man. 'I cannot sufficiently express my feelings of gratitude for your kindness . . . I love you and may God bless you . . . I do feel extremely grateful for the many lessons of religion and virtue I have received from you';[42] 'How delighted I am when I awake in the morning to find myself free . . . there is no trembling or shaking now when I meet a policeman, no, thanks to the Almighty, I can hold up my face';[43] 'I arrived in London quite safe with M———. We were together all night. Before retiring to rest we read the 51st Psalm; we then committed ourselves to God in prayer; nor did we forget those we left in affliction at Portland.'[44] Others however seemed to be losing the struggle whilst alone and unaided in the world: 'I am inclined to ask sometimes why does God allow me as it were to be bound down? I use the word bound because it exactly expresses what I feel. For first I am bound spiritually; I have but little or no appetite for spiritual things; I am mentally — I strive to exercise my mental faculties in attaining knowledge. I fail in duties which I am accustomed to do continually and which one would almost fancy had become habit. I am sometimes at a loss in this respect. I am bound morally: I have only to go to my corrupt mind to prove this; and I am physically too, for I am convinced that depressions of body and mind are inseparable. In fact, Sir, my whole energies appear deadened; almost everything I do is laborious as if it were fixed work, but at the same time the sensual appetites are very strong; I have no love or affection for any one or any thing.'[45]

These letters at least are evidence that the pursuit of intimacy and engagement by spiritual and stage reformists in convict prisons was not all in vain and that there were many who operated these systems with mildness and integrity. Thus a wife wrote: 'before he was taken away, although he was neither a bad husband nor father, he seemed as if he could not be happy in his own house. Sometimes I had to entice him to remain but I do not know what he had on his mind. Thank God he is quite another man now . . . my husband desires to be remembered to the assistant chaplain and with many thanks to you, Sir, for the books you sent to my children.'[46] Others wrote with requests for help or about particular events which had occurred after release. One man explained 'I arrived safely and have plenty of work. I am sorry to inform you when I enquired for my wife I found she was dead. My father in law and mother are dead also . . . I have lost a fond mother by breaking her heart through trouble in the family and a sister only twenty years old by drowning.'[47] Another wished to send his 'kind love to you and Mr. Hoskin' and to thank the chaplain for the 'little present you was so good as to send me by Mr. Cole, for that was a great kindness to me'.[48]

In general, these letters reveal a sense among the writers, and on occasion their relatives, that the recipients of their letters were deeply interested in their wellbeing and progress, and wished to know of events in their lives and to hear from them. 'I write to inform you of an event which I am sure you will not be surprised at hearing of, viz. the death of my poor dear boy . . . I beg to thank you for all the attention which . . . you have paid him and to present my thanks to the governor likewise'; 'Colonel Jebb whose kindness shall ever be remembered with gratitude told me when leaving that he wanted my father's address'[49]; 'I was very troublesome to Mr. Gibbs but he was ever most kind and attentive . . . your kind and affectionate admonitions have produced a lively effect on my mind and I often wish that I could still come and hear you';[50] 'God bless you, dear Sir, for your affectionate Christian kindness, for I really feel you have not only been my friend in the darkest day of man's adversity but still feel interested in my future welfare . . . when you can spare a few minutes do send me a line; they are truly prized and are like the reviving words of a dear parent to an excited orphan and prodigal son.'[51]

To Jebb these were clear evidence of the success of the mixed reformatory system of the convict prisons for he believed that these letters, which arrived in considerable quantities, showed a deep influence of prisoners and dedication of prison staff to convicts whose progress they followed 'with the deepest interest'. He added 'they often write with perfect openness relating their troubles and trials, their temptations and their success in resisting them . . . they are like the letters of affectionate children to a distant parent to whose firm and judicious training they feel they owe the prospects of happiness and success in life.'[52]

Juveniles and Women

Although reformatory schools for children who collided with the criminal law are outside the scope of this study, being a particular aspect of reformatory endeavour which has received its own special attention,[53] it is worth making more explicit some of the distinctions which reformists made between 1840 and 1860 in dealing with young offenders. In the first place the attitude to juveniles was ambiguous. On the one hand they were presumed to be more malleable in their attitudes than older prisoners with longer experience of vice and crime who were thus 'proverbially difficult to teach . . . a sapling may be trained while young and pliant but who can tutor the full grown oak?'[54] However, juveniles were also seen to pose particular problems because of their susceptibility to the influences of others, especially those of parents and other criminals, and it was in a somewhat undefined way believed that there was some point at which the impact of the background was so great that reform became much more difficult, that the inherent innocence and honesty of the child to which Christ had referred had been direly corroded by the corrupting nature of environment and the depraving nature of human personality, leading to a progressive decline into hardened criminality. 'No-one but those who have to deal with the very refuse of a vicious, ignorant and degraded class of boys can be aware of the difficulty of subduing the habits which have grown with their growth from early childhood';[55] 'the most difficult boys to reform are those taken from haunts of theft and drunkenness, but their reclamation is not nearly as desperate as that of young girls who have been seduced or are prostitutes'.[56] Notwithstanding this, reformists hoped that the spark of honesty and innocent desire for good could be rekindled by patient care. More than average attention was given to spiritual and moral education of young prisoners in order to exploit the presumed sapling-like pliable susceptibility to the influence of others. In particular, it was hoped that the quasi-parental prison staff would win their deepest loyalty. Thus much could be done to repair and refill small damaged moral vessels but because of youthful susceptibility it was difficult to be sure that during prison and after release, contrary influences — 'hardened and reckless boys' — would not undo all this good work, destroying the reformation achieved by separation and spiritual and moral instruction.[57]

Although all the assumptions regarding reform of criminals generally held by spiritual and stage reformists were also applied to juveniles, much attention was paid to preparation for release. Life in the colonies or in the army or navy was considered particularly satisfactory, for there it was believed that the lessons of industry, morality and obedience learned would bear singularly useful fruit. As the Governor of Parkhurst put it: 'It is to me a very gratifying sight to witness as I often do a well set up smart soldier or a weather browned seaman seated in his old bench in the Sunday School or the chapel, having availed himself of a pass from his commanding officer to come to visit those under whom he had been trained here (and to hear him say) "I know, Sir, that when I was at Parkhurst you had good cause to regard me as a very mutinous character. I am sorry now that it was so but I am thankful to say that it was the discipline I underwent and the drilling and schooling which I received at Parkhurst which have been the making of me".'[58]

Before the Reformatory Schools Acts of the 1850s magistrates were frequently disturbed by the fact that small children appeared before them for trifling offences whose backgrounds fitted exactly the profile of the criminogenic environment provided by such as Alexander Thomson and Matthew Hill. Normally such children would have been returned home after a short sentence but during the 1840s it became common in some areas to sentence such children to lengthier periods of imprisonment for its presumed good effect. Baffled prison staff were thus confronted with small children, who might either be so distressed as to cry persistently and desperately, or who must be allowed to play leap-frog in the prison yard or to look after the prison pets. 'We know not what to do with them . . . I have had three or four boys in whose cases we have been obliged to light their gas and leave the door of their cells open by night . . . I have had them really so small and tender that I have been obliged to put them in the female hospital to play with the kitten.'[59]

Some further light is thrown upon the approach to juveniles by the admittedly exceptional arrangements at Parkhurst which served as a prison for young convicts up to the age of eighteen. In the first place, the treatment based upon spiritual and stage reformist theory was naturally applied to them although adapted to the age group in question. Consequently, at Parkhurst a shorter period of initial separation was imposed (four months) although from this the 'little boys' were excused and immediately put into the junior group.[60] The prison, which held around five hundred boys from all over Britain, was divided into two further wards, for the older and younger age groups, and each of these wards was divided into three sub-classes. The great majority were between the ages of 13 and 18, although in 1845 there were two inmates under 10 and, in 1847, one.[61]

In this institution careful attention was paid to education, and the method of education known as the Glasgow Training System invented by the educationalist David Stow was practised. According to this method, children were instructed by adult teachers (contrary to the monitorial method of Lancaster and Bell) in large classes in galleries and a number of principles of Stow's approach were emphasised at Parkhurst. First, the emphasis was upon his belief that children learn most effectively when they are working out solutions for themselves rather than reciting by rote. Therefore individual blackboard space was made available for each young prisoner so that he might express in figures or words what he had learned in order to be open to correction — a method strongly advocated by Stow. Secondly, an attempt was made to integrate different disciplines in single lessons. For example in a geography lesson a single sentence replete with geographical information would form the informational basis of the lesson. However, the sentence would also be analysed grammatically and its spelling examined and the pupils then required to write out what they had learned on their blackboard space. Thirdly, great attention was paid to pictorial or verbal illustration of subjects — 'picturing out'

— so that the imagination would be enlisted as well as the memory. Fourthly and finally, Stow's emphasis on technical knowledge and on a moral and religious base to education was exemplified by the very detailed curriculum of subjects, including etymology, reading, grammar, mathematics and scripture, by the great library of nearly six hundred books, all of which dealt pointedly with religious and moral subjects, and by the prolonged emphasis upon hymns, bible reading, scriptural exposition and prayer on Sunday.[62] Each class within the ward was fixed at a particular stage of educational advancement and the boy allocated to his own level of competence. A large quantity of 'homework' was also undertaken in cells during the evening.

So concentrated was the educational endeavour at Parkhurst that it created the problem that the boys hoped for an occupation commensurate with their acquired skills after release in the colonies. Therefore in 1849 Jebb reduced this side of the work in favour of increased industrial training because he felt that the boys would be unlikely to secure clerical work on release no matter how academically competent they were.[63] In any event, Parkhurst had always tried to teach occupational skills and by 1850 nine specific trades were taught, such as tailoring, carpentry, bricklaying, and increased emphasis was placed on these. Yet, right up to the discontinuance of Parkhurst as a juvenile prison in 1864 and the placement of young male convicts firstly at Dartmoor and subsequently at Portland, detailed educational emphasis continued to be an important aspect of the reformatory endeavour there.

One of the main inducements to correct attitude and behaviour was, as with adults, the prospect of improving conditions by good behaviour (a better diet, for example) but also of securing early release. During its first fifteen years, all the boys served their term at Parkhurst as the reformatory phase of a sentence of transportation. If they behaved appropriately, they would be released in Eastern or Western Australia, Van Diemen's Land (Tasmania) or New Zealand, at first as apprentices to colonial families and later on a ticket of leave (usually also involving apprenticeship). Indeed the assumption was that these 'exiles' had been reformed in Parkhurst, although a Guardian of Juvenile Immigrants was appointed to coordinate apprenticeship arrangements in Western Australia and to report back on the safety and behaviour of the boys, fifteen hundred of whom were sent from Parkhurst to the colonies between 1842 and 1853.[64] In addition, some young prisoners were released in England to the control of the Philanthropic Society which in the early-1850s sought to arrange apprenticeships in the colonies or to the care of friends and relatives if it was deemed that they had strong prospects of success in Britain. Again the exact nature of disposal after the prison experience (whether release in England, a conditional pardon to Western Australia, ticket of leave to Southern Australia or more restricted conditions in Australia for those whose complete reformation was in doubt) greatly depended on conduct in Parkhurst.[65] This discretionary variation was seen as a highly important aspect of the reformatory approach.

In the early-1850s this complex system experienced difficulties. In the first place there arose substantial criticism that many British child emigrants were neglected in Australia. Specifically concentrating on the Parkhurst system itself, Mary Carpenter launched a swingeing and determined attack against the prison as part of her promotion of reformatory schools. Consequently, although she later retracted her remarks after a visit to the prison, Parkhurst's reputation suffered as a result of her hostile comparison of it with the reformatories of France and Germany, which she claimed to be based upon the Pestalozzian ideal of family groups, dedicated housemasters acting *in loco parentis*, with personal influence in creative and Christian activity and training. However, Parkhurst had been designed as a reformatory prison for young men and Joshua Jebb never intended that it be regarded as a school or non-penal institution. The prison was faced with an added problem when in 1853 transportation came to an end for all those sentenced to less than fourteen years (which included almost all juvenile convicts). By 1856 almost 300 of the boys had been released in Britain on tickets of leave[66] earned by good conduct. In any case, the remarkable expansion of reformatory schools (some 65 by 1865)[67] led to a reduction of young convicts so that in 1864 there were in penal servitude only 68 under eighteen and by 1875 only 2 under fifteen.[68] The same process of reducing numbers of juveniles in the prison system after the Reformatory Schools Acts of the 1850s is shown much more generally by their percentage decline relative to total numbers of prisoners in British prisons: from 1.5 per cent under-twelves in 1857 to 0.6 per cent in 1877, and from 8.5 per cent between twelve and sixteen in 1857 to 3.7 per cent in 1877.[69]

Lastly, throughout the life of Parkhurst Juvenile Prison attempts were made to assess the boys so that they could be allocated to the appropriate academic level and so that some prognosis of future behaviour might be made. Consequently chaplains and teachers laboured to find ways not merely of assessing educational standard on admission but of summing up the personality of each young prisoner during sentence so that his virtues might be utilised and faults attacked. Thus 'Number 19' was 'quiet, rather heavy'; 24 'calm, demure'; 36 'mild and quiet'; 40 'quick tempered'; 42 'calm, reserved'; 79 'frank, self possessed'; 86 'resolute, steady'; 87 'blunt, reserved'; 89 'excitable, morose', and 103 'heavy, sullen'.[70]

Some consideration must also be given to women prisoners for it was believed that these posed particular problems to the spiritual or stage reformist. Women in the convict prison system in the 1860s were subjected to a period of separation at Millbank before proceeding to a staged system at Brixton and finally to Fulham Refuge, a half-way house to freedom on ticket of leave — the nearest equivalent to the Irish intermediate prison in England.[71] It was believed that women often became criminals because they had been trained up for thieving by their mothers or because they had been lured into theft or prostitution when naïve and young by calculating and wicked men. The criminality of many women was thus an extension of that of men who were the instruments of their downfall. Furthermore, prison staff believed that women posed particular problems from a reformist point of view. In the main they were considered highly emotional and volatile if checked by prison staff. This trait was thought partly to be linked to the fact that prison disciplinarians were unwilling to punish them as severely as men in the event of indiscipline, and partly to a view of women as creatures of feeling and impulse rather than rationality and calculation. Much later in the nineteenth century, Arthur Griffiths referred to the smashing up of cells by women who had been angered by staff and to collective defiance in Millbank in its early years: 'a loud scream or huzza was heard among the females . . . at the next moment half a dozen prayer books were flung at the chaplain's head in the pulpit'.[72] In the 1850s Joshua Jebb complained that there were always a 'few very bad women' at Millbank who 'without reason or provocation suddenly break into acts almost amounting to frenzy, smashing their windows, tearing up their clothes, destroying every useful article within their reach, generally yelling, shouting or singing as if they were maniacs'.[73]

Reformists tended to identify a number of distinct types of female prisoner. The two extremes were represented by the passive demure victim of circumstance, who was vulnerable to her own emotional passions and therefore liable to become highly distressed if denied attention or failing to advance as speedily as she hoped in the stage reform system; and the woman seen as utterly depraved, a grotesque perversion of the ideal of feminine chastity, honour, wifely obedience and motherly love. Irredeemably ruined by alcohol and sexual vice, such women were the associates of thieves, violent, cynical and contemptuous of all that was good and true; 'as a class they are desperately wicked — deceitful, crafty, lewd and void of common feeling . . . all the vices under the sun are exemplified in these hundreds of women.'[74] However, in general reformists were convinced overall that a dominating unreasoning emotionality distinguished women criminals from men and that this had to be taken into account when working with them. For example if a woman wished to go to the easier conditions of the infirmary she might surrender to this wish regardless of consequence to bring this outcome about: 'a woman will coolly pound a piece of glass to powder, and bring on an internal haemorrhage, nay, often bring herself to the dark threshold of death's door for the mere sake of the change . . . stay laces will be twisted round the neck till respiration almost ceases; women more desperate still will run the risk of hanging themselves in the hope of being cut down in time and taken to the infirmary.'[75] In addition, apart from screaming, smashing cells and self-injuring behaviour, women were prone to foolish tricks characteristic of mischievous children.[76]

The problems presented when reformatory approaches were offered were perceived as formidable. Dominated by emotion, women lacked the rationality which was an important basis for the success of the stage reformist system. An enraged woman would repetitively 'scream like a hyena, dash at her cell door . . . curl her arms round her knees, and commence a series of violent swinging motions that brought her head rapidly against the wall.'[77] In the prison school they would show fierce resentment if their ignorance was shown up or others laughed at them, and indeed often women would warn matrons of the onset of extreme emotion in order to be locked up in their cells to avoid loss of remission. They would quarrel with each other over trifles, they would refuse bibles and moral texts and rather demand picture books or 'Jack the Giant Killer' or 'The Newgate Calendar' from the prison library.[78] They would form powerful and jealous relationships with other prisoners or with staff and would also undertake malevolent reprisals as a result of imagined or real slights. Thus one prisoner, resenting another's superior airs, bit the tail off a mouse which she had tamed and another suffocated the kitten of a matron with whom she was in dispute. One 'begged very humbly the matron's company for a few minutes; she had found such a beautiful verse in her bible, she said, if the officer would only kindly read it to her. Suspecting no treachery . . . the officer accompanied Kearns into her cell . . . the door was shut to on the instant and with a wild beast's spring Kearns was on the matron who . . . fell to the ground with the prisoner above her stabbing at her face and throat with a knife'. One 'Johanna Lennon . . . was adept in punching in the pit of the stomach those male officers who were sent to remove her to the refractory cell.' Others would delight in mockery of reformatory attempts: one prisoner, fond of caged birds, would alter the chapel responses to 'Lord have mercy upon us and incline our hearts to keep jackdaws.'[79]

Because of the belief among reformists that female prisoners were prone to outbursts of feeling, uncontrolled behaviour, sudden savage vindictiveness and intensity of emotion in their dealings with staff and other inmates, they emphasised, even more than with men, the appeal to the heart by understanding, intimacy and trust so that this emotionality might be held within bounds by loyalty won and the intensity turned to advantage in the relationship with strong figures of integrity and spiritual strength. As one writer remarked, much benefit would result from the use of a squad of 'extra matrons as it were; the flying division of warm-hearted, anxious, energetic women whose duty it is to pass from cell to cell acting as companion and associate for half an hour, not as a preacher but ever in the character of a friend for a prisoner to seek advice from, if necessary, and to be strengthened in her duties by'.[80] At Brixton the superintendent and the chaplain emphasised the importance of patience, sympathy and individual attention with such vulnerable creatures of passion.[81] Even Alexander Maconochie felt that his marks system would have to be adapted for women whom he believed were very easily wounded in their feelings, were often victims of others and lacked the self reliance of men. He insisted that female convicts should be treated with 'paternal kindness and solicitude' because women were naturally dependent, easily thrown into despair and loss of confidence, so needing especial encouragement. Furthermore they were more severely judged than men by the surrounding society because they had lost their virtuous reputation, and Maconochie believed that particular encouragement was needed on this count also.[82]

Despite determined spiritual and staged approaches (with

badges to be worn as a symbol of progress achieved, intimate engagement, moral lessons) it seems that at Brixton as at other prisons where there were large numbers of women, reformists felt particular problems faced them. Consequently, as with juveniles, they tended to place particular emphasis on post-release influences aimed to shore up these creatures of emotion and dependence on external circumstances and on a gradual return to society (as at Fulham Refuge). Furthermore, it seems that the almost exclusively male world of prison discipline theorists and analysts was never entirely at ease in its attitude to women prisoners. For one thing their sex required special provision of facilities, even the presence of their dependent children within the prison. Mayhew and Binny were astonished to find at Brixton 'a pretty grey eyed child and dressed the same as the other infants in the room in a spotted blue frock — the convict baby clothes' adding that 'at Millbank one little thing had been kept so long incarcerated (with her mother) that on going out of the prison it called a horse a cat (whilst another, on leaving the prison with the mother, remarked of a horse "look at that great big doggie").'[83]

Most of all, it was the belief that women prisoners displayed peculiar and disturbing attitudes and behaviour which really unsettled their custodians. As Griffiths put it, although they were 'more susceptible to gentle influences than men' and 'more impressionable, more sanguine, more easily depressed than men', they were also possessed of 'cold blooded cruel insensibility when their jealousy or other evil passions are aroused . . . notoriously imitative'. In general, they were subject in prison to 'unreasoning exhibitions of temper . . . prone to fits of grave and protracted insubordination', sometimes exploding in 'insensate rage, venting its whole force upon the nearest and most fragile things'.[84]

Reformatory Influence following Release

In connection with children and women, but also with prisoners generally, it is important in conclusion to refer in greater detail to the development of attempts to continue the reformatory influence over prisoners to a post-release stage, for well before 1860 there was a growing tradition of what came in the twentieth century to be called 'aftercare'. Much of this occurred alongside the concern regularly expressed much earlier in the nineteenth century that young prisoners were contaminated in unreformed prisons. It was felt better that these be diverted altogether from prisons by placing them in special institutions either under the supervision of magistrates acting *in loco parentis*[85] or under the control of committees of earnest worthy people who had associated to establish 'refuges' or 'asylums' designed for reformatory purposes. Warwickshire justices as early as 1817 set up an institution at Stretton to receive young men sent there without sentence by the courts or placed there after their prison sentence had expired. At this asylum, education, religious instruction, occupational training and eventual apprenticeship to employers of correct moral type were the basis of a system characterised by 'gentleness and good treatment . . . repentance and reform.'[86] By 1840 the growing number of these institutions for young ex-prisoners were exemplified by the Paradise Row School of Discipline, the Royal Victoria Asylum for girls and the Hackney Wick Asylum for boys. There was also, of course, the well known Reform set up long before in 1788 by the Philanthropic Society for the support of children of convicts and the reformation of young offenders[87] which became in the mid-nineteenth century a notable reformatory school.

In these institutions the aim was to inculcate the same kind of knowledge and skill as provided at Parkhurst. The experience was to be plainly based on tutelary intimate and respectful relationship between the grateful inmate and the superintendent, serving as a kind of half-way stage to freedom in which the exact pressures likely to undermine reformation in each case would be identified and reduced. To attain this serious individualised objective, lengthy assessment of propensity and need was undertaken (as at the Refuge for young prisoners established by the Prison Discipline Society) by masters and matrons 'well calculated to conduct and manage the untoward tempers of the children'[88] in an atmosphere of sombre industry, attainment and obedience. From such places all undue levity was sternly banished. The unambiguous emphasis upon religion, knowledge, occupational training and upon the daily repetition of action (with its attendant reward) would, according to the spiritual and psychological theoretical framework, combat the tendency to 'mere sensual gratification'[89] previously fostered by the defective moral environment of the child. Therefore permanent behavioural and attitudinal change would result from continuous impact in the direction of pleasure in industry, achievement, obedience and religion. Great emphasis was placed at Stretton on lectures given by reformed ex-inmates, on assessment of the 'bent' of the individual mind, understanding of the precise previous parental influences, and on the wish to 'open the mind, to amend the heart — in the seed time of life and when the soil is most tenacious of the good or bad it may receive — to scatter the principles of subordination and order, of industry and application, to inspire the love and fear of God and due respect and reverence for man.' Indeed it was particularly important to work out the precise moral effect of all activities undertaken: at Paradise Row 'we do not allow them skipping ropes or anything of that kind. It was introduced at one time but we did not find it suitable; it made them bold in their manners.'[90]

The emphasis of such schemes was either on wholesale reform, where the prison experience was itself one of further moral deterioration (as believed to hold good in the 1820s), or a continuation and strengthening of reformatory direction as in the case of the new penal regimes. Many, like William Brebner governor of Glasgow, emphasised the fundamental error of numerous short periods in prison which 'inure, harden and gradually train them to endure confinement without feeling it as a punishment'[91] as well as the dangers besetting malleable young offenders when returning from even a reformatory prison to the Thomsonian social environment. Consequently the refuges which were set up in the 1830s and 1840s[92] paid careful attention to the time when the children would eventually leave; plainly emigration, apprenticeship at home and the merchant navy or Royal Navy were favoured as guarantors of future discipline and maintenance for these young offenders. Overall, it seems clear that these endeavours, though small in number, were important forerunners of the Reformatory Schools of the 1850s which emphasised the need to subject the children to closer, more individual, intimate, quasi-parental disciplines than were possible in the new Parkhurst or other prisons.

Elizabeth Fry had particularly — at least for a time — caught the attention of polite society with her emphasis upon sincere religion and compassion in her approach to female prisoners and, for the same reasons outlined earlier, it was feared that they would prove fragile in the face of social pressures and might well take to prostitution as their only recourse. Therefore earlier in the nineteenth century evangelicals had turned their attention to the establishment of penitentiary refuges, which received girls either from prison or prostitution. At these, medical care and a firm morality underpinned regimes whose aim was to afford 'an asylum to females who having deviated from the paths of virtue are desirous of being restored by religious instruction and the formation of moral and industrious habits to a respectable station in society.'[93] Of the London Female Penitentiary refuge it was claimed that the reformatory effects were outstanding, comparable with those of the earlier established Magdalene Hospital,[94] and these institutions, managed by committees of pious local women, fitted well with the promotion of engagement with female ex-prisoners by the Ladies' British Society, whose local committees, existing in many parts of Britain by 1840, sought to emulate the work of Elizabeth Fry and to provide 'suitable posts for them or to help them to emigrate.'[95] By 1840 penitentiary refuges and houses of industry had been set up either wholly or in part for women ex-prisoners in a number of towns, for example in Exeter and Edinburgh. The latter refuge possessing a separate cellular unit where women went voluntarily to undergo a reformatory regime similar to that of the separation prisons.[96]

With regard to adult prisoners generally, by 1860 provision had been developed in some localities which was designed to prevent erosion of the reformatory aspect of penal discipline. One aspect of this was the emphasis on what Jebb called 'patronage' — the notion of a close involvement between the friendless, helpless released prisoner, eschewed by his former respectable friends and tempted to return to those evil companions who would at least accept him, and the established orders of society, involving the assertion of a special duty owed by the well-to-do to the prisoner.[97] Before 1850 special local societies 'for assisting destitute and deserving prisoners to obtain an honest livelihood on their release' were set up at many prisons such as Millbank or in some counties as a whole working to return prisoners to relatives and families where these were of good moral worth, finding employment for them and also often the promotion of emigration to colonies for reasons earlier made clear. There, at least, a use might be found for 'that restless activity' and need for excitement which often characterised the criminal.[98] The aim of these societies was that to suitable prisoners there would be offered a friendly presence to sustain, support, encourage and direct them, for, without this, previous reformation might be undermined.[99] Representing this approach, an association of gentlemen was formed in Surrey to support destitute prisoners who 'from want of friends or inability to procure employment were frequently driven almost by necessity to seek support in their former courses of profligacy'[100] and which for a time maintained a refuge to allow the consolidation of reformation in the new environment of quasi-freedom and the recovery of an honest reputation before unsupported living. In Edinburgh and Aberdeen similar committees established Houses of Refuge for male prisoners[101] and in Shropshire a society was set up to provide penniless ex-prisoners with money and to furnish clothes and work tools to those who needed these on leaving prison.[102]

The emphasis on provision of means for survival on leaving prison had been encouraged in legislation for many years.[103] From the beginning at Millbank a carefully organised system had been invented whereby clothing and subsistence were given to the convict on release (together with his earnings) and a further three pounds paid him if he could show that he had been in 'proper employment for one year' thereafter.[104] After 1840, the growth of societies for assisting discharged prisoners was seen increasingly as a means of retaining some reformatory influence after release. In the 1850s large Discharged Prisoners' Aid Societies were set up in London and Birmingham, with particular emphasis on emigration or arrangement of an occupation. Matthew Davenport Hill emphasised that the time of release was fraught with risk for prisoners who often became 'low spirited as the day of departure approaches' and needed the foster care of such societies in order to adapt to the demands and temptations of society and to their own uncertainties and anxieties.[105]

The advent of penal servitude further encouraged such societies whose representatives interviewed prisoners on release, provided clothing, lodgings and pocket money and regularly visited them after release[106] and, as described earlier, in 1857 the Directors of Convict Prisons agreed with the societies that those convicts who were to be under their care would receive their earnings or 'gratuities' in instalments at the discretion of the society in question, thus inviting a more effective control over licensees. In 1871 nearly half the male convicts released from penal servitude and over two-thirds of women were in contact with these bodies[107] and nearly a decade earlier legislation had been passed allowing local Quarter Sessions to make payments to these societies of up to two pounds per prisoner helped, thus further encouraging their spread.[108]

The extent of this aspect of reformation, which continued such influences beyond the confines of the prison itself, was uneven in Britain before 1860. In addition to those houses of refuge, asylums and penitentiary refuges which had sprung up, certain prisons and counties formed local aid societies to investigate and relieve needy ex-prisoners and to encourage them to settle to regular self-maintenance by labour. It must be emphasised, though, that despite parliamentary encouragement, many areas saw no such activity, whilst in others the exact shape of the endeavour very much depended upon the enthusiasms of a particular magistrate or chaplain. Consequently when the Prison Commission came into being in 1877 only 29 discharged prisoners' aid societies were in existence.[109]

As earlier suggested, this aspect of reformatory practice obviously had implications for prison staff, especially chaplains, who were often engaged in negotiations with such institutions and societies. The chaplain of Manchester Borough Gaol, for example, was especially struck by the waif-like homelessness and friendlessness of many children in his prison in the 1850s. He particularly viewed refuges as a kind of home for such children on release although he noted the grave problems encountered when agreement was reached with young prisoners to make application for reception. With one 12-year-old boy who had been defiant towards the officers he patiently cultivated a relationship until he was 'uniformly docile and even gentle . . . would listen to my instructions and assent to my wishes in everything.' On offering him a home in a refuge for destitute children 'the boy who was never known to give way to any softened feelings before burst into tears and sobbed convulsively as he assured me I should never have cause to regret it.' However the refuge could not at that point accept him and he was released, quickly to return to prison on reconviction only to commit suicide in the prison on his first night following a rebuke by one of the officers.[110] Like other reformist agents in Victorian prisons, those involved in 'aftercare' support and influence saw themselves as engaged in activities whose importance could scarcely be overemphasised or the difficulties exaggerated, pursuing a reinforcement of those benefits so strongly promoted by 1860 in the prison system generally, and acting as an outreach to sustain and influence beyond the judicial and architectural limits of the prison itself.

References

1. S. McConville, *English Prison Administration*, p. 374.
2. J. E. Thomas, 'A Good Man for Gaoler? Crisis, Discontent and the Prison Staff', in *Prisons Past and Present*, (ed.) J. C. Freeman, Heinemann, 1978, pp. 53–64; J. E. Thomas, *The English Prison Officer since 1850*,

Routledge & Kegan Paul, 1972, pp. 54–74; S. McConville, op. cit., pp. 218–467 *passim*.

3. M. E. De Lacy, 'Grinding Men Good?', p. 199.

4. S. McConville, *English Prison Administration*, p. 270.

5. J. E. Thomas, *English Prison Officer*, p. 39.

6. Lord Wharncliffe to Joshua Jebb, 12.11.1845, Jebb Papers. Quoted by S. McConville, *English Prison Administration*, p. 213.

7. S. McConville, *English Prison Administration*, p. 211.

8. J. E. Thomas, *English Prison Officer*, p. 57.

9. *RDCP*, 1860, PP, 1861, vol. XXX, p. 147.

10. J. E. Thomas, *English Prison Officer*, pp. 56–7.

11. Ibid.

12. S. McConville, *English Prison Administration*, p. 166.

13. At Bristol Borough Prison, *House of Lords . . . SC*, PP, 1863, vol. IX, p. 334.

14. These were clocks with revolving dials denoting quarter-hour intervals on which a warder had to press pegs to prove that they had correctly proceeded upon their patrol rounds.

15. S. McConville, *English Prison Administration*, p. 214.

16. C. Steedman, *Policing the Victorian Community: The Formation of English Provincial Police Forces 1856–80*, Routledge & Kegan Paul, 1984, p. 92.

17. J. E. Thomas, *English Prison Officer*, p. 81.

18. Ibid., pp. 65–6.

19. S. McConville, *English Prison Administration*, p. 461.

20. *SC of the House of Commons on Prison Discipline*, PP, 1850, vol. XVII.

21. Ibid., vol. XVII, pp. 151, 158.

22. *SC of the House of Lords on the Present State of Discipline*, PP, 1863, vol. IX, p. 204.

23. Ibid., pp. 383, 388–93. S. McConville, *English Prison Administration*, p. 313.

24. S. McConville, *English Prison Administration*, p. 238; *SC of the House of Lords on the Present State of Discipline*, PP, 1863, vol. IX, pp. 167–8.

25. *SC of the House of Commons on Prison Discipline*, PP, 1850, vol. XVII, pp. 405, 300.

26. E. Stockdale, *A Study of Bedford Prison*, Phillimore, 1977, pp. 164–5.

27. *Fifth RInsP*, Home District, PP, 1840, vol. XXV, p. 380.

28. *SC of the House of Commons on Prison Discipline*, PP, 1850, vol. XVII, p. 141.

29. For example *Penny Magazine*, 1836, vol. 5, pp. 182–4; *Edinburgh Review*, 1847, vol. 85, pp. 320–40.

30. *SC of the House of Commons on Prison Discipline*, PP, 1850, vol. XVII, p. 341.

31. M. Ignatieff, *A Just Measure of Pain*, p. 3.

32. Hepworth Dixon, *The London Prisons*, pp. 143–4.

33. See description of the crank cited in Chapter 4, reference 62.

34. *Report of the Commissioners appointed to enquire into the condition and treatment of prisoners confined in Leicester County Gaol and House of Correction*, PP, 1854, vol. XXXIV, p. viii.

35. *Report of the Commissioners appointed to enquire into the conditions and*

treatment of the prisoners confined in Birmingham Prison, PP, 1854, vol. XXXI, p. vi.

36. Ibid., pp. vii, viii, ix.

37. Ibid., p. xi.

38. J. Mitchel, *Jail Journal or Five Years in British Prisons*, Cameron and Ferguson, 1876, pp. 66, 101.

39. *RDCP 1854*, PP, 1854–5, vol. XXV, p. 168.

40. Ibid., pp. 169, 170, 172. *RDMCP*, Lt. Col. Jebb, PP, 1854–5, vol. XXV, p. 150.

41. *RDCP 1854*, PP, 1854–5, vol. XXV, pp. 220, 223; *RDMCP*, Lt. Col. Jebb, PP, 1854–5, vol. XXV, pp. 155–6.

42. *RDCP 1854*, PP, 1854–5, vol. XXV, pp. 174–5, p. 175; *RDCP 1854*, PP, 1854–5, vol. XXV, pp. 221, 224, 225.

43. *Report of the Surveyor General of Prisons*, PP, 1854, vol. XXXIII, p. 120.

44. *RDMCP 1853*, PP, 1854, vol. XXXIII, pp. 120–1.

45. Ibid., p. 152.

46. *Report on the Discipline and Management of the Convict Prisons and Operation of the Acts, 16 & 17 Vict. Cap 99*, Lt. Col. Jebb, Surveyor General of Prisons, PP, 1854–5, vol. XXV, p. 158.

47. Ibid., pp. 158, 170.

48. *Sixth RCGPP*, PP, 1847–8, vol. XXXIV, p. 46.

49. Ibid., pp. 45, 46.

50. Ibid., p. 47.

51. *Seventh RCGPP*, PP, 1849, vol. XXXVI, p. 18.

52. *Report on the Discipline of Convict Prisons for 1856 and 1857*, Lt. Col. Jebb, PP, 1857–8, vol. XXIX, pp. 82–3.

53. J. Manton, *Mary Carpenter and the Children of the Streets*, Heinemann, 1976; I. Pinchbeck and M. Hewitt, *Children in English Society*, vol. 2, Routledge and Kegan Paul, 1973.

54. *RDCP 1857*, PP, 1857–8, vol. XXIX, p. 213.

55. *Report on the Discipline of Convict Prisons for 1856 and 1857*, Lt. Col. Jebb, PP, 1857–8, vol. XXIX, p. 64. See also J. J. Tobias, *Crime and Industrial Society in the Nineteenth Century*, Pelican, 1972, pp. 90–1.

56. G. de Beaumont and A. de Tocqueville, *Système Pénitentiaire aux Etats Unis et de son Application en France*, Société Belge de Libraire, 3rd edn, 1837, vol. 2, p. 27.

57. *Papers relating to Parkhurst Prison*, PP, 1847–8, vol. XXXIV, p. 10.

58. *RDCP 1861*, PP, 1862, vol. XXV, p. 102.

59. *SC of the House of Commons to enquire into the Execution of the Criminal Law*, PP, 1847, vol. VII, p. 283; *SC of the House of Lords . . . Gaols and Houses of Correction*, PP, 1863, vol. IX, p. 152.

60. *Parkhurst Papers, for 1845*, PP, 1846, vol. XX, p. 4.

61. Ibid., p. 4; PP, 1847–8, vol. XXXIV, p. 3.

62. *Parkhurst Papers*, PP, 1839, vol. XXII, pp. 20–3, 23–7; 1846, vol. XX, pp. 19–21.

63. *Parkhurst Papers*, PP, 1850, vol. XXIX, p. 5.

64. *Parkhurst Papers*, PP, 1849, vol. XXVI, pp. 21–2; 1852, vol. XXIV, pp. 94–101. Pinchbeck and Hewitt, *Children in English Society*, vol. 2, p. 548.

65. *Parkhurst Papers*, PP, 1846, vol. XX, p. 4.

66. *RDCP 1855*, PP, 1856, vol. XXXV, p. 44.
67. *Eighth Report of the Inspector of Reformatory and Industrial Schools*, PP, 1865, vol. XXV, pp. 19–26.
68. S. McConville, *English Prison Administration*, pp. 428–9.
69. Ibid., p. 337.
70. *Parkhurst Papers*, PP, 1844, vol. XXVIII, p. 49.
71. *Minutes of Evidence before Penal Servitude Acts Commission*, J. Jebb, PP, 1863, vol. XXI, pp. 57–8.
72. A. Griffiths, *Memorials of Millbank and Chapters in Prison History*, Henry King & Co., 1875, vol. 1, p. 200.
73. *RDCP 1853*, PP, 1854, vol. XXXIII, p. 88.
74. F. W. Robinson, *Female Life in Prison by a Prison Matron*, Hurst & Blackett, 1862, vol. 1, pp. 47–8. In fact Robinson was a Victorian journalist and novelist and the work is not that of a prison matron even though many of his contemporaries (like Mary Carpenter) believed that this was the case. Nevertheless, these writings were based on 'actual records' (DNB Supplement January 1901–December 1911, vol. 1, p. 216). Furthermore, it seems likely, given Robinson's detailed knowledge of prison regulations, that he not only consulted records but interviewed matrons of female convict prisons.
75. Ibid., vol. 2, p. 42.
76. Ibid., vol. 2, pp. 45–6, 49.
77. Ibid., pp. 58–9.
78. Ibid., p. 128.
79. Ibid., vol. 1, pp. 160, 154–5; vol. 2, pp. 144, 180, 284.
80. F. W. Robinson, *Prison Characters Drawn from Life*, Hurst & Blackett, 1866, vol. 1, p. 203.
81. *Report on the Discipline of Convict Prisons for 1856 and 1857*, Lt. Col. Jebb, PP, 1857–8, vol. XXIX, pp. 50, 51, 53.
82. Captain Maconochie, *Thoughts on Convict Management*, pp. 128–30.
83. H. Mayhew and J. Binny, *The Criminal Prisons*, pp. 190, 191.
84. A. Griffiths, *Secrets of the Prison House*, Chapman & Hall, London, 1894, vol. 2, pp. 25, 27, 9–10, 20.
85. J. Eardley Wilmot, *A Letter*, 1827, pp. 14, 16, 18–20.
86. *SC of the House of Lords . . . Gaols and Houses of Correction*, PP, 1835, vol. XII, pp. 427–39.
87. *Reports of The Philanthropic Society*, 1790, 1799, 1814, 1818, 1819, 1821, 1822, 1823, 1825.
88. *Report of the SC of the House of Commons on Gaols*, PP, 1819, vol. VII, p. 155.
89. *SC of the House of Lords . . . Gaols and Houses of Correction*, PP, 1835, vol. XII, p. 514.
90. Ibid., pp. 428–9, 435, 485.
91. W. Brebner, *A Letter to the Lord Provost on the Expediency of a House of Refuge for Juvenile Offenders*, Smith, 1829, p. 5.
92. For example, *Report by the Directors of the Glasgow Society for Repressing Juvenile Delinquency*, 1839.
93. W. Hale, *An Address to the Public upon the Dangerous Tendency of the London Female Penitentiary*, W. Nicholson, 1809, p. 11.
94. *2nd Report from the Commons Committee on the State of the Police of the*

Metropolis, PP, 1817, vol. VII, p. 332.

95. *SC of the House of Lords . . . Gaols and Houses of Correction*, PP, 1835, vol. XII, Appendix 17, pp. 550–8; A. F. Young and E. T. Ashton, *British Social Work in the Nineteenth Century*, Routledge & Kegan Paul, 1967, p. 158.

96. *Second RInsP*, S & W, PP, 1837, vol. XXXII, p. 2; Scotland, PP, 1837, vol. XXXII, pp. 127–8.

97. *Report on the Discipline and Management of the Convict Prisons*, J. Jebb, PP, 1854–5, vol. XXV, p. 29.

98. PRO HO-20-8, Millbank Superintending Committee to the Home Office, 23 Dec. 1839; *Fourth RInsP*, Home District, PP, 1839, vol. XXI, pp. iii–iv; *Third RInsP*, PP, 1837–8, vol. XXX, p. 111.

99. *Fourth RInsP*, Home District, PP, 1839, vol. XXI, p. 394.

100. *Gaols: Reports and Schedules (B) transmitted to the Secretary of State*, PP, 1826, vol. XXIV, p. 248; 1826–7, vol. XIX, p. 226.

101. *Second RInsP*, Scotland, PP, 1837, vol. XXXII, pp. 127–8, p. 34.

102. *First RInsP*, S & W, PP, 1836, vol. XXXV, p. 60.

103. 4 G IV Cap. 64, Sec. 39.

104. 56 G III Cap. 63, Sec. 19; see also S. McConville, *English Prison Administration*, pp. 143–4.

105. *Second Report from the SC on Transportation*, PP, 1856, vol. XVII, pp. 22, 24.

106. S. McConville, *English Prison Administration*, pp. 424–5.

107. Ibid.

108. *25 & 26 Vict. Cap 44.*

109. A. F. Young and E. T. Ashton, *British Social Work*, p. 161.

110. *17th RInsP*, N & E, PP, 1852–3, vol. LII, pp. 42–4.

6
A New Direction for Prisons
1860 – 1864

The Growth of Opposition to Reformatory Prisons

During the 1840s and 1850s there had been those who had, from differing points of view, watched the rise of reformatory prisons with considerable alarm and anger. They had so far been unable to make any substantial headway against the system, even though in their number were to be found some well known and influential politicians, writers and philosophers. Their dislike of the burgeoning reformatory endeavour took various forms and no single united philosophy or political party supported their opposition. To some, like Peter Laurie and Charles Dickens, it had earlier been the nature of separation which seemed so offensive. These considered it to be a cruel and unnatural system, suspect constitutionally because it relied upon experts wielding vast powers established by legislation depending upon new interventionist principles, and deriving its existence from a mixture of official humbug and claptrap whose main result was precisely to induce prisoners to various impostures in order to obtain the praise of their custodians.[1] On the same grounds, *The Times* newspaper was suspicious of the concentration of power in official hands and, after initial hesitation, felt with Charles Dickens that separation might unbalance the mind. Indeed *The Times* conducted a long campaign against separation which its editor called 'this maniac making system' which 'sometimes terminates in insanity, oftener in idiocy and still more frequently in permanent weakness and imbecility of mind'.[2] The sustained attack on the basis that separation caused madness had been successfully withstood by the prison system up to 1860, but throughout the previous twenty years separation had remained unpopular with many who saw it as a strange, unnatural punishment subjecting prisoners to an 'immense amount of torture and agony . . . a depth of terrible endurance'[3] and which encouraged them to perform like religious monkeys but left the heart untouched.

Separation was continually criticised in its heyday by those who believed it had so changed prisons as to defy the basic requirements of less eligibility. In 1849 Lord Brougham described Reading as 'of the nature of a public nuisance' which 'might rather be called Reading University' and demanded that prisons should be places of 'terror to the indolent'.[4] In the 1840s and 1850s there was a body of opinion which detested what was seen as the growing sentimentality towards criminals of self-righteous philanthropists. This opinion was strongly expressed by Thomas Carlyle, the historian and philosopher, in 1850. He vilified the folly of those who believed that human misery could be cured by philanthropy and 'the indiscriminate mashing up of right and wrong into a patent treacle of the philanthropic movement'. He found it preposterous that a determined reformatory attempt had been made at all since it was plain that criminals were in the main 'miserable distorted block heads . . . ape faces, imp faces, angry dog faces, heavy sullen ox faces, degraded underfoot, perverse creatures, sons of indocility, greedy mutinous darkness . . . base natured beings on whom in the course of a maleficent subterranean life of London scoundrelism the Genius of Darkness (called Satan, Devil and other names) had now visibly impressed his seal and had marked them out as soldiers of Chaos and of him'.[5] Prisoners were not our brothers but 'enemies', a fact confused by 'this universal syllabub of philanthropic twaddle' and should be subjected not to the 'eloquent Mr. Hesperus Fiddlestring denouncing capital punishments and inculcating the benevolences' but to unmistakeable retribution, itself the law of God. If the distinction between right and wrong became blurred by Liberal environmental regenerative interventionism then all would 'bellow and bray of universal misery' and 'the astonishing new phallus worship' of French Revolutionary false gods come among us with their 'sacred kiss of peace for scoundrel and hero alike'.[6]

Ironically, the theme of retribution (in the sense of suffering visited upon the illdoer in order to enable crime to be expiated and a new beginning to be made) also developed as an issue amongst a few spiritual reformists themselves in the early 1860s because separation seemed to be in defiance of certain theological truths.

Mary Carpenter became convinced that before reformism could reap its harvest of regenerated souls in adult prisons it was of paramount importance to subject prisoners to 'a condition of privation and suffering following sin as will lead to the knowledge that man's government is in harmony with God's government'.[7] In the same vein, John Clay's son, Walter Lowe Clay, suggested that prison discipline in particular and society more generally had fallen into two major theological errors. There had developed an adoption of 'half heathen theology and philosophy which knows no higher aim than the protection of society' — such as the liberal theory which sought to adjust social institutions to securing the maximum pleasure and minimum pain — and 'on the other the hyper Christian philanthropy which, obliterating the eternal difference between right and wrong, regards the criminal as merely suffering from a moral disease'.[8] To Walter Clay it was clear that God's model of justice was a substantially retributory one and that 'to stir up such repentance God has provided no means so sure as bitter punishment — punishment of which the sinner acknowledges the justice, even while he groans under the infliction'.[9]

The ranks of reformists themselves, therefore (and both Carpenter and W. L. Clay were reformists, the former in practice and theory, the latter in theory alone), contained those who believed that the system had become detached from its pure theological base. Although separation emphasised the need for the offender to experience sorrow as a precondition of repentance, the system had given itself over to a philanthropy which excluded retributory pain.

Well before the early-1860s, therefore, there had been disquiet at the direction taken over the previous twenty years, but between 1857 and 1863 a very much more general distrust of reformatory prisons surfaced so that during the early 1860s discontent with them became a major feature of debate about the workings of the penal system. In 1863 two extensive inquiries were completed, one into the operation of the Acts of Parliament relating to Penal Servitude and Transportation, the other investigating the state of discipline in the gaols and houses of correction of the boroughs and counties; the appointment of both committees was stimulated by fears about rising crime rates. The reports issued by these two bodies exercised a most important immediate influence on the prison system and, in the first place, one of them declared that the reformist base of borough and county prison discipline was almost entirely erroneous in principle, whilst the other recommended

143

that a more stringent system of penal servitude be created which, whilst continuing to include an unmistakeable stage reformist element, would be more plainly based on a deterrent philosophy of punishment.

It must be said at the outset that this change of direction has received a recent flurry of attention from modern writers, who have concentrated upon the relationship between violent crime and public opinion, and have taken differing views. Davis in 1980 argued that outbreaks of robbery in 1862 in which a garotte was used to render the victim powerless or unconscious, created an entirely new climate of opinion towards reformists and prisoners. A widespread outcry ensued, condemning reformatory treatment of offenders and this undoubtedly 'facilitated the effective dismantling of the reformative penal system by its critics . . . and its replacement by a punitive model of convict treatment'.[10] A new consciousness developed that there existed a distinct class of criminals irreconcileable in their hostility to society, physically and perhaps psychologically different from the rest, and dedicated to cruelty and crime. Other writers have been quick to point out that Joshua Jebb, for example, had been widely criticised since the 1850s for his sympathy towards prisoners ('my family of eight thousand')[11] and that the concern about the relationship between garotting, more general crime and the granting of tickets of leave may be easily traced back to the later-1850s,[12] although admittedly it died down during the period before the 'garotting epidemic' in London of 1862 – 3.[13] Accordingly, it is argued that the changes in penal direction need to be set in the context of a lengthier development of public concern about crime rates since at least 1855.

It is often difficult to show precisely the extent of changes in public attitudes but it is certain that, whatever its antecedent strength in the late-1850s, there existed by 1863 a strong belief that violent crime was on the increase and it is equally clear that this belief played an important part in the direction of penal policy in the mid-1860s, notwithstanding the various criticisms of the prison system prior to 1862. Recent research has pointed to the substantial fear of crime generated by newspapers and weekly magazines with large circulations which emphasised a wave of violent crime and the existence of a vile predatory criminal class in the early-1860s.[14] Now although the idea of a criminal class did not originate in the early-1860s (or 1850s for that matter), this research does substantiate the argument that a very real increase in fear of violent and other crime had been created by the late-winter of 1863. This was plainly linked to a substantial parliamentary campaign against reformatory prisons which, it was said, formed part of the cause of rising crime rates. That campaign resulted in major changes in law and administration, beginning to reverse the general direction of the policy of the previous quarter century.

On 19 February 1863, the fourth Earl of Carnarvon, later Colonial Secretary under both Lord Derby and Disraeli, rose to address the House of Lords on the subject of prisons and crime. There had been, he declared, 'a very startling increase in crime' of almost all kinds but in particular he asserted this in respect of crimes of violence such as murder, rape and robbery with violence to the person or property. Adverting to 'insecurity in the streets of London' which had recently been 'too dangerous to walk about after nightfall', he suggested two inferences about this apparent rise in crime. Firstly 'in a large proportion of the gaols and houses of correction in the kingdom there was an insufficiency of penal discipline', and in the second place there was an entirely unacceptable dissimilarity between the systems of discipline practised from area to area throughout Britain. In some prisons, indeed, owing to 'the interference of well intentioned theorists who thought it practicable to make moral influences a substitute for hard labour the visiting justices had come to the conclusion that the best mode of solving the difficulty was to give the prisoners no work at all' and in many 'meat was given to the prisoners every day in the week . . . there were certain luxuries, certain comforts . . . which made it a very grave question whether the dietary generally given to prisoners was not in excess of what it ought to be.' Therefore, unlike the lot of the common man who must resist privation and hardship unaided, that of the prisoner was one of comfort, liberality, 'an object of desire' and he concluded that although he would not 'exclude all idea of moral reformation . . . it was perfectly idle to put into operation all the elaborate machinery provided in gaols for the instruction and reformation of prisoners', ideas which were 'fanciful theories' likely to invite the criminal to commit crimes in the sure knowledge that there merely awaited him a good diet, warm bed and light, often voluntary, labour.[15]

Lord Carnarvon was raising issues which had troubled him for some years following visits to continental prisons in his late-twenties (between 1857 and 1860) and which had disturbed him in his capacity of Chairman of the Judicial Committee of Hampshire Quarter Sessions in which county a separate prison system was in full operation at Winchester. He had spoken out vehemently

145

against 'the utter introversion of the prison discipline at Winchester'[16] where 'various relaxations and indulgences . . . had
broken into the prison system such as exercise in the open air,
extra clothing, extra bedding and libraries of entertaining knowledge',[17] and he viewed the Winchester regime as 'cruel to the
prisoner because it really does him no good . . . cruel to the
country because it acts as an incentive to crime . . . expensive to
the ratepayer, unjust to justice and unjust to honest poverty'.[18] He
had become convinced that the apparent rise in local crime was a
direct result of this mitigation of penal severity in the name of
reformation and indeed subsequently brought pressure to bear
upon Hampshire Quarter Sessions to enforce 'continuous labour',
'an uninviting diet' and a 'real and unquestionable severity of
punishment both in amount and kind'.[19] Carnarvon was thus
denying the wisdom of that rationality which for over a quarter of
a century had led to the conclusion that the moral reconstruction of
the prisoner was an essential (or realisable) part of any prison
discipline system. In general, indeed, he detested what he saw as
an over-dependence on intellect and reason in social and moral
matters in Europe subsequent to the French Revolution. He was
deeply conservative in his respect for time-honoured social institutions and for gradual organic change in a primarily rural stratified
society bound together by orderly co-operative reciprocal relationships. This society was one of the 'ideal country gentleman', of
'tenants . . . agricultural labourers . . . gardens and allotments, of
meadows, cow runs and small holdings' with tenants as 'valued
friends' to whom he would be 'their unfailing resort . . . for advice
and help', a paternal superior whose 'sayings and doings were
followed with the deepest interest'.[20]

Nor was Lord Carnarvon only concerned about the county and
borough prisons, for over a year later in a debate on penal servitude
he referred to the 'failure of our penal' system as a result of 'so
much vacillation and so much misplaced tenderness evinced
towards great and notorious criminals'.[21] He was not alone in his
views. In both Lords and Commons a growing opinion was
expressed that in local and convict prisons there was insufficient
rigour, that prisoners were better fed than military personnel or
labouring folk, that sentences of penal servitude were too short,
that no control or surveillance of ticket of leave prisoners was
exercised and that in general there was a laxity in prison discipline
which was connected with the growth of reformatory theory and
which deterred few offenders from committing crimes. Bound up

with this view was the unmistakeable suspicion that the great local differences in penal practice were an obvious evil in the prison system and were connected with this lack of severity and rise in crime.

It would be wrong to assume that Lord Carnarvon and those who argued alongside him were entirely unopposed in their analysis of the link between comfortable prisons, reformation and higher crime rates. Lord Wodehouse, for example, suggested that, 'quite unintentionally he was sure', Carnarvon had misled the Lords because, taken over a fifteen-year period, crime had actually decreased.[22] Earl Cathcart reminded them that if prisoners at hard labour were underfed they would die and in the Commons Mr Neate denied that a nation which 'professed to the most Christian, the most religious, the most moral and the most prosperous community in the world' ought to proceed towards 'a return to greater savagery of past times' whilst other European nations 'were steadily pursuing a more humane and gentle system'.[23] However, it was plain that many members of both houses were disturbed about the current state of the prisons of Britain, despite the striking differences of opinion about such matters as the operation of tickets of leave, the relationship of such licences to outbreaks of street robberies in London, the desirability of more central control of local magistrates, the ending of transportation, and the workings of the stage reformist system in the convict prisons. Most seemed to agree with C. B. Adderley, whose views had substantially hardened since the 1850s, that 'he would make punishment to be punishment. Reformation should be concurrent with it as far as possible but he would make punishment, that is the suffering of something disagreeable in consequence of crime, the sole object of penal law . . . for the first time in a long period the criminal class would entertain some fear of punishment': elsewhere he added that 'the criminal part of the population suppose the country laid open to their depredations.'[24]

These debates, which heralded two new Acts of Parliament in 1864 and 1865,[25] were but a small part of a discontent which had been growing in strength for more than a decade. As has been said, the late-1850s and 1860s were punctuated by a number of panics that crime was not only growing but was also becoming more brutal, and the view of a crime increase was linked by many to the increasing practice of releasing convicts on tickets of leave before the expiry of the term pronounced by the court. *The Times* remarked: 'the other day, in a case before Mr. Boreham, it came

out that three ruffians had been heard, over their supper, talking
about their attempt at garotting a man as others talk of shooting
pigeons or spearing salmon. It was just their profession or one
form of their profession. Now it is clear that these men, when they
come out of prison, or from penal servitude, must betake themselves to robbery, burglary or some other violent misdeed.'[26] The
belief that gangs of ex-convicts on licence were prowling the streets
of London and other large cities, bent on robbery by use of the
garotte or any other weapon, was not reduced by the disclosure
before the 1863 Penal Servitude Commission that only $12\frac{1}{2}$ per
cent of convicts so released were reconvicted (the vast majority for
offences not involving violence).[27] It continued to be strongly held
by many who questioned the claim put forward that penal servitude reformed convicts, and that anxiety was heightened by the
decline of transportation to Western Australia in the late-1850s.
Now the entire criminal population was to be contained within the
British Isles and 'prison discipline must become more than ever
material to us when the prisoner by and by will be at large in our
own country'.[28] Nor was the fear lessened by administrators from
Ireland extolling the marks system and pointing out that English
convict prisons were arranged on false premises so that liberated
convicts, far from having been reformed, returned at once to their
old trade to prey upon society 'as ostensibly and nearly as openly
as honest men ply their vocation.'[29]

During the late-1850s and early-1860s there developed a widening discontent with the actual efficiency of British prisons in promoting the objective of prisoner reform, quite apart from the
disputes between reformists of various schools which have already
been discussed. These doubts were felt amongst administrators
within the system as well, long before the 1863 enquiries into
English prisons and penal servitude. Captain Williams, a prison
inspector, coldly remarked of Reading: 'the system of instruction
which takes place . . . is simply the getting off by heart whole
chapters of the Bible and in some cases where I tested it I found
that the prisoners understood little of what they had acquired',[30]
while a troubled Director of Convict Prisons worried that prisoners
released from prison to their old environment 'would turn out
quite or nearly as bad as they were before'.[31] Many administrators
who, like Williams, accepted the validity of an associationist
reformist base to prison discipline, nevertheless urged that the
deterrent aspect of prison discipline was in fact of great importance
and pointed out that the reformation of the majority of prisoners

by any means was a most difficult undertaking, given the very bad social backgrounds from which they came. Confidence was not enhanced either amongst people outside the system when confronted with the findings of journalists who had made it their business to investigate reconviction rates among released prisoners subjected to spiritual reformist discipline at Reading. These indicated that official figures were entirely erroneous and that many described as 'living an improved life' had in fact been convicted of further offences whilst the rates of reconviction for Reading were higher than the national average.[32]

Parliamentary Investigation

The growth of anxiety about the effectiveness of British prisons and their link to rising crime rates eventually led to the appointment of a Royal Commission to enquire into penal servitude. It reported in 1863 and the commissioners accepted that the 'present system appears not to be sufficiently dreaded either by those who have undergone it or by the criminal classes in general'.[33] In the evidence which was given to that body there clearly emerged a number of features of the working of the convict prison system which were disturbing to those who saw a decline in severity as linked to an increase in crime. The Clerk of the Western Assize Circuit showed that there had been a marked decrease in the average length of sentences of penal servitude since 1854;[34] Walter Crofton, the Director of Irish Convict Prisons, strenuously urged that the reformation of convicts could not be achieved without subjection to longer periods of convict discipline.[35]

Apart from 'the injurious shortening of the punishment of convicts',[36] other criticisms were levelled at the system. Some witnesses felt that the real antecedent history of a convict never actually came to light either at the court or during sentence so prison staff were working blind, a most serious difficulty given the assumption that all reformatory discipline required individual knowledge of the prisoner.[37] In addition, there were substantial problems surrounding the assessment of prisoners' progress during penal servitude. As the ex-deputy governor of Chatham explained, the assessment of the character and performance of a prisoner required great impartiality and determination, neither of which could be guaranteed. In the first place the officer was paid in part according to the performance of the convicts, whose industry he was therefore likely to record as very good. An equally serious flaw was the propensity of most officers to be 'influenced generally by the character of individual prisoners, who are disposed to commit assaults, in the records which they put down of their work'.[38] Thus the daily record of progress which was intended to act as the artificial incentive to repetitive obedience might well be inaccurate and create an entirely inappropriate reward for an aggressive attitude or mere inertia.

Another ground for criticism concerned the operation of the ticket of leave system. The debate over this issue aroused strong feelings not just amongst the witnesses before the 1863 Commission but also in the Members of Parliament, who subsequently passed the law stemming from its recommendations. During the 1850s those convicts released on tickets of leave were not required as a condition of licence to submit themselves to the continuous supervision of any person or body, being released on the basis that if they breached the conditions of the licence they rendered themselves liable to recall if this were discovered. In fact only 69 licences were revoked for non-criminal breaches of the licence condition such as frequenting places where other criminals were to be found (public and common lodging houses).[39] The theory was indeed that mere compliance with licence terms was a sufficient final part of the convict prison sentence and that there was no need to catalyse further effort among licensees.

There was indeed much objection to any further attempt to stimulate effort and control behaviour of licensees. Such control which would have been exercised by the police appeared to many to be unconstitutional in that powers of recall would be exercised on the basis of secret reports provided by supervising agents, 'the most mischievous and pernicious of all forms of espionage'.[40] There was also a marked fear that the police would in various ways make it more difficult for a man to re-establish himself. If he had found work the police would presumably contact his employer, who might well regard him thenceforward in a wholly different light. Indeed, in France, where such supervision operated, 'it tends to form them into a separate class distinguished from the rest of society in that after a certain time when they become known as belonging to that class and are watched by the police no-one will employ them and they are driven back again into crime'.[41] There was then much uncertainty on both constitutional and operational grounds as to whether supervision ought to be introduced into penal servitude (and in what way). But there was universal agreement, rightly or wrongly, that no effective supervision was in fact exercised over licensees, and that the Home Secretary had been exceedingly cautious in use of those powers he did possess. As Sir Richard Mayne, Commissioner of the Metropolitan Police, pointed out: 'with regard to those released on ticket of leave the police were directed not to notice them as they were looked upon as persons who must be considered reformed and therefore the police were not to notice them lest it might make them known and interfere with their getting employment'. When a police officer visited taverns or lodging houses he might indicate known thieves to the owner of the premises but never ticket of leave men;[42] in other words, as the Lord Chief Justice remarked, 'it has been the reverse of supervision'.[43]

Throughout the late-1850s and early-1860s there were suggestions as to how these problems of constitutionality and inherent impediment to individual progress could be resolved. Matthew Davenport Hill suggested that convicts ought to be released on licences with very clear conditions which could only be revoked after a case alleging failure to keep such conditions had been heard before magistrates, thus answering the problem of the secret machinery of state withdrawing individual liberty.[44] Others put forward the idea that convicts should be obliged by law to report to the police, rather than be subject to police surveillance of their places of accommodation and employment, as this would prevent them being discovered to be on licence by landlords, employers and workmates. The subject remained controversial and Jebb himself was most uncertain about the desirability of supervision. He drew the sharp reproof of one parliamentary committee on transportation because his evidence appeared to be contradictory — on the one hand seeming to oppose the idea on the basis that harm to the licensee might result, and on the other apparently suggesting release under supervision as part of a more stringent system of penal servitude.[45] He later developed the latter idea into supervision by the convict prison system rather than the police, especially of those 'atrocious criminals whose crimes and antecedents or whose conduct in prison gave no hope of amendment'.[46]

Although of course in Ireland the greatest confidence was expressed in active supervision, whether carried out in Dublin by James Organ or elsewhere by the police, and although the problems of restriction of individual progress by surveillance and of resentment by convicts themselves were said to be of little real significance there, in England there was a great deal of perplexity about the issue of supervision. Two particular objections to the entire ticket of leave system (with or without supervision) were held by a number of judges. One held that it created uncertainty regarding the meaning of the punishment ordered by the court and was an incentive to hypocrisy. One of the Judges of Common Pleas, Sir Creswell Creswell, remarked that 'criminals will always indulge the most favourable view of the future and hope to escape with a light punishment . . . a man goes into gaol and by playing the hypocrite for twelve months succeeds in getting the good opinion of the chaplain and the gaoler and has a fair prospect of a ticket of leave which relieves him from any further suffering under the sentence'.[47] However, the most swingeing attack came from Lord Chief Justice Cockburn, a member of the 1863 Penal Servitude Commission who sternly criticised penal servitude for its lack of severity, pointing out that licensees with or without supervision were allowed to roam unchecked the haunts of crime and vice. This was a self-evident absurdity since 'the reformation of the offender is in the highest degree speculative and uncertain and its permanence in the face of renewed temptation exceedingly precarious . . . suffering inflicted as the punishment of crime and the fear of its repetition are far more likely to be lasting and much more calculated to counteract the tendency to the renewal of criminal habits.'[48] He urged the abolition of licences because these undermined the certainty of punishment in the mind of the prisoner and rejected supervision on the additional ground that it made employment and a settled life less likely for honest ex-convicts to obtain. Furthermore, he added, the most dangerous convicts were frequently the best conducted in prison and the entire idea of personal reformation was wholly unproven; indeed, if prisons were more penal and sentences inflexibly enforced, the length of sentences could be reduced by judges.

Cockburn believed that Western Australia ought to be retained as a convict colony and in his general view about the inefficiency of reformation he was echoed by another sentencer who favoured transportation, Sir Archibald Alison, Sheriff of Lanarkshire. Alison condemned the entire ticket of leave system in the most unambiguous terms. This, he said, 'has had the very worst possible effects in Scotland . . . it has sent back the most talented, the most dangerous, and the most formidable class of depredators . . . they are the centre of all the great crimes that have been committed in Scotland within the last four or five years . . . I have the greatest doubts whether there can be produced in an adult . . .

by any course of discipline that a prison can give him, any real moral reformation.'[49]

This growth of scepticism about reformation in the early-1860s among those connected with the administration of criminal justice stretched beyond the convict prisons into the entire county and borough prison system. In February 1863 a select committee of the House of Lords was appointed following the lengthy debate in which Lord Carnarvon had spoken about the undesirable laxity of the prison system. Under his chairmanship there began the first major parliamentary inquiry into the county and borough prisons since the Commons inquiry of 1850 which had decisively sup-ported reformation as a substantial basis of prison discipline. This committee of fifteen members of the House of Lords included at least three who had spoken in support of Carnarvon in the House, as well as Lords Cathcart and Wodehouse who had urged caution in drawing conclusions. The witnesses called before it were drawn from prison administration at all levels throughout England as well as from groups closely connected with the system.[50] It rapidly became clear that the committee was mainly interested in two aspects of the system: the degree to which it was administered symmetrically throughout the realm and the amount of severity felt by prisoners subjected to it.

A study of the very lengthy and detailed evidence given to this committee reveals several of the preoccupations of penal adminis-trators. It is clear that a strong reformist approach was advocated by one party, led by one of the two Inspectors of Prisons, John Perry, who argued most strongly for separation, individual instruction and training of prisoners under a spiritual reformist model of prison discipline. Indeed, Perry, who had replaced Francis Bisset Hawkins as Inspector of Prisons for the South West in 1842 when separation was in its early days and when there were altogether five inspectors, had long been a convinced separatist. He had conducted an unflagging struggle in favour of converting all prisons in his area to this system[51] and he also believed that the state required substantial legal powers to compel local areas to reform their prisons. Thus by 1863, after twenty years in which he had promoted separation, Perry was able to tell the Lords that 'all the prisons that have been rebuilt or materially altered within the last eighteen or twenty years are upon the Separate System'.[52] Perry staunchly defended the reformist ideals of the system and claimed that the major evil was the survival of small borough prisons which were often little changed from John Howard's day.

A New Direction for Prisons 1860–1864

He made the widest claims for reformation as the primary purpose
of prisons and expressed much scepticism about the value of
deterrence. 'Reformation is the main object . . . if that could be
brought about without punishment I should be very glad to see
such a change . . . the time they have had for reflection . . . the
good advice and encouragement that they have received from
benevolent and zealous chaplains and governors have contributed
to make them lead good lives afterwards.'[53]

Perry objected to all severities which were not essentially
reducing the prisoner to a sense of his own forlorn suffering,
brought about by his own sin. He repudiated hard labour
machines, for example, as mere irritants which rendered the
prisoner hostile to his superiors and obstructed their best influences. This was to meet a very different kind of reception from that
accorded to his views by the 1850 Commons Committee, however.
Now he was confronted with scepticism and irritable sarcasm.
'Would not your answer come to this, that except for the purpose
of reforming offenders it would be better to abolish prisons
altogether than to go to the expense and trouble of maintaining
them?' To this he replied, with some ingenuousness: 'It would still
be necessary to restrain them by imprisonment. I said before that
if it were possible to reform a man without inflicting pain I should
conceive it to be our duty to do so, but that, as pain to a certain
extent is necessary to produce reformation in the present constitution of the human character, pain must be inflicted; but we do
not do it for the purpose of inflicting punishment but to make
punishment a means of improving the prisoner.'[54]

Perry was also at odds with the committee when he criticised the
practice of appointing ex-military personnel to the governor and
staff grades of prisons, suggesting that promotion to governor
ought to be on merit and to be from serving prison officers. Ex-
military men tended not to study 'the characters of men' so as to
individualise treatment but to govern 'by rules rather than individual means'.[55] To the suggestion that military officers were
people of 'gentlemanlike feelings and views' and possessed a great
deal of experience of commanding men as well as a good education, Perry replied that he preferred 'practical experience to
polished accomplishments'.[56] Collective, severe and coercive discipline in the hands of ex-soldiers and naval officers had to him a
tendency to 'stir up all the bad feelings of a man against the
authorities and therefore to produce a deterioration of his moral
character'.[57]

Perry was supported by the separatist magistrate from Berkshire, William Merry, who reiterated to the Lords the details of Reading prison. 'Get a man shut up in a separate cell and you can do a great deal with that man . . . I recollect a special instance of a man who had read through half his bible in a fortnight.'[58] As he proceeded in his evidence the committee became increasingly angered by the absence of any compulsory hard labour. When challenged on this, Merry showed that, after twenty years, separation in its purest reformatory form still operated at the prison with its voluntary labour, moral and religious instruction and distrust of deterrence.[59]

The bulk of the evidence, however, was entirely contrary to this optimistic reformist view of the nature of criminals and in particular a number of experienced prison governors were closely questioned about their view of deterrence as the basis of prison discipline. Major Fulford, Governor of Stafford Prison, argued that the 'system of moral reformation' was almost wholly valueless, that even the very few who were genuinely comforted by the chaplain were people who would not return to crime in any event, and that for the majority of criminals prison was an occupational hazard, 'just as in the case of a man hunting who breaks his collar bone'. Suggesting that corporal punishment for those who reoffended and rigorous severity in general were important to deter prisoners, he agreed without reservation with the committee member who observed: 'it comes to this, does it not, that if there were severer punishment all over the country there would be greater hesitation about committing offences'.[60] Indeed, in a number of prisons which maintained rigid isolation of prisoners from one another, staff told the committee that it was the *deterrent* aspect of separation which was its primary value; at Leicester, where hard labour on cranks was performed in separate cells, it was believed that 'the separate system conjoined with hard labour is a very powerful element of deterring them'.[61]

A third group of witnesses was drawn from a variety of related medical and administrative groups to whom may be added the other inspector of prisons, Herbert Voules, whose area comprised the Midlands, the North and Scotland and who had also served as a Director of Convict Prisons. He was, like Jebb and most other directors, an ex-military officer. Voules agreed with Perry that many borough prisons should be entirely rebuilt but, while he did not repudiate entirely the moral effects of separation, he criticised what he termed the 'ultra-philanthropy' which led offenders to see themselves as 'aggrieved parties . . . they have more or less a craving for notoriety and the sympathy which has of late been shown towards great criminals has encouraged this feeling with all classes of prisoners'.[62] This theme of the moral ineffectiveness of separation was developed by a number of witnesses but it was left to Jebb to suggest an alternative system of discipline which could be imposed in local prisons.

Jebb realised that the associationist reformist aspirations which pervaded the convict prison system were inapplicable to the local prisons because the sentences served therein were often only of a few weeks' length, very seldom more than twelve months. Therefore the prisoners were not held for sufficient time to enable the intended substantial reorientation to occur. He began his recipe for change by entirely accepting that isolation of prisoners within separation was an indispensable part of prison discipline. However it was essential, he urged, that prisons be administered on the basis of uniformity throughout the country and that it ought to be plainly recognised that reformation of a prisoner undergoing a short sentence was impossible. To prevent contamination separate isolation, far from being a mistaken policy over the last two decades, was 'essential as the basis of discipline'.[63] However, it ought to be used as a deterrent rather than in a reformist way and should include 'the enforcement of distasteful hard labour of a penal character with a view to deter'.[64]

Jebb then turned to the model of the military prisons of which he had been inspector general for many years. These held soldiers and sailors who had infringed military regulations or committed minor civil offences, and in them separation as a moral reformatory discipline had been rejected as early as 1844. In place of this an exceedingly harsh form of discipline had been devised consisting of hard labour, nocturnal cellular isolation and a system of three stages as in the convict prison system.[65] The hard labour was wholly unlike that of the convict prisons, however, and consisted of an activity called shot drill: 'a row of shot are laid on the ground . . . in a line. The men are formed up in the rear of the shot and on a signal they stoop down and take the shot up and then face to the right or left, march three or four paces to where the next shot was and set it down again; on a signal they take up the shot again, march back and replace them where they took them from.'[66] This system also involved the winning of softer conditions by obedience: the lowest class might have a bed only every third night and had to undertake three hours' shot drill (with a 32 lb shot) together with four hours' drill daily; the next class up had to work with a lighter shot, had a bed every two nights, and so on. This was naturally a highly deterrent system for short-sentence prisoners and at no point was any reformist base urged for it other than that promotion depended upon 'quiet, orderly habits and general good conduct under punishment'.[67] Jebb particularly pointed out that in the convict prison system labour was quite different and that there 'the deterring influence' was 'loss of liberty'.[68]

Jebb's proposal, then, was that in local prisons there ought to be uniformity of severity throughout the land, a deterrent basis of 'hard labour, hard fare and a hard bed',[69] a model based upon military prison regimes in which the objective was that of deterrence by rigour, and he suggested for civil prisons the use of treadmills and cranks, rather than shot drill, should characterise the system. Additionally, there would be nocturnal isolation and a rigid prevention of all communication between prisoners, who would be kept in isolation at all times when not working on treadmills, which in any event would be designed with separate cubicles for each prisoner.

Furthermore, the Committee of Lords heard evidence from Captain Maxwell Luckraft, who governed the new naval prison at Lewes, to the effect that this strict and severe discipline was especially useful for securing 'activity and readiness to do that which is right and proper' amongst those undergoing it.[70] This emphasis upon deterrent impact as the main basis of future local prison discipline was echoed by Crofton, who added that the addition of marks to Jebb's scheme would make prisoners less intractable towards the system. Since juveniles were now being diverted from the prisons to the reformatories, it was desirable to take most stringent measures against adults serving short sentences because often these would have had the benefit of commitment to reformatories earlier in their lives and had failed to take advantage of this.

Medical experts argued that, where a large diet was given to a prisoner who did not have to exert himself, much of the food failed to be 'assimilated' and that, given severe labour, it would be the case that all the elements in a 'vegetable and farinaceous diet' would be entirely utilised by the body which would no longer therefore require as much meat and would in any event be healthier and more 'vital'. Another doctor urged that severe and monotonous labour 'is not at all unwise' in terms of dietary assimilation and claimed, as a result of experiments with German dogs, that although treadmill labour increased bodily waste this in no way meant that the meat given to prisoners needed to be increased.[71] This evidence was particularly important given the widespread complaints that, in reformatory prisons, fat and lazy prisoners spent their time dining well at the ratepayers' expense.

The Change of Policy

It was unsurprising, given the weight of the evidence, that the committee reported unambiguously against the evangelical reformist school of prison discipline and plainly implied that associationist reformist hopes were most unlikely to be fulfilled in local prisons where sentences were so short. In the first place the members complained about 'an inequality, uncertainty and ineffi-ciency of punishment productive of the most prejudicial results' and, with the impatience born of over forty years of legislation intended to create a symmetrical system, demanded that there be established 'without delay a system approaching, as nearly as may be practicable, to an uniformity of labour, diet and treatment'.[72] Secondly, it was emphasised that severe labour 'is the chief means of exercising a deterrent influence' and that this was best carried out by means of the crank and treadmill rather than by 'industrial occupation' or trade instruction, whether accompanied by the voluntarism implicit in separation or not. Although separation was to become the essential basis of all prison discipline, the Lords were clearly of the mind that this would not be the system of spiritual revival of Crawford and Russell. Instead, it was to be a severe, bleak and painful experience in which the isolation would be merely one of the pains of imprisonment to be accompanied by a coarse and barely sufficient diet, plank bed and corporal punish-ment for infractions of rules. They declared that 'the reformation of individual character by any known process of prison discipline is frequently doubtful' for although prisoners may be open to encouragement and reward so as to affect their conduct within the prison, the Carnarvon Committee did 'not consider that the moral reformation of the offender holds the primary place in the prison system; that mere industrial employment without wages is a suffi-cient punishment for many crimes; that punishment in itself is morally prejudicial to the criminal and useless to society, or that it is desirable to abolish both the crank and treadwheel as soon as possible.' The remedy was for the first three months to be served in conditions of hard labour and greatest severity and that thereafter graduation to a higher class would be earned by marks so that a 'strictly progressive' system operated based throughout on a theory of deterrence with a few carrots to encourage obedience from those serving more than three months.[73] Furthermore the Home Secretary ought to be given the power to compel boroughs to make a contract with the county authorities for the reception of their prisoners in the larger county prisons where appropriate and a body of rules ought to be given the mandatory force of law for every prison in the country. The efficiency of the sentencing system ought to be improved by automatic photography of criminals in order to ensure that previous convictions were attributed to the offender at time of sentence and the entire system should be based on the need for 'those offenders who are commencing a course of crime' to be made aware 'that each repetition of it duly recorded and proved will involve a material increase of punishment, pain and inconvenience to them'.[74]

The passage of the legislation stemming from this major reappraisal of the prison system proved by no means easy to accomplish, primarily because of objections to attempts to deprive town councils and county magistrates of some of their traditional powers to govern their prisons as they saw fit within a loose framework of parliamentary law and the guidance of the inspectors. Some felt that the Lords had overlooked the substantial progress towards uniformity which had been made, that over sixty separate system prisons now existed in Scotland and nearly eighty in England,[75] whilst others questioned the suitability of hard labour for women. However, as indicated, the major resistance was against 'a new principle . . . the worst species of centralisation'[76] which would result if the Home Secretary acquired powers to make rules at will, an attempt to supersede the powers of magistrates and to 'arm . . . every Secretary of State, we know not whom, with an indefinite power of overriding the discretion of the justices'.[77] At the time in question there had been much controversy over the desirability of encouraging Roman Catholic priests to minister to Catholic prisoners and some feared that the government was asking for great powers over local prisons as a Trojan horse concealing within it the secret introduction of numerous priests of Rome.[78]

The 1865 Prisons Act[79] made plain the new uniform severity which was to characterise the prison system. The Secretary of

State was given authority to close persistently inadequate prisons and to withhold financial grants of aid in respect of other less recalcitrant authorities; hard labour was defined and demanded; 14 prisons were closed and 104 new rules required by law to be obeyed in every prison in England and Wales. The new system was without exception to depend upon isolation by night and hard labour of the treadmill, shot drill, stone-breaking kind by day, with the possibility of promotion to a less arduous stage by obedience and docility. Henceforth the county and borough prisons must have as their central objective the deterrence of the prisoner and the follies of such places as Reading must speedily become a thing of the past.

Throughout 1863 the Royal Commission had also been in session. This was investigating the system of penal servitude, some of the evidence before which has already been discussed,[80] and the members of this body, whilst in general more favourable to the spiritual and associationist reformism which pervaded convict prisons, concluded that sentences of penal servitude needed to be lengthened from a minimum of three to one of seven years and that the sentence ought to be more severe for convicts who were reconvicted. So as to reduce the incidence of criminality in England the Commission proposed that all fit adult convicts ought to be sent to Western Australia as part of the discipline and that other convicts released in England should be subjected to close active supervision and surveillance by the Convict Prison Directorate, despite the possible impediments which individuals might suffer that had been foreseen by the anti-supervision group. Lastly the members suggested that marks be introduced to the convict prison regime so that, in order to obtain class promotion and ticket of leave release either in England or Western Australia, prisoners must unequivocally demonstrate spirited diligence and effort. The suggestion that the actual daily impact of penal servitude was insufficiently severe was rejected: 'the life of the prisoners is exceedingly monotonous. Having been used in most cases to constant change and excitement they are debarred from all pleasures and amusements, they are compelled to pass their time in a dull unvarying routine of distasteful labour and at the close of each day's work they return to the cheerless solitude of their cells.'[81] The intention was therefore to increase rigour by extending the total amount of time spent in such incarceration, to substitute marks to be earned rather than allowing mere inert passage from one stage to another, to introduce active supervision

160

and to remove as many as possible to a convict colony. Undoubtedly these measures were based upon a desire to increase substantially the deterrent base of the system but they also were suggested
as an enhancement of the reformatory efficiency of convict
prisons. It was felt that marks would stimulate positive exertion
and consequent rewards and that such an attitude would bear fruit
in a land of sparse population and much opportunity, where there
was a need for labour — a view held even by the most pronounced
deterrent member of the Commission, the Lord Chief Justice.

The immediate problem that arose with this was that a number
of the other Australian colonies were opposing transportation on
the grounds that the entire continent ought to be protected from
being overwhelmed by hordes of criminals from the mother
country. So strong had been the representations that the government lost confidence in Western Australia as a homeland for ex-
convicts. Parliament was therefore confronted with legislation
which merely considered release of convicts in England on tickets
of leave and very great disappointment was expressed. Some
members questioned the right of other Australian colonies to have
any say at all in what was done in Western Australia and suggested
that surrender to these colonial associations was wholly wrong in
principle. Lord Houghton mourned that 'the abandonment of
transportation' was 'one of the greatest social misfortunes which
have ever fallen upon this nation'.[82] Notwithstanding this, and the
lengthy attacks on the supervised ticket of leave as unconstitutional, the Act of Parliament passed on 25 July 1864 created a substantially more rigorous sytem of penal servitude than had
previously been the case.[83]

The minimum period of penal servitude which could be passed
upon a convict was increased though not to the seven years which
had been suggested by the Commission (with Western Australia in
mind), but to five years. Any person who had previously been
found guilty of a felony was to receive a sentence of penal servitude
of not less than seven years. In the second place, the government
introduced a compulsory system of monthly reporting to the police
by all holders of tickets of leave in an attempt to meet the argument
that a prying surveillance would damage the progress of the
licensee in the eyes of employers and others. But also included in
the Act was a stipulation that the licence would be 'forthwith forfeited' if convicted for such failure before magistrates. Thirdly, the
Act suggested that the conditions of penal servitude licences should
be more closely defined. A licence model was therefore included

in a schedule; the licensee must produce his licence to any Justice or constable on demand, abstain from any crime, 'he shall not habitually associate with notoriously bad characters such as reputed thieves and prostitutes' nor 'lead an idle and dissolute life without visible means of obtaining an honest livelihood'. Commission of a further crime or failure to report rendered him liable to serve the entire unexpired portion of his penal servitude sentence and breach of the other conditions was made a summary offence punishable with three months' imprisonment. Finally, special conditions might be inserted in licences where considered appropriate.

One somewhat ironic feature of all this was that it had been forcefully argued in both Houses of Parliament that, over the long term, crime had decreased and that in any event the belief that ticket of leave offenders were a common feature of court calendars had been greatly over-subscribed. As Lord Naas remarked: 'a succession of outrages by men, who were called ticket of leave men but had no right to that name, had induced a belief that the system created a class the most dreaded of all the dangerous classes'. That view was underlined by another Member of Parliament, who remarked: 'a year ago the country was alarmed with the prodigious increase of crime, especially of crimes of graver descriptions. It was difficult to trace the causes of that increase but the country, I think hastily, jumped at the conclusion that it was all owing to tickets of leave.'[84] It seems clear that even though the supposed crime rise was entirely contradicted by a longer-term statistical view, the mood prevailing among Members of both Houses was, with few exceptions, a pessimistic one regarding the reformation of offenders. The fear remained that they continued after release to stalk the cities of England in search of prey, despite the fact that 'no sufficient case has been made out for coupling increased intensity of punishment with increased duration'.[85] Doubtless the bleak fact that transportation was now admitted by government to be in its death throes stimulated this fear, but it was clear that many were worried that the reformatory endeavour had been based upon naïve optimism and that criminals had enjoyed an immunity from severity which had allowed them to flourish in vice and crime unchecked. As confidence in penal reformation declined, various schemes were designed aimed at the incapacitation of the criminal, either by creating huge settlements of 20,000 convicts on remote islands or by proposing campaigns against those who sustained or housed criminals so as to render the very survival of the criminal in society an impossibility.[86]

In conclusion, it is important to note that during 1863 the reformist base of the Irish Convict Prison system was also vigorously and publicly attacked by the Reverend C. B. Gibson, who was a chaplain within that system, and by C. P. Measor, who published a tract ominously entitled 'Irish Fallacies and English Facts'.[87] Both sought to undermine the belief that Crofton was the architect of the Irish convict system and suggested that this 'prison plagiarist' was merely implementing ideas which had their origin in the English convict system established by Joshua Jebb, pointing out, for example, that prisoners working in groups outside the prisons in intermediate conditions could be seen in England at Dartmoor where moor reclamation was an established feature of prison discipline.[88] The thrust of the argument of both men was that the Irish convict system lacked sufficient rigorous severity. As the Reverend Gibson expressed it: 'When I saw two or three young fellows — who had been working in some other part of the city — returning at dinner time to Smithfield . . . and taking two or three of the prison steps at a bound, I could not but soliloquise "those young fellows take to reformatory prisons as young ducks take to water" '.[89]

Gibson was concerned to destroy the belief that some extra-ordinary new reformist system was radically reducing Irish crime and he itemised the misconceptions which had arisen. He implied that the educative work of such people as James Organ was beset with difficulties, quoting a schoolmaster of Mountjoy Prison that the prisoners in such classes were 'fidgetty, peevish and irritable',[90] and further suggesting that the labour required of prisoners was so light as to instruct them in idleness. Gibson, who desired reformist prison discipline to be based on a more strict separatist basis, declared that dormitory accommodation in some of the Irish Convict Prisons led to corruption and deflected moral and spiritual reflection. He was convinced that those who claimed that this system of instruction, marks and final intermediate conditions, followed by active supervision, plainly led to reduction of crime had misled the public with confusing statistics. The bare fact was, he concluded, that 'the great advantage possessed by the administrators of Irish Convict Prisons over those of England may be summed up in one sentence — the facilities we possess of disposing of our convicts. The Irish nation, since the famine, have become as migratory as the Northern Hordes that overran the Roman Empire. They go down to their emigrant ships in crowds.

An Irishman with a five pound note in his pocket, a blackthorn stick in his hand and his luggage in a pocket handkerchief will go to America hoping . . . By this love of emigration, in which consists the cure of many of our social evils, the reconvictions among Irish intermediate convicts has [sic] been reduced to at least one half, for which Sir Walter Crofton gives his intermediate prisons credit, and the public Sir Walter Crofton credit.'[91] Thus began the discrediting of the third and most recent jewel in the reformist crown (after separation and English stage reformism, with or without marks) — another sign that the great days of reformist nostrums were fast ending.

References

1. P. Laurie, *Prison Discipline*, 1837; C. Dickens, *American Notes*, pp. 117 – 19, 130 – 1.
2. *The Times*, 29 Nov. 1843, p. 4. *The Times*, 6 Apr. 1844, p. 4.
3. C. Dickens, *American Notes*, p. 118.
4. *Parliamentary Debates*, Third Series, vol. 106, cols 1368, 1370, 1375.
5. T. Carlyle, 'Latter Day Pamphlets', Centenary Edition, *The Works of Thomas Carlyle in Thirty Volumes*, vol. XX, Chapman & Hall Ltd, 1898, pp. 50, 55.
6. Ibid., pp. 66, 68, 70, 81, 82.
7. M. Carpenter, *Our Convicts*, Longman, 1864, vol. 1, p. 103.
8. W. L. Clay, *Our Convict Systems*, p. 367.
9. Ibid., p. 369.
10. J. Davis, 'The London Garotting Panic of 1862: A Moral Panic and the Creation of a Criminal Class in Mid Victorian England', p. 191, in *Crime and the Law — The Social History of Crime in Western Europe since 1500*, (eds) V. A. C. Gatrell, B. Lenman and G. Parker, Europa, 1980, pp. 190 – 213.
11. M. Heather Tomlinson, 'Penal Servitude 1846 – 65: a system in evolution', in V. Bailey (ed.), *Policing and Punishment in Nineteenth Century Britain*, Croom Helm, 1981, pp. 126 – 49.
12. Peter W. J. Bartrip, 'Public Opinion and Law Enforcement — the Ticket of Leave Scares in Mid Victorian Britain', in V. Bailey (ed.), *Policing and Punishment*, pp. 150 – 81.
13. Ibid., p. 166.
14. S. J. Stevenson, 'The Criminal Class in the Mid Victorian Century', D. Phil., Oxford, 1983, pp. 42, 48 – 52.
15. *Parliamentary Debates*, Third Series, vol. 169, cols 476, 477, 478, 480, 483.
16. Sir Arthur Hardinge, *The Fourth Earl of Carnarvon 1831 – 90*, OUP, 1925, vol. 1, p. 196.
17. Ibid., p. 196.
18. Ibid.

19. Ibid., pp. 201, 213.
20. Ibid., vol. 1, p. 76; vol. 3, p. 326.
21. *Parliamentary Debates*, Third Series, vol. 175, col. 893.
22. Ibid., vol. 169, col. 487.
23. Ibid., vol. 180, col. 124.
24. Ibid., vol. 173, col. 747; C. B. Adderley, *A Century of Experiments on Secondary Punishments*, Parker, Son & Brown, 1863, p. 3.
25. *27 & 28 Vict., Cap. XLVII; 28 & 29 Vict., Cap. CXXVI.*
26. *The Times*, 6 Jan. 1857, p. 8.
27. *Report of the Commissioners appointed to inquire into the operation of the Acts relating to Transportation and Penal Servitude*, Written evidence, J. Jebb, PP, 1863, vol. XXI, pp. 146–7.
28. *First Report from the SC on Transportation*, PP, 1856, vol. XVII, p. 42.
29. W. Crofton, *The Immunity of Habitual Criminals*, Gill & Daldy, 1861, pp. 17–18.
30. *Report from the SC on Prison Discipline*, PP, 1850, vol. XVII, p. 52.
31. Ibid., p. 105.
32. Ibid., p. 649.
33. *Penal Servitude Acts Commission*, PP, 1863, vol. XXI, p. 23.
34. Ibid., Minutes of Evidence of Sidney Gurney, p. 152.
35. Ibid., Minutes of Evidence, p. 307.
36. Ibid., Report, p. 24.
37. Ibid., Minutes of Evidence of J. Weatherhead, p. 427.
38. Ibid., Minutes of Evidence of C. P. Measor, pp. 438–40, 464.
39. Ibid., Minutes of Evidence of J. Jebb, p. 30.
40. *Parliamentary Debates*, Third Series, vol. 175, col. 894, words of Lord Carnarvon.
41. *Penal Servitude Acts Commission*, PP, 1863, vol. XXI, Minutes of Evidence of H. Waddington, p. 34.
42. Ibid., pp. 130–1.
43. Ibid., Report, p. 83.
44. *Second Report from the SC on Transportation*, PP, 1856, vol. XVII, p. 12.
45. *First Report from the SC on Transportation*, PP, 1856, vol. XVII, pp. 101, 120–1.
46. *Penal Servitude Acts Commission*, PP, 1863, vol. XXI, Minutes of Evidence, p. 85.
47. *Second Report from the SC on Transportation*, PP, 1856, vol. XVII, pp. 101–2.
48. *Report of the Penal Servitude Commission*, PP, 1863, vol. XXI, pp. 85–6.
49. *Second Report from the SC on Transportation*, PP, 1856, vol. XVII, pp. 29, 37.
50. *SC of the House of Lords . . . Gaols and Houses of Correction*, PP, 1863, vol. IX.
51. W. J. Forsythe, *A System of Discipline: Exeter Borough Prison 1819–1863*, pp. 79–81.
52. *SC of the House of Lords . . . Gaols and Houses of Correction*, PP, 1863, vol. IX, Minutes of Evidence, p. 13.
53. Ibid., Minutes of Evidence, pp. 62, 67.
54. Ibid., Minutes of Evidence, p. 70.

55. Ibid., p. 31.
56. Ibid., pp. 41, 42.
57. Ibid., p. 61.
58. Ibid., pp. 238–9.
59. Ibid., pp. 241, 243.
60. Ibid., pp. 155, 160.
61. Ibid., p. 167.
62. Ibid., p. 203.
63. Ibid., p. 108.
64. Ibid., p. 111.
65. See *Report on the Discipline and Management of the Convict Prisons, 1850*, PP, 1851, vol. XXVIII, pp. 62–5.
66. *SC of the House of Lords . . . Gaols and Houses of Correction*, PP, 1863, vol. IX, Minutes of Evidence, p. 114.
67. Ibid., p. 113.
68. Ibid., p. 116.
69. Ibid., p. 125.
70. Ibid., p. 229.
71. Ibid., Evidence of Dr W. A. Guy, p. 351; of Dr E. Smith, pp. 73–82.
72. Ibid., Report, pp. iii–iv.
73. Ibid., Report, pp. iv, xii, xiv, xiii.
74. Ibid., Report, p. xvi.
75. *Parliamentary Debates*, Third Series, vol. 175, col. 2047.
76. Ibid., col. 2055.
77. Ibid., col. 2065.
78. The passage of this legislation is summarised in S. McConville, *English Prison Administration*, pp. 378–80.
79. *28 & 29 Vict., Cap. CXXVI.*
80. Ibid., PP, 1863, vol. XXI.
81. Ibid., PP, 1863, vol. XXI, p. 41.
82. *Parliamentary Debates*, Third Series, vol. 175, col. 885.
83. *27 & 28 Vict., Cap. XLVII.*
84. *Parliamentary Debates*, Third Series, vol. 173, cols 752, 787–8.
85. Ibid., Third Series, vol. 174, col. 1256.
86. *2nd Report from the SC on Transportation*, PP, 1856, vol. XVII, Evidence, p. 38. W. Pare, *A Plan for the Suppression of Predatory Classes*, pub. Effingham Wilson, 1862.
87. C. P. Measor, *Irish Fallacies and English Facts*, W. Ridgway, 1863.
88. Ibid., p. 22.
89. C. B. Gibson, *Irish Convict Reform: the Intermediate Prisons A Mistake*, McGlashan and Gill, 1863, p. 32.
90. Ibid., p. 12.
91. Ibid., p. 60.

7

The Scientific Approach to Criminal Man 1860–1890

The Scientific Challenge

The 1840s and 1850s had seen the zenith of the reformatory ideal, based upon the notion that the criminal was in the main a product of the environment in which he had lived. A plethora of literature had been published by reformists emphatically declaring that vile sanitary and immoral domestic or social conditions created surroundings in which children, men and women were precipitated into membership of the criminal class. Alexander Thomson's earlier cited works[1] depicted the expected general results of pollution, overcrowding, bad sanitation and drunkenness, which demanded vital social action by the strong and well-to-do to repair, by education, sanitary measures and a moral dedication. To these had been added the works of others which highlighted the widespread and social destabilising debauching of the lower orders, showing not only that such misery and crime were intolerable within a Christian nation but that by vigorous social action all might yet be made well. Mary Carpenter in the 1850s forcefully led the campaign for reformatory and industrial schools so that the community would become 'the fathers and mothers of these moral orphans'.[2] These were the ones who had either fallen into membership of the 'dangerous' (i.e. criminal) class or who were, as members of the 'perishing' class, 'almost certain from their ignorance, destitution, and the circumstances in which they are growing up to do so'.[3] She echoed the belief of one of the Common Sergeants of London that potent causes of crime were 'the absence of parental care and the exercise of parental misrule and unkindness . . . the want of the fostering care of a mother' so that children 'run wild, idle, unheeded and untaught in the streets where they form acquaintances, congregate and stumble on others expert in all the Arts of crime',[4] most obviously in the large industrial cities and London. Yet despite the terrifying vision of a social pyramid standing upon a foundation of 'materials often decaying and rotting away, whose corrupting influences are perpetually spreading upwards'[5] or of 'the miserable state in which thousands are lodged, the degrading and demoralising effect of this upon the character'[6] the belief that the causes of crime were essentially lodged in post-natal experience of a deficient environment which could be changed and remedied had given a strong optimistic flavour to much of this work. It was exemplified by the title of one collection of writings on such matters, 'Meliora — or Better Times to Come'.[7] And, as these writers had never ceased to proclaim, such conditions would give way in the face of the 'kindly feeling betwixt the various classes of society' so that the rich and poor would be bound by ties of mutual knowledge, respect and endeavour; above all by Christian devotion.[8]

These calls to arms had been further supported during the mid-century by copious references to earlier well known figures who had begun the mighty work of moral reconstruction, and in the prison field attention was frequently drawn to such figures as the humbly born Sarah Martin of Great Yarmouth. She captured the mid-century imagination as one who carried the moral-spiritual message of true Christianity to the inmates of her local prison between 1819 and 1843 and never faltered in her commitment to such work despite the intense pain which she suffered as a result of the illness from which eventually she died.[9] If the endeavour could be made, all might change:

> When deep concern for others on me lie
> Whose guilt and wretchedness cause many a sigh
> Let me still seek their interest here
> And in the world above.[10]

The accounts of Sarah Martin's life contained numerous descriptions of her encounters with prisoners, the compassionate and firm spirit, active and reforming in a forlorn and vicious world of the unloved and rejected: 'when I told her the motive of my visit, her guilt and her need of God's mercy she burst into tears and thanked me whilst I read to her the 23rd chapter of St. Luke — the story of the thief on the cross . . . "do you frequently think me personally

severe then?'' ''We do'', he replied, ''and the prisoners talk of it.''
''But if they feel offended at the moment they are convinced of the
justice of it afterwards?'' ''That'', said he, ''has been my own
case[11] . . . bad as they all three are, they make each other worse
and are all so poor and ill fed when out of prison that their living in
it is better''.'[12]

In the midst of this general environmentalist spiritual/moral
approach to the criminal and the notion of an essentially fluid
criminal class whose recruitment resulted from social conditions
and whose reduction might be hoped for, just as it would later be
claimed that 'juvenile crime as it existed twenty years ago has been
absolutely annihilated' by reformatory schools,[13] there appeared a
book which attracted no particular attention and which suggested
that matters were not so simply to be resolved. The writer,
Thomas Plint, was interested in the relationship between crime
and environmental circumstances and he gathered large quantities
of statistical information in his investigation. Thus he appeared to
be conducting a familiar sociological enquiry into criminogenic
social surroundings, expounding the idea that the criminal class
was formed as a result of 'a sequence of errors in the frame and
working of social institutions or as a moral cesspool into which all
the offscourings and dregs of the community settle down and
corrupt'.[14] However he also suggested that in fact little was known
about criminals and observed that, far from being creatures of circumstance, 'a large majority of the class is so by descent and
stands as completely isolated from the other classes, in blood, in
sympathies, in its domestic and social organisation . . . as it is
hostile to them in the whole ways and means of its temporal
existence.'[15] He argued that detailed empirical knowledge of this
class was necessary in order to base remedies upon such knowledge
and it seems clear that Plint was influenced by the growing body of
opinion which required more than the unproven evangelical or
associationist assumptions about criminal man which had prevailed previously.

This work is a long-forgotten and minute part of what Greenleaf
saw as the increasing importance of the scientific approach in the
'formation of general attitudes'. In this, there grew an assumption
that 'real or genuine knowledge is only possible on the basis of
matter of fact, carefully observed, catalogued or categorised in
some way and, if possible measured, quantified and subsumed
under a law or functional generality', with the onset of a positivism
which consisted of 'the attempt to apply causal scientific analysis

to as wide a range of data as possible'.[16] Such an approach to social and human problems possibly received much impetus from the sociological writings, which had become available in Britain in the 1830s, of Auguste Comte. The latter argued that there were three stages in human development: the theological (in which man believes in invisible gods and spirits), the metaphysical (in which his gods and spirits become abstractions) and the scientific (in which 'the religion of humanity supplants that of Christianity').[17] Between 1820 and 1859 (the year of *Origin of the Species*) a remarkable intellectual emphasis on rigorous and impartial observation and empiricism grew, as metaphysical speculation was abandoned in favour of patient collection of facts which might allow accurate description and prediction. Furthermore there occurred dramatic 'breakthroughs in geology, palaeontology and prehistory [which] opened the door to interpretations which accentuated natural processes rather than catastrophic interventions by the creator'.[18] Thus it was found that dinosaurs had existed long before the reported creation of the world in Genesis, strange African tribes were discovered and their head shapes measured by the new discipline of craniometry to establish an anatomical basis for description of different human types, and skeletal remains discovered which suggested a more primitive type of man resembling the higher apes discovered. Between 1820 and 1860 the study of ethnology flourished in which tribal physical and biological characteristics were carefully observed and the intellectual climate began to be influenced by two notions. First it became plain that the time-span within which man had existed was far shorter than the life of the planet, but secondly it became well known by 1845 that there was an increasingly serious question as to whether man was in some way descended from other species.

The extraordinary growth of positivistic enquiry (indeed Darwin's voyage on the *Beagle* was completed as early as 1836) naturally led by 1860 to a conviction among many that reason and scripture had come into direct conflict.[19] As Professor Owen Chadwick remarked, whilst at the beginning of the nineteenth century religion and morality 'were inseparable',[20] by the end of the 1870s faith in the literal truth of the Bible had been deeply unsettled, and to certain people it even appeared that it was a matter of 'science versus orthodoxy, science versus a semi-barbarous Hebrew cosmology, day versus night . . . the philosophy of scientific light versus religious darkness.'[21] However, for the majority of Victorian thinkers and students it was not the simple apparent conflict between biblical revelation and scientific discovery which was most disturbing, but the gradual unfolding of a complexity, a huge unsuspected prehistory which made them in their inmost selves far less certain 'what God was like'.[22] It left them at the edge of an almost infinite time and space in earthly history, revealed by science, and apparently brooded over for unknown millennia before man first made an appearance by a God who was content to make do with dinosaurs rather than humans. At the very least the creation of man less than a week after that of the earth and the direct decision of God a few thousand years later to send Christ because man had not understood His will as the central two events around which all else turned might not appear now in quite the same starkly dramatic interventive light.

The growth of positivist science, rooted in detailed measurement, classification, apparent absence of *a priori* judgement and observation of fact, had, well before 1859, intersected with a strengthening evolutionist — or at least transmutationist — approach to man's origins. This was unsettling to the religious view of man as a specially modelled and beloved creature of God for such an approach seemed to suggest that he was not distinctly separate, a special category of creature uniquely created by God as quintessentially different from other life. He might, instead, be descended from the animal kingdom, merely a kind of mammal whose distant past history had involved substantial physiological change and whose future physiological structure might not indeed be safely predicted. The notion of creatures evolving over huge periods of time was by no means new in 1859 and it had been notably developed by Jean Baptiste Lamarck, who died in 1829 'believing himself to have demonstrated with certainty how one species could change into another [so that] the development of medical and biological science in the thirty years after his death brought the relationships of species ever more into the argument and with them the animal nature of man'.[23]

In 1859, Charles Darwin's *Origin of the Species* was published and, as is well known to subsequent generations influenced by his view of man and his world, he sought to explain the changes which occurred in life forms. He argued that man was descended from higher forms of animal life which were themselves descended from the lower and that across the time in which life had existed on the planet it had developed from an original homogeneity at the time of its first existence to an increasing heterogeneity and complexity. In part (although not entirely so, as Lamarck had maintained) the reason why this occurred lay in the interaction between life forms and their environment. Over time, life forms either adapted functionally to survive in their changing environments (and to compete for that environment) or they adapted insufficiently and tended towards extinction because, as Malthus had urged, the environment is not sufficient for the survival of all life forms. Survival was therefore largely determined by adaptability (although it ought to be added that, unlike Lamarck, Darwin believed that there was also a 'spontaneous variation . . . regardless of environmental conditions').[24] Each succeeding life form therefore developed characteristics which made its survival more likely and, no matter how minute the changes, tended to bequeath them to the next generation, thus enabling the future chance of survival to be strengthened. Indeed within the higher species like tended to mate with like so as to reproduce more efficiently their hard-won capacities for survival, 'the pairing of the strongest and best armed males . . . with the most vigorous and best nourished females.'[25]

Darwin's work needs to be treated with caution because of its great complexity and, indeed, it is worth noting two qualifications. First, although Darwin believed that he was approaching the world as a disinterested scientist, he apparently felt that the increasing heterogeneity of life and eternal change had an overall long-term tendency towards progress and improvement,[26] although he was less optimistic in this respect than had been Lamarck. Secondly, whereas at first sight it may appear that he was emphasising competition with other living beings and hereditary variations in the 'general and specific gifts' of individual men (just as the length of a polar bear's hair or a bird's wings varied from its fellows),[27] he did in fact make clear that strong and weak creatures of the same type were capable of co-operation and that the effect of education and religion upon 'the moral qualities' should by no means be discounted.[28]

Darwin's views were contrary to the earlier prevailing notion of the world as a place of animate and inanimate phenomena which were fixed in their characteristic, orderly and distinctive harmonious development according to God's intention for the phenomenon in question. Together with his contemporary Alfred Wallace, Darwin made it clear that living existence was a changing, striving experience in which man's present position as the highest form of mammal might well be only temporary. He emphasised the infinite variation of life forms in the struggle for survival, the restless changing nature of the environment, the

descent of species from other species, eternal and endless interaction and competition. Man was therefore no longer a unique
creature standing between animal and God, separated in his
essence from other creatures by a distinct, changeless moral or
intellectual superiority. He was in all aspects part of a general con-
tinuity of life which at one point included a bird, another a fish,
another a bee, another a man, the future shape of which would be
determined by the capacity to compete and adapt in order to
improve survival chances. In this process the least fit would decline
and die out and morality would be established by species largely in
accordance with the demands of the environment.[29]

Three points ought to be made explicit. First, Darwin's *Descent
of Man* (1871) did not necessarily controvert the associationist
theorising of the later-nineteenth century, for associationist
psychology was during this period itself moving (again) towards
'an increasingly physiological character . . . that the reaction of
faculty with the environment could produce some memory of
itself. It could in fact be incorporated into the individual's
heredity';[30] thus associationist processes within the individual
might be seen as having an evolutionary component predating
birth. Secondly, Darwin's work further undermined the biblical
interpretation of nature. Thirdly, although between 1863 and
1867 'discussion of science and religion changed its character . . .
because of Darwin' Darwin himself was 'not so much the cause as
the occasion' in that the way had already been paved for very widespread attention to be given to his work by scientific development
for at least two decades before publication of *Origin of the Species*, and
between 1840 and 1860 'there was a growing acceptance of the idea
of biological evolution which Darwin synthesised in the *Origin of the
Species*'.[31] Darwin therefore emphasised the already strengthening
tendency to see social process as scientifically explicable and
provided a thoroughly grounded framework for such an approach;
thus, for example, contemporary anthropologists could study
African tribes in terms of physique and morality appropriate to an
earlier stage of evolution.

The Application of Science to Criminal Man

Although Darwin expressed approval of the work of Francis
Galton, whose 'admirable labours' came to link his work to
crime,[32] the relationship between Darwin's ideas and the Social

Darwinism of the later-nineteenth century is a most complex one. It has recently been analysed by Dr Greta Jones, who has suggested that 'Social Darwinism . . . reasserted many of the traditional ways in which survival of the fittest and population pressure had been used before Darwin.'[33] Darwinian evolutionism was readily utilised to explain the existence of groups within society which appeared to be either above or below the norm. In his first major work, *Hereditary Genius*, published in 1869, Galton summarised arguments, which he had rehearsed since 1865, that man's abilities are chiefly inherited and that by selective breeding it would be possible to produce a highly gifted race of men. He offered a most detailed analysis of descendants of well known gifted people, observing that 'the range of mental power . . . between the greatest and least of English intellects is enormous'. In conclusion he suggested that, in order to assist evolution and to protect the evolving strength of the English race, those of weak capacity should be kindly received 'in celibate monasteries or sisterhoods'.[34] This notion of interference with the evolution of human beings so as to improve the strength and vitality of human society received further attention fourteen years later when Galton published *Inquiries into Human Faculty*. Here he set out to show how it might be possible to replace 'inefficient human stock' with better, in order 'to further the ends of evolution'.[35] He drew a disturbing picture of the criminal, the insane and the pauper. These, he argued, possessed mental and moral qualities which were not only far inferior to those of notable competence but obviously inferior to the norm. 'The ideal criminal has marked peculiarities of character. His conscience is almost deficient, his instincts are vicious, his power of self control is very weak and he usually detests continuous labour. The absence of self control is due to ungovernable temper, to passion or to mere imbecility . . . he has neither sympathy for others nor the sense of duty both of which lie at the base of conscience . . . their vagrant habits, their illegitimate unions and extreme untruthfulness are among the difficulties of the investigator. It is however easy to show that the criminal nature tends to be inherited.'[36]

It must be noted that some of these observations could be easily found in much earlier-nineteenth-century literature about criminals, and indeed the reference to 'sympathy' puts one in mind of Bentham himself and of associationists generally. However, one aspect which was explicitly Darwinian in this was the importance attributed to inheritance of characteristics, and to their constitutional presence within the creature from birth. Whereas evangelical and associationist theorists had emphasised an environment which affected the individual after his birth, Galton was emphasising that the environment interacted with families and races over centuries to shape moral, mental and physical characteristics which were materially bequeathed to individual human beings and were present within the baby at the instant of birth. Now it must be added that Galton was not saying that all criminality may be so explained, and indeed he referred to education and other post-natal environmental influences as necessary within society. However he had no doubt of the 'vastly preponderating effects of nature over nurture' (after conducting detailed studies of twins) and plainly he was asserting the biological existence of 'a countless number of abortive seeds and germs . . . crippled, insane, idiotic and otherwise born incurably imperfect in body or mind.'[37]

Galton knew that the problem was more than merely one of subnormal and fixed criminal, pauper and insane groups at the bottom of society which were likely to be selected out by nature fairly swiftly, for evolutionary selection was a process which, albeit operating eternally, achieved only very small changes in the short run. He therefore went on to consider whether the energy and intelligence of man, having discovered these basic laws, might accelerate the speed of their operation. By careful and rigorous study of individuals by scientific means Galton believed it would be possible to discover the sturdy and strong and the subnormal and to 'devise means for favouring individuals who bore the signs of membership of a superior race'. That would allow the introduction of 'an element of forecast' as to who were 'most likely to stock the world with healthy, moral, intelligent and fair natured citizens'.[38] As for the rest, 'the stream of charity is not unlimited and it is requisite for the speedier evolution of a more perfect humanity that it should be so distributed as to favour the best adapted . . . I have not spoken of the repression of the rest, believing that it would ensue directly as a matter of course'[39] if artificial maintenance of this group were withdrawn or greatly reduced.

Without such steps there might be little evidence of this selective process in the short term. The general theory of inherited predisposition was tested in America in the 1870s by R. L. Dugdale, who investigated the descendants of a couple known as the Jukes. The results not only were believed by Galton to show the profound truth of Social Darwinian Theory but to show that the criminal and vicious were procreating their own kind at a deeply disturbing rate and that of 'the infamous Jukes family . . . a frightful number degraded into criminality, pauperism or disease'.[40] Thus it might well seem to many, especially those of a Malthusian or political economic turn of mind, that the natural social environment of men had been so altered since 1750 by state action towards the poor that Darwin's theory of natural selection might be in danger of suspension, that by protective institutions of social policy such as the Poor Law the harsh laws of evolution might cease to operate and the vicious and criminal be saved from extinction to procreate their own kind, even perhaps to overwhelm the normal and their superiors. Nor was this grim vision of a social armageddon likely to be effaced by Galton somewhat weakly repeating that those would 'deserve better of their county . . . who determine to live celibate lives through a reasonable conviction that their issue would probably be less fitted than the generality to play their part as citizens.'[41] To the generations who had absorbed the dire prediction of Malthus that if natural restraints such as death from hunger or disease induced by vice were removed by the social policies of the state, population would outstrip food supplies, it was little surprising that protection of the criminal by charity or whatever might transform natural selection and extinction into fearful increase by procreation. And for this case the Jukes were powerful witnesses.

The rapid growth of positivist and Social Darwinist approaches to human behaviour tended therefore to contradict most strongly any idea that social action of an evangelical or associationist kind would lead to substantial spiritual or moral changes within inferior human creatures. Increasingly it was maintained that human characteristics were established at a much deeper level than merely the result of foul sanitation or unchristian parents. Furthermore it appeared that the criminal might well be one whose characteristics were normal for an earlier evolving age and were plain evidence of an inability to exhibit that evolution displayed by the sturdy and the strong. He was, in effect, an anachronism blindly moving towards his eventual extinction during the millennia ahead provided that human arrangements did not alter the laws of nature. Darwin had therefore validated scientifically some of Malthus' most disturbing intuitions about human viciousness and virtue.

The idea of anachronistic characteristics seems certainly to have been in the mind of the theorist Herbert Spencer, whose early work was written entirely independently of Darwin, being founded in Lamarckian theory, but who quickly came to believe that Darwin's contribution to knowledge was of the profoundest importance. Spencer in his numerous scientific writings on psychology, sociology and biology analysed 'mental evolution in its higher stages'[42] in terms of 'one long process of mankind's adaptation to the requisites of perfect life . . . [he] attempts to show how progress in all spheres — sociology, biology, psychology and astronomy conforms to an identical pattern consisting of a transformation from a chaotic homogeneity to an ordered heterogeneity'.[43] He further believed that all living things evolved towards a higher perfection, and inherited their characteristics. He described the most highly evolved men as thoughtful and self-critical in judgement, appropriately hesitant and careful in action, possessed of 'a judicial intellect' in contrast to the uncivilised man whose intellect was 'sudden in its inferences, incapable of balancing evidence and adhering obstinately to first impressions'. More evolved man would be detectable by 'the degree of remoteness from primitive reflex action' as well as by well-developed nervous systems, larger brains and frequently exercised 'lines of nervous communication'.[44]

However bright was the ultimate future, Spencer's description of natural evolution towards more perfect psychological, biological and sociological complexity also implied a biological and psychological inferiority within certain groups at any given time. His portrayal of 'the savage character — unsociable, improvident, unutilitarian, unpredictable' implied change as arising 'from relatively unmanipulable, steadily evolving factors'.[45] Spencer was able to argue that social policy which aimed to alter moral behaviour was based on erroneous assumptions, for a higher morality naturally arose out of organic movement towards complexity and heterogeneity, that in the profound world of natural change lay an evolution not merely psychological, sociological and biological but also moral.

These positivist and evolutionist theories brought again into the foreground that interest in physiological psychology which had been present earlier in the nineteenth century but which had not achieved the widespread acceptance of spiritual or associationist approaches to the problem of crime. One particular earlier school of thought had been that of phrenological positivism pioneered by Franz Joseph Gall (1758–1828) who had sought to correlate specific behavioural functions with particular regions of the brain. In Britain the psychologist George Combe had produced a lengthy exposition of this branch of psychology, and argued that 'the brain consists of a congeries of organs, that each organ manifests a particular mental faculty and that . . . the power of manifesting each faculty bears a proportion to the size of its organ.'[46] Combe had classified human faculties into animal, moral and intellectual, and described the location of each of these within the brain. So 'the organs of intellect lie in the anterior lobe of the brain. In the coronal region there are organs which manifest emotions or feelings called the moral sentiments viz. benevolence, veneration and conscientiousness. The power in any individual of experiencing each of these emotions bears a relation . . . to the size of its own organ.'[47] God had intended a balance between these classes of faculties but in many human beings an imbalance was detectable. A man with an enlarged animal and a small moral organ of the brain, for example, would be predisposed to impulsive crime in pursuit of his desires and all abnormal behaviour might be understood precisely in terms of enlargement or diminution of these organs in relation to one another. Furthermore the brain structure was inherited and an examination of workhouse children showed predictably that they were 'palpably inferior in temperament and in size of brain' and 'spring from parents who are the refuse or dregs of the community'.[48] By this it was obvious that men were not equal rational creatures but 'in the case of persons possessing the lowest class of brains, we are presented with beings whose tendencies to crime are naturally very strong and whose powers of moral guidance and restraint are very feeble.'[49]

Combe had rejected deterrence as ineffective for such people and, although he had proposed a corrective strategy based upon the need to stimulate the underdeveloped parts of the brain to activity, the overwhelming inference to be drawn from all his work was that the criminal was the natural result of inherited brain structure. He revealed that the brain structure of a person was indicated by the physical shape of the head: 'when firmness is large and conscientiousness small the head slopes at an acute angle downwards from firmness'.[50] In fact, he had identified 35 aspects of mind and feeling which he clustered in four main categories. Each aspect had its seat in a defined part of the brain, the size of that part in relation to others determining the extent to which the man was 'conscientious', 'combative', 'acquisitive', 'amative', 'benevolent' etc.[51] It is worth noting that Combe did believe that brain organs might develop in an imbalanced manner if small children were ill trained by their parents. If, for example, the animal organs were 'presented with objects calculated to call them into vivid action, while his moral sentiments . . . receive no proportionate training',[52] this would have a lasting effect. But, overall, the theory was one of 'the hereditary predisposition'[53] amongst habitual criminals and additional stimulated imbalance — whose correction was most difficult — among other abnormals.

Since head shape revealed the brain structure of the case in question it was not long before Combe and his followers had begun to appear at British prisons in order to measure the capital characteristics of inmates. Thus at Newcastle-on-Tyne in 1835, 'T.S., aged 18 . . . destructiveness is very large, combativeness, secretiveness and acquisitiveness are large; intellectual organs fairly developed; amativeness is large; conscientiousness rather moderate, benevolence is full and veneration rather large. This boy is considerably different from the last. He is more violent in his disposition; he has probably been committed for assault connected with women. He has also large secretiveness and acquisitiveness and may have stolen';[54] George Laval Chesterton was 'staggered' at Coldbath Fields in 1852 when, by use of a 'magneto-scope', a phrenologist accurately assessed characters of prisoners: 'my judgement was led captive, all latent scepticism vanished'.[55]

Positivistic phrenology did not in the period before 1860 become a major preoccupation of penologists. Indeed, at the publication of Combe's first work in 1819 his views seemed absurd to the great majority of readers. By mid-century, however, it was accepted that brain structure had an influence on conduct, although most psychological theorists hesitated about the precise details of phrenology itself and continued to emphasise environment as the major determinant of conduct.[56] Nevertheless, the notion of more general inherited constitutional predisposition steadily gained ground after mid-century and was given great impetus by the work of Darwin, Galton and Spencer as their work gradually became known and respected. In particular, Galton was deeply involved in the pioneering of anthropometric measurement, seeking to show that cultural and other behaviour was linked to cerebral physiology and that cranial measurement might indicate evolutionary stage. There emerged in the 1870s and 1880s a much more influential positivistic psychology than phrenology itself, based upon a widely held view that criminal man was not only different from normal in terms of his head shape and more general physiological structure but represented an earlier more primitive organism, an atavism resembling the remote ancestors of man, carrying with him a savagery generally characteristic of a bygone era long since passed by evolution. Furthermore, as earlier noted, associationist psychology had itself now entered the realm of heredity so that associationist impacts upon mind might theoretically be bequeathed biologically and did not stand in opposition to these new endeavours to explain criminal behaviour and attitude.

In the criminal justice field this period showed these influences gaining considerable ground. Dr Bruce Thompson of Perth Prison explained in two articles in 1870: 'the physical organisation of the criminal is marked by . . . a singular stupid and insensate look . . . a bad complexion and harsh angular and clumsy outlines . . . a devil, a born devil on whose nature nurture could never stick . . . a set of coarse, angular, clumsy stupid features . . . the women are ugly in face and action without the beauty of colour or grace or regularity of features and all have a sinister and repulsive expression in look and mien.'[57] In 1869, Dr George Wilson reporting 'on moral imbecility of habitual criminals as exemplified by cranial measurement' found over-represented cranial underdevelopment in a sample of nearly 500 criminals and asserted that 'habitual criminals were cranially deficient, especially in the anterior lobes of the brain'. There were other physical abnormalities: 'bullet heads, low brows, projecting ears, weazel eyes' and a 'morbid condition of the brain or other organs in the shape of tumours, cancers, ulcerations or irritating secretions which have fully accounted for mental or moral defects'.[58] Other well known medical and psychological experts such as Alexander Bain or David Nicholson also began to develop the image of the criminal mind as impulse-dominated, indifferent to pain, unable to retain memory of consequence, utterly failing to learn from experience and inherently defective. In a general analysis of the physiology of the criminal the medical officer of Millbank by 1868 had become convinced that most of the invalid convicts in Millbank were so as a result 'of originally feeble constitutions . . . over which they have had no control' rather than damaged by 'vicious or irregular habits'.[59]

The primitive unevolved habitual criminal was most fully identified for positivist science by Cesare Lombroso in Italy. In fact Lombroso altered his views somewhat during his life and by 1899 he was clear that the 'organic factor'[60] only affected around 40 per cent of criminals. However, at the outset of his work in 1870 he 'found in the skull of a brigand a very long series of atavistic anomalies, above all an enormous middle occipital fossa and a hypertrophy of the vermis analogous to those that are found in inferior vertebrates. At the sight of these strange anomalies the problem of the nature and of the origin of the criminal seemed to me to be resolved; the characteristics of primitive man and of inferior animals must be reproduced in our times. Many facts seemed to confirm this hypothesis, above all the psychology of the criminal.'[61] Lombroso then went back 'not only to savage men but also to animals and even to [insectivorous] plants . . . to find the origin of this atavistic phenomenon'[62] and arrived at a physiological and psychological view of the characteristics of the born criminal whom he saw as a distinct anthropological type, initially an atavistic survival in advanced societies of the savage, a concept to which he later added that of a diseased degenerate phenomenon which had fallen below normality. Born criminals, whom he at first believed to be 70 per cent of all criminals, might thus be detected by anthropometric measurement for they would possess particular physical characteristics of an earlier evolutionary stage — 'the small skull, the developed jaw . . . the retreating forehead, the voluminous ears . . . low cranial capacity . . . thickness of the bones of the skull' as well as some characteristics not those of earlier man but of animals — 'the prominence of the canine teeth, the flattening of the palate . . . occurring among criminals as with the lemurs and rodents, as also the prehensile foot'.[63] Born criminals possessed many other physical and psychological characteristics which enabled them to be known. They were relatively insensible to pain, they possessed 'moral insensibility . . . they talk like savages because they are veritable savages in the midst of this brilliant European civilisation',[64] and they exhibited 'great agility . . . blunted affection . . . great vanity, a passion for gambling and alcoholic drinks, violent but fleeting passions, superstition'.[65]

Lombroso made it clear that he believed crime to be influenced by many factors such as sex, race, climate and he also identified a group of criminals whom he called criminaloids who 'differ from born criminals in degree not in kind' having a 'less intense . . . organic tendency'[66] as well as another group of 'occasional criminals'[67] who showed no particular abnormality. Even in the later stages of his work, he remained highly suspicious of reformatory strategies and believed that both born criminals and criminaloids who had given evidence of recidivistic tendencies ought to be held in perpetual custody or executed for 'the fact that there exist such beings as born criminals, organically fitted for evil, atavistic reproductions not simply of savage men but even of the fiercest animals, far from making us more compassionate towards them . . . steels us against all pity.'[68] This left 'the so called causes of crime being often only the last determinants and the great strength of congenital impulsiveness the principal cause'.[69] Lombroso urged preventive measures, such as a better trained police force, anthropometric testing, burglar alarms and criminal photography as important social responses to criminality rather than any particular way of dealing with criminals whilst they were in prison.

The Change in General Approach

The growth of such approaches to psychology, sociology and ethnology influenced the attitudes of both social explorers and administrators increasingly after 1860 and evidence of this influence may be seen in the 1850s. This is not to suggest that social explorers all began to search around for human apes or tribal types, for they did not apply a rigid theoretical framework to their descriptions. What did occur was that positivist and evolutionist theories, often only partially understood or absorbed from the press or wider intellectual climate, interacted with a general increasing disillusionment with reformism to reinforce the tendency (probably always present in all ages) to make firm unbridgeable distinctions between occasional and habitual offenders, respectable and undeserving poor, curable and incurable insane. In other words, the optimistic emphasis on universal human value and worth wilted in the face of a pessimistic scepticism strengthened by rising crime rates and reformist failure; most notably the sciences seemed to offer an objective validity and a general framework for the understanding of such marked differences. In the general field of management of the poor, Christian reformers such as Canon Barnett or William Booth emphasised the need for a crusade which excluded none from universalist social action, but the mainstream belief, reflected in the Charity Organisation Society, was that the poor could be sharply divided into two groups: those who would (or had the capacity to) respond and those who did not or could not; so entirely different approaches were adopted. A growing awareness of deeply rooted human characteristics became established, and this especially applied to the predatory inhabitant of foul urban slums who appeared to exhibit a clear difference in terms of civilisation and who could be contrasted with the settled, well-behaved poor amongst whom he lived. In respect of the former group it became self-evident that moral change would not follow sanitary or educational reconstruction because there was an inherent difference in the repetitive criminal whose 'race' or 'tribe' also collectively exhibited traits which were separate from the encircling society and could be studied, catalogued and debated.

The influence of the new climate is detectable in the work of the well known journalist and social explorer, Henry Mayhew, who began to publish reports about the London poor in 1849.[70] He concentrated his attention particularly on criminals in the late-1850s when he and a collaborator, John Binny, were preparing an exhaustive account of the London prisons. Mayhew followed the well-trodden paths of the Thomsonian moral environmentalists in denigrating 'self conceit' in 'the social and moral differences of our nature'.[71] To this Binny added: 'thousands of our felons are trained from their infancy in the bosom of crime . . . born in the homes of habitual thieves . . . familiarised with vice from their earliest years . . . carried to the beershop or gin palace on the breast of worthless drunken mothers . . . they soon learn to be deceitful and artful'.[72] In point of fact, Mayhew and Binny were not penal reformists, nor did Mayhew believe that 'the criminal classes care about prison discipline . . . trouble their heads about it',[73] sarcastically ridiculing education of offenders by pointing out that he had observed prisoners at Millbank laboriously attempting to work out the interest on £2726.1s.4d at $4\frac{1}{2}$ per cent per annum over three years and 154 days.[74] For the purposes of this study, however, the relevant fact is that Mayhew had derived from contemporary theorists an interest in ethnology which he added to his general account of the poor and the criminal of London.[75] At the very outset he divided the poor into two races, observing that 'of the thousand million of human beings that are said to constitute the population of the entire globe there are — socially, morally and perhaps even physically considered — but two distinct and broadly marked races, the wanderers and the settlers, the vagabond and the citizen, the nomadic and the civilized tribes'. He then observed that all civilised peoples have 'some wandering tribe'[76] within them and he attempted to identify the characteristics by which members of this tribe were detectable. In the first place they would have distinct physiological structures, greater jaw bones and cheekbones, indicating 'a more ample extension of the organs subservient to sensation and the animal faculties'. The settled classes, by contrast, would exhibit 'a greater expansion of the brain and consequently of the intellectual faculties'[77] compared to the unsettled, with their tendency to immediate gratification, idleness, slang language, pugnacity and 'utter want of religion'.[78] Furthermore, the immediate environment created by this horde wandering within the great cities of civilised Europe was characterised by 'a system of depravity, atrocity and enormity which certainly cannot be paralleled in any nation, however barbarous, nor in any age however dark'.[79]

Mayhew was arguing that some humans are clearly settled and civilised, others are nomadic predators, although he did also imply that there was a category sharing the characteristics of both. Mayhew and Binny advanced these ideas further in *The Criminal Prisons of London* which appeared in 1862, some thirteen years after Mayhew's first letters on London's poor in the *Morning Chronicle*. The two authors assured their readers that in their very midst there dwelled a class of determined habitual criminals (whom they distinguished from casual offenders who had fallen into crime by circumstance) which was spawning 'a criminal epidemic — a very plague as it were of profligacy — that diffuses itself among the people with as much fatality to society as even the putrid fever or black vomit'.[80] Calling to their aid anthropological knowledge they remarked that all settled races are beset by barbarous predators (the Kaffirs have their Fingoes, the Finns have the Lapps and so forth). So European civilisation had its 'Prigs' and 'Cadgers'.[81]

However, when they attempted to identify more precisely the characteristics of members of this class, Mayhew and Binny produced a plethora of ideas with no coherent theoretical relationship to one another. Thus at one point images of parasites and hosts were invoked: 'the predatory maggot . . . within the social nut . . . the criminal ovum . . . in the very bosom of the plant';[82] at another human biological knowledge: 'we can discover microscopically the new tissue in the course of being secreted from the blood and see little spiculae of bone thrown down one after another, from the same mysterious fluid in the wonderous and beautiful efforts of nature to repair a limb — in like manner can we behold with the enlarged vision of experience how the young criminal tends to renovate the wasted ranks of the old offenders';[83] at another anthropological. Yet in the end Mayhew and Binny confessed themselves defeated and again reminded the readers of the urgency of the discussion because of the social perils involved.

Whatever the precise process involved they assured their readers that moral, psychological and sociological characteristics were inherited as were Jewish or gypsy traits and criminals were possessed of a distinct appearance 'a peculiar lascivious look . . . short thick kind of neck which is termed bull and which is generally characteristic of strong animal passions'.[84]

More generally the growing tendency to objectify the appearance and fixed traits of the criminal began to influence observers and explorers during this period towards a pessimistic attitude to the lowest class which might not be consciously theoretically supported by constitutional psychological or evolutionist theory but which plainly at least in part depended upon it, a potent mixture of ill-digested scientific concept and unmistakeable fear. This interest in the physiological or psychological fixed characteristics of criminals may be seen at large in the literature of the 1860s and 1870s. As early as 1850, Hepworth Dixon referred to 'the criminal countenance' characterised by 'a certain monotony and family likeness which is at once repulsive and interesting . . . occasionally the eye rests upon a cranium of superior order . . . such low misshapen brows, such animal and sensual mouths and jaws, such cunning, reckless or stupid looks'.[85] Later, Montague Williams referred to 'a peculiar look about the London pick pocket . . . he is small in stature . . . a sharp terrier like look about his face',[86] while another writer referred to 'these morbid sprouts of the body politic'.[87] Increasingly the description of the habitual criminal revealed a fear that there existed distinct, menacing creatures to be observed and reported but not appealed to or changed, denizens of a lower world.

By 1880 the optimism of the early-nineteenth century had been eroded by approaches which emphasised the relatively unchanging nature of the lowest classes, those of the pauper and habitual criminal. These were sharply differentiated from the classes of the poor who shared the same moral universe as their rulers — the docile, deferent and unfortunate to whom charity was both productive of good results and was due from Christian obligation. This prowling residue 'would remain. The filthy would be filthy still; the thieves would still be thieves'.[88] In the areas where they lived might be found 'slipshod, haggard looking women and prematurely old children . . . vice, filth and poverty . . . teeming inhabitants who stare sullenly from the fetid cellars', cruel unrelenting criminality which would 'filch the last penny from the pocket of the poorest woman . . . the halfpenny from a starving child', malevolent predators awaiting their victims: 'the tigers are for the most part quiet in their lairs; slinking, watchful, crouching cruel beasts who wait there sharpening their claws and looking with hungry eyes for the prey'.[89] The vagrant pauper was thus a 'moral leper' to whom 'no foreign heathen can compare . . . in his utter disregard of religion, in his obscenity of language and in his utter brutality and filthiness of life and action . . . let us be deaf to their most importunate clamours and . . . shake off these dead weights from our wheels . . . dislodge these swarms of vermin from our State.'[90]

These writers and many social explorers expressed a common view of sharp differentiation between the repetitive pauper and criminal, who formed a dangerous and irreclaimable class, and the unfortunate poor or offender overwhelmed by temptation and weakness who deserved the compassion of his society. The latter was himself a victim of the criminal class who dwelt in his midst, generating crime and obstructing the economic system by their habits of casual labour when opportunities for crime did not occur. The opinion grew that this lowest class possessed characteristics which were objectively different and dangerous and they increasingly saw these as the result of inherent tendency. The characteristic differences were not in the grimness of the revealed conditions or the polluting moral vileness of the lowest class, because both of these are present within nineteenth-century social survey literature throughout. What was new was the deep pessimism which characterised all but the small number of explicitly universalist Christian theorists, and the sense that there existed a different human type, awareness of which had been derived, however vaguely, from the new scientific ethos. This had enabled the development of analyses which, in the short run at least, offered little hope of improvement in habitual criminal behaviour but which seemed to show rather that such people were characteristically both individually and collectively different. They were of a lower moral order which recreated itself from generation to generation, established in their own social environment rather than having been brought into being by the problems of a contemporary changing society. So Ribton-Turner insisted that much crime and vagrancy represented the anachronistic survival of forms of social response appropriate to savage medieval society. James Greenwood, a prolific writer on London's poor, revealed an almost Mayhew-like confusion, commenting on the one hand that the habitual criminal was treated by society in the late 1860s 'as though he had ceased to be human and had degenerated into the condition of the meanest and most irreclaimable of predatory animals'. On the other hand he declared that in every one hundred and fifty of us was 'a human bird of prey . . . a wily cunning wolf-man . . . so many rats . . . pests of every civilised community'.[91] The well known historian of crime, L. O. Pike, had few doubts however: large numbers of criminals were possessed of inera-dicable inherited 'instincts' and tendencies towards conduct which suited a bygone age of barbarism. With Ribton-Turner, he argued that crime was in the main 'an inheritance from past ages; many if not all of the criminals of today are the offspring . . . of more numerous and more brutal criminals who lived in days gone by'. Pike was convinced that, although society was gradually evolving progressively and exercising an overall sympathetic effect upon savage human instincts through continuous evolutionary inter-action, in some an atavistic barbarous character survived to be handed down biologically to offspring. Criminals were representa-tive of an anachronistic savage violent human character type whose existence was explained by evolutionary theory as having 'the propensities of the savage which have been handed down from generation to generation'.[92] Prison discipline could have little reformatory effect therefore.

The overall impact of positivism and evolutionary theory conse-quently played a substantial part in eroding further the optimism of those who surveyed and accounted for crime and reinforced deep fears that a malignant, subhuman, pitiless enemy dwelled within the bowels of the social order for whose reclamation or regeneration no substantial hope remained. The habitual criminal class was not in essence a fluid entity recruited as a result of the environmental circumstances surrounding the individual, but rather a separate distinct social category which owed much to inheritance and which created and thrived in its own horrific con-ditions. By reference to positivism and evolutionary frameworks of theory its members could be identified. Now it must be repeated that the notions of the habitual criminal and a class of criminals are continuously present in the literature from at least 1830, but there is a substantial difference after about 1860 in the meaning of the terms. Under evangelical or associationist theory each was circum-stantially created by environment and might therefore be reclaimed by a new environment. By 1880 the prevailing ethos, absorbed however vaguely from science, was that there was a relative constitutional fixedness which could not be changed in the short run by optimistic remedial methods. This inherently distinguished type of habitual criminal was inferior mentally or organically, collectively displaying habits and obeying social norms relentlessly and irreversibly in conflict with those of the surrounding society. Frederic Hill was able, when describing the Gorbals in Glasgow in 1837 as a 'fortress of crime and disease',[93] to offer hope that this could be ameliorated by better prisons and environmental change. By 1880 such optimism was greatly reduced.

This change of attitude occurred slowly and hestitantly and the surveyors of the period were often self-contradictory. They were themselves influenced by both old and new approaches and were in the process of being influenced by new ideas. Thus Greenwood in the 1860s, despite his pessimistic view of habitual offenders, presented a lengthy analysis of environmentally-created vice and crime in London, together with reclamatory programmes at least for youthful offenders and a call for political action. Yet a decade later he was reduced to weary descriptions of the hopelessness of attempts to help juveniles towards a reclaimed life.[94] In the end he descended to regaling his readers with long anecdotal accounts of London criminals pulling 'a mug as long as a musket' in order to convince prison chaplains that they were 'dead set on for paths of honesty' and 'a dreary repetition of the story of the misdoings of drunkards, wife beaters, begging impostors, petty larcenists, pick pockets and burglars with an occasional spice of bloodshed and murder'.[95] Between 1869 and the 1880s he had moved away from political and social environmentalism to reportage of the evil deeds of the criminal class although he was at pains to deny that this was his intention, having himself posed as a pauper on numerous occasions in order to discover the conditions within workhouses. Lord Carnarvon was with the tide when he remarked to the 1872 International Penitentiary Congress held in London that the habitual criminal class 'feed upon society like animals of prey . . . the one and only remedy is imprisonment for life'.[96]

After 1870 the notion of institutional reformation of the lowest social order of criminals and vagrants, described by one surveyor of vagrants as similar to the 'minutest parasitic forms of life . . . human parasites',[97] was being increasingly undermined. Most commentators saw a self-evident absurdity in the pursuit of reformation either as a primary or substantial purpose of prisons. Greenwood captured this discontent when he explained that the young criminal swiftly learned of the prison governor's pet theories of crime and responded accordingly. To the governor who believed that smoking caused crime, he would say 'It is all through smoking, Sir. I never knowed what bad 'abits was afore I took to bacca'; to another, attributing it to cheap magazines, he would say 'it was them there penny numbers what I used to take in, Sir'; a third, who believed that the mention of a mother's love would reduce criminals to sorrow was given an appropriate response when 'they all most dutifully wept, in some cases bellowed as loudly as the stern restriction of the silent system would permit, as soon as the delicate subject was broached'.[98] Increasingly it was felt, as Hepworth Dixon had earlier said, that there was a foolishness in 'great brawny fellows dawdling over texts of which they understand not the beauty and care not for the meaning'.[99] Ribton-Turner made a similar point when sarcastically reported, regarding gangs of tramps coolly preparing detailed surveys of those in their locality whose religious convictions could be exploited (and whose pets might be savage): 'Ugly bull dog. Family pious. Ask for reading matter, say your father was a minister. Don't ask and you may get something.'[100]

In this altered intellectual climate, powerfully articulated by Havelock Ellis[101] at the end of the century, it was to be expected that the centrality of the prison chaplain and the flourishing of spiritual reformism in prisons would be questioned on theoretical grounds and that chaplains would fairly soon find themselves edged towards the periphery of such institutions. These new approaches also implied (with Lombroso or Ribton-Turner) a necessity for the pursuit of unambiguous penal rigour (feared by both human and subhuman alike) as well as an emphasis upon efficient, unmanipulable, mechanical containment according to regulations. It is therefore to the prisons of the later-nineteenth century that attention must now be directed in order to assess the degree to which reformatory aspiration and practice survived the developments in policy, law and theory hitherto described.

References

1. See also *Lecture on Sanitary Reform*, King, 1859; *Our Treatment of The Lower and Lowest Classes*, Parker, 1853; *Prevention Is Better Than Cure*, Parker, 1853, all by Alexander Thomson.

2. Mary Carpenter, *Juvenile Delinquents, Their Condition and Treatment*, Cash, 1853, p. 7.

3. M. Carpenter, *Reformatory Schools for the Children of the Perishing and Dangerous Classes*, Gilpin, 1851, p. 2.

4. J. Mirehouse, *Crime and its Causes*, Cleaver, 1840, pp. 16, 18.

5. A. Thomson, *Our Treatment*, p. 18.

6. G. Godwin, *London Shadows*, Routledge, 1854, p. 13.

7. Viscount Ingestre (ed.), *Meliora, or Better Times to Come*, Parker, 1853.

8. A. Thomson, *Sanitary Reform*, p. 34.

9. See Mrs C. L. Lucas, *A Sketch of Sarah Martin*, Cash, 1854.

10. Sarah Martin, *Selections from the Poetical Remains of the Late Miss Sarah Martin*, Denew, 1844, p. 44.

11. *Sarah Martin — The Prison Visitor of Great Yarmouth*, Religious Tract Society, 1872, pp. 51, 109.

12. *A Brief Sketch of the Life of the Late Miss Sarah Martin*, Barber, 1844, p. 97.

13. E. Pears (ed.), *Prisons and Reformatories at Home and Abroad*, Longman, 1872, p. 681.

14. T. Plint, *Crime in England: its Relation, Character and Extent*, Gilpin, 1851, p. 153.

15. Ibid., p. 153.

16. W. H. Greenleaf, *The British Political Tradition, Volume 1: The Rise of Collectivism*, Methuen, 1983, pp. 237, 239, 257.

17. T. H. Leahey, *A History of Psychology*, Prentice Hall, 1980, p. 146.

18. F. W. Voget, *A History of Ethnology*, Holt, Rinehart & Winston, 1975, p. 111.

19. O. Chadwick, *The Victorian Church*, Adam & Charles Black, 1966, vol. 1, p. 572; see also A. D. Gilbert, *Religion and Society in Industrial England*, Longman, 1967, pp. 184–5.

20. O. Chadwick, *The Secularization of the European Mind in the Nineteenth Century*, CUP, 1975, p. 229.

21. O. Chadwick, *The Victorian Church*, vol. 2, pp. 12, 14.

22. O. Chadwick, *European Mind*, p. 188.

23. Ibid., p. 135.

24. G. Jones, *Social Darwinism and English Thought: the Interaction between Biological and Social Theory*, Harvester, 1980, p. 79.

25. C. Darwin, *The Descent of Man*, John Murray, 1901, p. 340.

26. D. Ospovat, *The Development of Darwin's Theory: Natural History, Natural Theology and Natural Selection 1838–59*, CUP, 1981, pp. 212–13, 228.

27. Gardner Murphy, *Historical Introduction to Modern Psychology*, Routledge & Kegan Paul, 1964, p. 117.

28. C. Darwin, *The Descent of Man*, p. 945.

29. P. H. Barrett, *Darwin on Man*, Wildwood House, London, 1974, p. 218; see also I. G. Barbour, *Issues in Science and Religion*, SCM Press, 1968.

30. G. Jones, *Social Darwinism*, p. 15.

31. O. Chadwick, *European Mind*, p. 170; F. W. Voget, *A History of Ethnology*, p. 162.

32. C. Darwin, *The Descent of Man*, see Note 20, pp. 159, 205, 41.

33. G. Jones, *Social Darwinism*, p. 8.

34. F. Galton, *Hereditary Genius: An Inquiry into its Laws and Consequences*, Watts, 1950, pp. 1, 22, 348.

35. F. Galton, *Inquiries into Human Faculty*, Dent, 2nd edn, n.d., p. 1.

36. Ibid., pp. 42, 43.
37. Ibid., pp. 217, 196.
38. Ibid., pp. 211, 219.
39. Ibid., p. 219.
40. Ibid., p. 43.
41. Ibid., p. 219.
42. H. Spencer, *The Principles of Psychology*, vol. 1, Williams & Newgate, 2nd edn, 1878, p. 582 (1st edn published 1855).
43. J. D. Y. Peel (ed.), *Herbert Spencer on Social Evolution: Selected Writings*, University of Chicago Press, 1972, pp. XX, XXII.
44. H. Spencer, *The Principles of Psychology*, vol. 1, pp. 581, 584, 582.
45. J. D. Y. Peel (ed.), *Herbert Spencer*, pp. XXXIII, XXVI.
46. G. Combe, *Lectures on Moral Philosophy*, Simpkin, Marshall & Co., 1840, p. 12.
47. Ibid., p. 28.
48. Ibid., p. 262.
49. Ibid., p. 278.
50. G. Combe, *A System of Phrenology*, Maclachlan, 5th edn, 1843, vol. 1, p. 418.
51. Ibid.; see the phrenological map opposite the title page.
52. G. Combe, *Lectures on Moral Philosophy*, p. 286.
53. Ibid., p. 267.
54. G. Combe, *A System of Phrenology*, vol. 2, p. 55.
55. G. L. Chesterton, *Revelations of Prison Life*, vol. 2, pp. 292, 286.
56. See for instance Sir B. Brodie, *Psychological Enquiries*, Longman, 2nd edn, 1855, vol. 1, pp. 239, 226–7.
57. C. H. S. Jayewardine, 'The English Precursors of Lombroso', *British Journal of Criminology*, vol. 4, Oct. 1963, pp. 165–6.
58. Ibid., p. 167; also W. Tallack, *Defects in the Criminal Administration and Penal Legislation of Great Britain*, F. B. Kitto, 1872, pp. 100–1.
59. *RDCP 1873*, PP, 1874, vol. XXX, p. vii; also W. Tallack, *Defects in Criminal Administration*, p. 101.
60. C. Lombroso, *Crime: its Causes and Remedies*, W. Heinemann, 1911, p. 376.
61. Ibid., Introduction by Maurice Parmelee, p. xiv.
62. Ibid., p. xiv.
63. Ibid., pp. xviii, 365, 368.
64. Ibid., p. xx.
65. Ibid., pp. 365–6.
66. Ibid., pp. 374, xxvii.
67. Ibid., p. xxvii.
68. Ibid., p. 427.
69. Ibid., p. 376.
70. R. Kent, *A History of British Empirical Sociology*, Gower, 1981, p. 44.
71. Henry Mayhew, *London Labour and the London Poor*, Cass, 1967, vol. 1, p. 320 (first published 1851).
72. Ibid., vol. 4, p. 273.
73. *Second Report from the SC on Transportation*, PP, 1856, vol. XVII, p. 151.
74. H. Mayhew & J. Binny, *The Criminal Prisons*, p. 250.

75. K. Williams, *From Pauperism to Poverty*, Routledge & Kegan Paul, 1981, pp. 237–77, has a penetrating discussion of Mayhew's approach.

76. H. Mayhew, *London Labour*, vol. 1, p. 1.

77. Ibid., p. 1.

78. Ibid., p. 2.

79. Ibid., p. 412.

80. H. Mayhew & J. Binny, *The Criminal Prisons*, p. 80.

81. Ibid., pp. 89, 384.

82. Ibid., p. 381.

83. Ibid.

84. Ibid., pp. 356–7, 165.

85. W. Hepworth Dixon, *The London Prisons*, pp. 138, 245.

86. M. Williams, *Leaves of a Life: Reminiscences of Montague Williams Q.C.*, Macmillan, 1890, vol. 1, p. 161.

87. W. Hoyle, *Crime in England and Wales*, Effingham, 1876, p. 49.

88. M. Williams, *Leaves of a Life*, vol. 1, p. 169.

89. T. Archer, *The Pauper, The Thief and the Convict*, Groombridge, 1865, pp. 11, 25, 122, 128.

90. C. J. Ribton-Turner, *A History of Vagrants and Vagrancy and Beggars and Begging*, Chapman & Hall, 1887, pp. 668, 670, 672.

91. J. Greenwood, *The Seven Curses of London*, Rivers, 1869, pp. 92, 85, 86, 121, 431.

92. L. O. Pike, *A History of Crime in England*, Smith, Elder & Co., vol. 1, 1873, pp. 421–2; vol. 2, 1876, p. 509.

93. F. Hill, *Crime: its Amount, Causes and Remedies*, 1853, p. 383.

94. J. Greenwood, *The Seven Curses of London*, p. 177; J. Greenwood, *The Wilds of London*, Chatto & Windus, 1881, Chs 20, 23.

95. J. Greenwood, *The Policeman's Lantern*, Walter Scott, 1888, p. 121; J. Greenwood, *The Prisoner in the Dock*, Chatto & Windus, 1902, p. vi.

96. E. Pears (ed.), *Prisons and Reformatories*, p. 359.

97. J. Flynt, *Tramping with Tramps: Studies and Sketches of Vagabond Life*, Fisher Unwin, 1900, p. ix.

98. J. Greenwood, *The Seven Curses of London*, pp. 178–9.

99. W. Hepworth Dixon, *The London Prisons*, 1850, p. 405.

100. C. J. Ribton-Turner, *History of Vagrants*, p. 656.

101. Havelock Ellis, *The Criminal*, Scott, 1914 (1st edn 1890).

8

The Decline of Reformation in British Prisons 1865–1895

Centralisation, Reformation and Edmund Du Cane

Between 1865 and 1895 the prison system of Great Britain underwent considerable administrative change. In the first place on 1 April 1878 the shires and boroughs were deprived of their legal duty to maintain prison discipline; this was now to be vested in a central commission. The long erosion of the autonomy of magistrates and councillors in prison discipline had been completed after at least fifty years of growing interference in their prisons by central government. From 1877 to 1895 this Prison Commission was under the chairmanship of Edmund Du Cane, like Jebb a Royal Engineer, who had lengthy experience of the management both of transportees in Western Australia and of convicts as a convict prison director in England. Indeed since 1869 he had been Chairman of the Directors of Convict Prisons. The convict prisons remained distinct from the prisons earlier administered by the local authorities and now transferred to the new central commission, and the Convict Prison Directorate continued as a separate legal administrative entity, but in practice the two systems were locked into one another in a more uniform way and the principles upon which each sector operated were more closely aligned under the dual chairmanship of Du Cane. In Scotland a new prison commission, set up in the same year, completed the process of central prison control which had begun in 1839 with the creation of the General Board of Directors of Scottish Prisons. Lastly, there occurred two substantial state inquiries into prisons in 1877–8 and 1895, known respectively as the Kimberley Commission on Penal Servitude and the Gladstone Departmental Committee which examined prisons generally.

After 1865 it is clear that in the convict prison sector there was a strong tendency towards collective rigour and a growth of distrust of individualised reformation as a major element of prison discipline. Daily congregate chapel services were discontinued and replaced by the reading of prayers in hallways to prisoners locked in their cells; provision of religious literature was reduced; the weekly half-day of education ended and education relegated to the evenings; writing materials were restricted; the Fulham 'refuge' for women was transformed into a prison; and reduced importance given to chaplains' recommendations for the award of tickets of leave.[1] Although, of course, reformist approaches had always been based upon rigour as well as individualisation, there was a notable increase in the severity of the convict prison system. Thus the period which must expire before a life-sentence prisoner would be considered for release was increased from twelve years to twenty, gratuities and diets were reduced, labour was made more severe, cell doors were kept bolted at all times during the nine months' separation (previously opened after two months), with a general 'increased stringency' that was said to create poorer health among convicts.[2] Indeed, by 1873 the entire convict prison system required prisoners to earn large quantities of marks to proceed through the various stages which followed separation and was aimed at ensuring 'hard never-ending work on hard fare with none of the small luxuries which even the poorest enjoy from time to time'.[3] Labour was increasingly defined solely in terms of its value to the state[4] and licensed release was made more difficult to obtain.

In the Scottish convict prison at Perth, distrust of reformation as a major penal aspiration also grew. As early as the 1850s the Board of Directors of Scottish Prisons had concluded that separation there was insufficiently deterrent in its reformist form and had emphasised the importance of hard labour machines. In the mid-1860s at Perth 'the tendency of recent changes has been . . . that the use of the mask has been gradually abolished. Open pews have been substituted for the separate stalls in the chapel and open yards, where the prisoners walk around in circular pathways, have been substituted for the separate airing yards which were each fitted to contain one prisoner at a time'.[5]

This desire that penal servitude should become 'the last and most dreadful result of heinous offences'[6] with a lifer held 'if it be so determined until his death',[7] the convict prison as 'a terror to evil doers'[8] also influenced the local prisons, which had in any

event been placed upon a more general footing of collective deterrence by the 1865 Act. As earlier noted, after 1877 the new Prison
Commission swiftly implemented a drastic reduction in the
number of local prisons.[9] A system of initial cellular confinement
with hard labour was introduced and subsequent detailed gradations of severity from class to class were made on a uniform basis
throughout England. At each stage was laid down the number of
days a mattress might be placed on the plank bed, amount of
gratuity and exercise, severity of labour and so forth. The marks
system was imported into the local prisons as the means by which
prisoners gained their promotion and the entire system was regulated by directives and standing orders emanating from London,
with local discretion reduced decisively.

The growing suspicion of reformation as a primary purpose in
prisons may be illustrated with reference to Edmund Du Cane
himself, although it must be made clear he was not entirely anti-
pathetic to the reformatory aspiration as a presence in prison discipline. Plainly he viewed the earlier spiritual endeavours of the
1840s and 1850s as based upon naïvety, remarking in 1885 that
Reading Gaol had been the 'final climax of burlesque absurdity.
The Bible was made the principal lesson book . . . and a reformatory influence was supposed to be achieved by requiring the
criminals to commit large portions of the Testament to memory',
adding that one man, disappointed that he had only got as far as
Ephesians, deliberately reoffended so as to complete his learning.[10]
Du Cane was also suspicious of the shape of earlier educational
approaches as a reformatory device. He preferred that reformatory
instruction should be seen as a subsidiary part of the business of a
prison, although he wished illiterate prisoners to be taught to read
and write because these skills were necessary to self-maintenance,
and he made mastery of them one means of obtaining promotion
to a higher stage. Consequently although he by no means tried to
exclude chaplains from prisons he eschewed the long earnest discussions of moral lessons or theological doctrine which he believed
had characterised separation in its earlier stages. His view of
religious and moral education was that its presence should not
undermine the deterrent severity of a prison although he did not
disregard reformatory techniques. For example, he had a commitment to prisoners' aid societies and refuges, such as the two run by
voluntary organisations for women released from Fulham,
together with some willingness to offer special facilities where
appropriate (i.e. the provision of a deaf and dumb teacher to a

young offender at Pentonville).[11]

Du Cane's chief emphasis was on the importance of marks and cellular isolation as the reformatory part of prison discipline. Under his rule the Prison Commission maintained a belief in a system of progressive stages. Thus marks and stages promoted 'the formation of ideas and habits which may have a useful reformatory effect on prisoners after their discharge',[12] and he reiterated that the self-direction which was essential to the obtaining of better conditions would enable the prisoner to understand that such effort allowed improvement of conditions in life generally. Du Cane also saw cellular isolation as 'a severe penal discipline during which the prisoner's mind is thrown in upon itself . . . he is put in that condition when he is likely to feel sorrow for the past and to welcome the words of those who show him how to avoid evil for the future.'[13] In addition, he emphasised that prisoners would have the opportunity to understand that the rigour which they suffered was to some extent in their own hands so that good conduct and industry might be stimulated.

The staged conditions of the Du Cane system were promoted on grounds which would have been understood by Jebb, but Du Cane would have claimed that he had stripped reformatory pretensions of their earlier ingenuousness and arrogance whilst yet allowing associationist and spiritual themes effective scope in his prisons, freed from the preposterous visionary utopianism of Crawford, Russell and Jebb. Such methods not only proved 'a mode of influencing prisoners to good conduct in prison',[14] but enabled the linkage of good behaviour with progressive amelioration of conditions in his detailed staged system to bring about an improvement of attitude and conduct, and in a number this would prove lasting.[15]

It is most important — given Du Cane's reputation for hostility to individualisation and reformation — to be clear that he saw reformatory influences as having a part to play in a prison and was convinced that all who could benefit from such influences would have them available. However, two aspects of his approach to reformation also stand out. In the first place, one of his major preoccupations was with the construction of a prison system which would run with mechanical uniformity exactly according to the requirements of law, economy and regulation, that prisons would operate with the precision of machines. It is partly in this context that his dedication to the elimination of disease and foul conditions in prison may be seen (often being frustrated in his crusade against these by the bureaucracies with which he had to deal, e.g. the War Office in respect of the Gibraltar Convict Settlement).[16] Consequently, the thrust of prison discipline led inexorably towards the exact implementation of rules which were not likely to sit easily beside the individualisation and flexibility which reformation required. It is clear from all his writings that although he retained cellular isolation and staged promotion/demotion, he mostly valued them as instruments upon which precise uniformity and primary deterrent purpose could be based and only secondly as pure reformatory techniques. Therefore he fully utilised the structures developed previously but viewed their primary purpose in a different way from Russell, Crawford or Jebb.

Secondly, Du Cane was consistently much more sceptical of the reformist aspiration than had been Jebb. In part this was because he was influenced by the intellectual climate which had developed during his period as a Convict Prison Director and Prison Commissioner. In the first place therefore he had little doubt that there would be large numbers of prisoners 'whom it is impossible to influence and who must be dealt with in course of law, not for much result on themselves, but to carry out the principle of justice and mainly to deter others. Such characters may probably be set down as in a certain sense mentally deficient.'[17] Despite accepting that habitual criminality was likely to be encouraged by a criminogenic environment, he also maintained an interest in contemporary theorists who were engaged in analyses of constitutional predisposition towards criminality. Du Cane frequently referred to Alexander Bain's discussions of a constitutional basis for incapacity, to make appropriate links between experience and conduct, and the work of the mental positivist David Nicholson. It was plain that Du Cane considered that many prisoners were of a 'type' unlikely in fact to be altered by any discipline. He used Nicholson and Bain to show that they 'form a class of fools whom even experience fails to teach. The lessons of the past profit them not as guides for the future . . . their natural proneness to evil . . . their memory has no record of the pain or the feeble residue which it preserves of it goes for nothing in the face of the emotion or other cause of misconduct': although some offenders might be positively influenced, Du Cane felt that the habitual criminal was characterised by a moral weakness of will, an incapacity to reflect, an inability to retain lessons. He quoted Bain and Nicholson frequently in his official reports and books and summarised his own conclusions to the Gladstone Committee in the last year of his career: 'the class from which criminals are drawn is a class mentally, physically and morally below the average of the population'. At an earlier point he had underlined their swift forgetfulness of 'advice, instruction and . . . punishment', their response to 'the expediency of the moment' and their fixed 'moral weakness . . . possibly . . . moral depravity'. Insisting that they were incapable of controlling emotions which 'a deliberative volition' would master with ease, he indicated a psychological condition which was often 'radically incurable',[18] and this analysis bore much resemblance to the Spencerian account of the primitive unevolved personality.

Du Cane was also sceptical of the environmentalist analysis of the aetiology of crime although, like almost all English prison discipline theorists, his suspicions also extended to the Lombrosian school of criminology. As early as 1875 he wondered whether habitual criminals might be 'examples of the race reverting to some inferior type . . . [having] characteristics . . . of the inferior races of mankind — wandering habits, utter laziness, absence of forethought or provision, want of moral sense, cunning, dirt; and instances may be found in which their physical characteristics approach those of the lower animals.' It appears that, without subscribing to the more extreme forms of Lombrosian positivism, he was, like most of his colleagues, influenced by what Janet Saunders called a 'biologism', the notion of a hereditarily flawed 'stage army of habitual and weak minded offenders' whose moral faculties were defective and who 'go criminal as the insane go mad, because they cannot help it'.[19]

It follows therefore that Du Cane held that there was a deep-seated incapacity in large numbers of prisoners which sharply distinguished them from people of normal self-control or ability. Logically, although he was willing for reformatory agents to be available in prisons, he was far from optimistic about this aspect of prison discipline. He was sure that the infliction of regulated, economic, efficient deterrent severity should be his primary objective — a 'uniform course of penal deterrent discipline' — and he doubted that reformatory approaches could achieve great changes. He came to believe that the major reason many persistent criminals desisted from crime was that after the mid-thirties they tended increasingly to desire 'a quieter life than the risk and excitement of crime can offer'. If offenders could be incapacitated in prisons until they were over forty, he believed much of the crime problem would be solved and that severe imprisonment of 'those who have an incurable tendency to crime' also might deter those less-flawed individuals who were considering commission of crimes.[20]

Convict Prison Staff and the Kimberley Commission

Du Cane was suspicious of the numerous international penitentiary congresses held throughout Europe after 1872, believing along with other prison officials that these tended towards a sentimental reformist approach. He disseminated his more pessimistic views through numerous articles. He wrote for journals such as *Nineteenth Century* and expounded his ideas through the National Association for the Promotion of Social Science, which had been set up in the late-1850s to investigate the knowledge base upon which social reform might be founded. However, in the main the tendency towards deterrent uniformity was promoted through the more tightly organised post-1877 prison system, meticulously controlled from London. This distrust of reformation was entirely with the grain of legislation and contemporary thought; in one sense, then, Du Cane was less the initiator of a new policy than the administrator of a system whose priorities had been established in the 1860s and validated by the greater pessimism about the nature of criminal man which characterised almost all writing on the subject in the late-1860s and 1870s.

The loss of faith in reformation may be seen amongst many other officials who, although they accepted that some prisoners were members of 'the more respectable class . . . the professional man, the commercial clerk, the post office man', often tended to see by 'far the greater number' as members of the habitual class. For that reason the Kimberley Commission was greatly concerned that a special class of convict 'against whom no previous conviction of any kind is shown to have been recorded' should be kept away from other convicts who might exercise evil influence over them.[21] Pessimism among prison officials had by 1895 become generally characteristic. Du Cane's successor as Chairman of the Prison Commission and of convict prisons in 1895, Evelyn Ruggles-Brise, observed 'that a large proportion of the prison population is mentally weak . . . I think I should call it moral imbecility'.[22] Medical men, both in and out of the prison service, increasingly drew attention to the distinct inferior criminal type whose reformation could not realistically be anticipated. Bevan Lewis, for twenty years Superintendent of Wakefield Asylum, regarded 'the habitual criminal . . . as simply a degenerate offspring of a very degenerate stock . . . both insanity and crime are simply morbid branches of the same stock'.[23] John Campbell, a convict service medical officer, maintained that 'vagrancy like crime is often hereditary . . . a class who may not inappropriately be termed permanent criminals . . . thoroughly debased and hardened as to resist any system of treatment . . . the semi imbecile class [who] when not undergoing sentences in prison depend on doles or indulge their criminal propensities by acts of theft, mischief and outrage.'[24]

Campbell was sure that within prisons there were those who were not within this class and that even the most hopeless of criminals possessed qualities which might be admired, but even so the general agreement was that a substantial proportion (probably a majority) of prisoners formed a distinct mental or moral category, separated from others by characteristic features which would not respond to reformatory method. This tendency was further theoretically supported by a growing conviction among medical personnel that habitual drunkenness, which some believed was associated with three-quarters of recidivism, was, in its extreme form, an identifiable moral psychological condition. The dipsomaniac was said to suffer from 'a disease uncontrollable by the individual', the result of which was that 'self control is suspended or annihilated, moral obligations are disregarded, the decencies of private and the duties of public life are alike set at nought' whilst habitual drunkards produced children who had a great chance of being idiotic, lunatic, physically deformed, 'liable to be a lower order of being . . . dwarfed and puny'.[25]

Although little was to be hoped for in terms of behaviour change among prisoners who in the main were characterised by a 'want of power to resist the very slightest temptation that is thrown in their way',[26] rigorous severity might at least provide a general deterrence of casual offenders. It would also emphasise the revulsion of the state towards crime and reverse that impression of public sympathy for criminals which reformists had so erroneously propagated. The convict prison sector in the 1870s and 1880s was marked by a general strengthening suspicion of reformatory techniques of the preceding era, a collective belief that pious and naïve men had propagated reformation under a misconception regarding the problematic nature of criminal man. Arthur Griffiths, for example, a well known official in the Convict Prison Service and

a writer of popular stories and military histories, was scathing in
his criticism of the reformatory period of English prisons. Griffiths
is usually cited at length in histories of the prison system and it
needs to be remembered that he was often writing about events
which had occurred around fifty years earlier. So, although he
made use of the official records of such institutions as Millbank, his
approach to them was that of a much later prison official who lost
no opportunity to ridicule the spiritual reformist ethos. He
described early Millbank as a 'bear garden' in which pious and
naïve amateurs attempted to convert highly aggressive and
predatory convicts, who then lost no opportunity to wreak revenge
upon their captors if their least whim was thwarted. Consequently
there was 'continuous warfare between ruffianism and constituted
authority which is inevitable when the latter savours of weakness
or irresolution . . . it is easier to tame a wolf into a house dog than
make a thief into an honest man.' Griffiths excoriated what he
believed had been a proneness to leniency in earlier prisons which
he felt encouraged violence, fraud, insult, manipulation and
cruelty, citing numerous examples of such things, the most well
known of which (cited also by Ignatieff) was the destruction of a
hated warder's cat:

> You see yor cat is hung And
> you Have Been the corse of it
> for yoor Bad Bavior to Those
> arond you. Dom yor eis, yoo'l
> get pade in yor torn yet.[27]

Griffiths was also most critical of Jebb and his colleagues who
'sought to gain their object by reward and encouragement rather
than by strictness and terror . . . [he] like others who had gone
before was hopeful of reformation by purely moral means . . .
[Jebb] had formed too high an opinion of the criminal class. He
was too hopeful, too ready to accept the shadow for the substance
and to view the outward whitewashed semblance of purity for the
radical transformation of the inner man.'[28]

Griffiths' work was in line with the suspicions of his day and
needs to be treated as such. He was himself clear about this,
observing that 'I may be called hard hearted if I point out that all
my experience points to the utter futility of these processes (of
moral reformation) and state my deliberate conviction that to
search for reformation by such means is to follow a mere will o' the

wisp which has constantly evaded and betrayed its well intentioned followers'.[29] It is also noteworthy that he, like Du Cane, had a critical attitude to the positivist stereotypes of Lombroso and was aware that scientific enthusiasm might be short-lived. He felt concerned at the implication for the social treatment of criminals if the idea of Lombroso's criminal men of 'ape like agility . . . stealthy loping walk like that of wild and wily animals' or that of the Russian Professor Babinski's 'psychopath' were universally adopted.[30] Nevertheless, Griffiths himself was quite clear that in his experience criminals were not in the main reformable. They were characterised by cunning, recklessness, secretiveness, self-indulgence, intractability and swift surges of rage, 'easily moved to wrath . . . generally incorrigible',[31] who would commit any foolish act to relieve boredom yet who also showed laudable emotion on such occasions as the deaths of convict friends in prison.

The decline of the reformatory aspiration led inevitably to conflict between prison chaplains, who were unwilling to relinquish any of their spiritual and moral influence within prisons, and the staff who were now approaching their charges in a more pessimistic way. One chaplain as early as 1865 gently warned that 'it is not by severity or harshness that these poor outcasts are to be reformed or brought to a sense of their moral degradation. This was not our Lord's mode of dealing with sinners'.[32] Before the 1878 Kimberley inquiry it emerged that there had been a good deal of tension between governors and chaplains in some of the convict prisons; a number of chaplains were feeling considerable anxiety about what they saw in these institutions. Thus Ambrose Sherwin of Pentonville reluctantly remarked that some officers were 'of a peevish disposition' and prisoners were on occasion beaten 'so hard that streams of blood have come from the top of their head'.[33] At Dartmoor the chaplain found that he was quickly at odds not only with his governor but also with the responsible convict prison director when he complained that prisoners were being ill-treated and subjected to harsh punishment for minor infringements of discipline. 'The relations between myself and the governor became so exceedingly strained and the visiting director appeared to me to give his whole countenance and influence to the governor in what I regarded from my standpoint as incorrect treatment that, finding that I could get no power of representation I left the service.'[34] It was further alleged that convict prison directors were beginning to exclude reports of chaplains from publication in their annual reports. In general among the convict prison chaplains such as the Roman Catholic and Protestant chaplains at Millbank there was a strong feeling that a return to classical separation would reintroduce the serious individualised moral purpose of prison discipline which was being jeopardised in the regulated collective discipline which prevailed in the public works system.

During the late-1870s there began to emerge a strongly argued case that in many of the eleven male and two female convict prisons reformation had ceased to occupy a place of any importance. There were perceived in these prisons some disturbing developments which were described in detail to the Kimberley Commission. First some ex-prisoners deposed that there was a good deal of unnecessary violence to prisoners: 'I saw Pearce use his truncheon to a man while he had his handcuffs on. I should say that he was about six foot four inches or six foot three, a big robust man. I have seen him take up his truncheon and knock them down as you would knock a bullock down. I have seen four officers go into a man with gray hairs whose gray hairs might have appealed to their humanity if they ever had any.'[35] Secondly, it was argued that institutionalised over-reaction to the slightest suspected disrespect was typical; thirdly, it was said that conditions were frequently degrading and cruel; fourthly, that staff who protested were rapidly forced out of the service; fifthly, that the Convict Prison Directorate was evasive and obstructive in the face of enquiry by interested groups such as the Howard League; and, lastly, that convict prison medical staff had devised ways to test malingerers such as the infliction of electric shocks or use of red hot irons. Certain prisons such as Parkhurst were said to be especially notable for these practices whilst at others, such as Pentonville, conditions were better. Yet at the former places prisoners never complained for fear of reprisals: 'I was struck at Chattenden once [a satellite of Chatham] . . . he struck me with his fist . . . the ground was that I was not expeditious enough in filling a basket with coke on a Sunday morning . . . I never did complain of an officer and there is no doubt that it was owing to my non complaining of officers that I escaped reporting.'[36] Prisoners added that these things were particularly prevalent at prisons which were, like Chatham and Chattenden, unpopular with officers and that in general it was the habitual criminals who did best in the system. These apparently understood its unwritten rules and knew 'the discipline and the prison proceedings so well' that they were 'able to help the officer in his duty'.[37]

The Kimberley Commissioners were well aware of three features of prison discipline as they heard these accusations. Firstly they knew that throughout the nineteenth century there had arisen in some prisons, both local and convict, allegations that behind the public mask of sober grave reformation and regulated deterrence there had been cruelty to prisoners. For example in the early-1820s it had been established that at Ilchester Prison, the governor, William Bridle, had shown himself 'wholly unfit to hold the situation' because of the various physical cruelties he had committed on prisoners, having shortly before been praised by one prison reformer for his enlightened attitude.[38] That cruelty had flourished, too, at Birmingham, where Maconochie's system had been perverted, whilst at Millbank an eleven-year-old boy had died after repeated confinement in dark punishment cells for matters such as calling an officer 'a big bugger'.[39] Secondly they knew that prisons contained political prisoners, whether political radicals such as Henry Hunt at Ilchester, or Fenian Irish nationalists like Michael Davitt (who in fact gave evidence to the Kimberley Commission); such prisoners might have a particular interest in discrediting the institutions of the British state. Thirdly, however, they were aware that staff in all prisons were at times faced with dangerous, degrading and difficult situations and that violence to staff had since the late-1850s been an increasingly problematic aspect of convict prisons. Convict directors had in fact always responded most severely to any riot or strike, such as those at Chatham and Portland, and had ordered ringleaders to be flogged with the cat o' nine tails after the militia or army had restored order. When prisoners had attacked officers at Portland, several convicts were shot during the ensuing battle.[40] Although any kind of strike or attempt to seize control of prisons was most strongly resisted, and seen in any case by Jebb as having originated from particular special causes (unfairness in licence award, bad officers imported to Chatham from the prison hulks), assaults on individual convict prison officers continued to be a feature of prison life. In 1866 at Chatham and in 1869 at Portland, officers were murdered, and in 1874 the puzzled directors remarked that 'at Portland for no apparent reason the number of assaults on the warders increased considerably'. Furthermore, the growth in self mutilation — for example by prisoners throwing themselves under locomotives in order to lacerate limbs so as to be excused labour at Chatham — was also reported as a disciplinary problem.[41]

With these aspects in mind the commissioners enquired about allegations that such serious overthrow of regulation and penal purpose had occurred in part of the convict sector. Nevertheless, they showed notable caution, being aware that some of their witnesses at least might have obvious axes to grind. They were suspicious, for example, of the credibility of William Tallack, Secretary of the Howard League since its inception in 1866, who had given much support and publicity to prisoners who had complained of cruelty. To the commissioners he made sharp criticisms of the evasiveness of the convict directors and the 'reign of an excessive military regime, reign of an unduly rigid discipline and etiquette'[42] which prevented abuses being reported by junior staff. The commissioners questioned him in considerable detail and eventually concluded that he could substantiate none of these allegations, most of which had been told to him by criminals, and were plainly most cautious of his evidence. A number of convict prison officials were also closely questioned and each of these produced either a reasoned denial or suggested that incidents had been misunderstood or exaggerated. Thus prisoners alleged to have died from negligent treatment were said by medical staff to have expired as a result of illness, and allegations of violence or gross physical ill-treatment were explained as exaggerated. Medical staff denied that 'they can strap you down, they can keep you groaning and shouting and make you mad and then punish you for being mad', maintaining that the medical treatment of the hereditarily degenerative 'race of the criminal class'[43] was exceedingly difficult. Use of electric batteries was claimed as a reputable treatment for immobile limbs and was not used to test malingerers surrounded by prison staff and doctors who 'laughed and gloated' over the contortions of the patients so treated.[44]

The Kimberley Commissioners approved of the fact that the penal servitude system had since 1864 become an object of greater fear among criminals and they also expressed conventional concern about contamination of inexperienced prisoners, adequacy of facilities for weak-minded and invalid offenders, and at the weakness of arrangements for supervising and surveying licensees despite the commitment of the 1863 Penal Servitude Commission to active supervision and the increase of police powers over licensees in the Habitual Criminals and Prevention of Crimes Acts of 1869 and 1871.[45] However, the Commission did take a most unusual step which, although based in part on their anxiety about the constitutional concentration of power in the hands of the

Convict Directors, was also a result of their anxiety about these discreditable allegations. They recommended that 'it would conduce to public confidence in the system and would be a valuable safeguard against any abuses creeping into it if means were taken to secure the inspection of the prisons from time to time by persons appointed by the government but unpaid and unconnected with the prisons department.'[46] That recommendation was subsequently implemented, although the medical commissioner Dr William Guy dissociated himself from it for 'there is in my opinion no government establishment in which it is so necessary as in the convict department to fix and concentrate responsibility and none in which it is more needful to discourage rash experiments from without professing to represent that public opinion which it is so easy to create and stimulate by appeals to feeling and so hard to correct by a resort to reason and experience.'[47]

The Experience of Prisoners

It seems clear that after 1877 uniform severity, cellular isolation during the early part of the sentence, marks, meticulously detailed regulated gradations of severity did, as the Prison Commissioners repeatedly claimed, come to characterise all British prisons, although of course many prisoners in local prisons were serving less than 28 days and therefore did not advance beyond the most severe cellular isolation stage of sentence. It is worth noting also that there were nearly 9,000 men and 1300 women in penal servitude in 1878, added to a daily average of around 20,000 in local prisons.[48] There did exist during the late-nineteenth century a body of literature, glimpsed by the Kimberley Commissioners, which was prepared by a tiny number of those who had experienced this system; their work throws some light upon the regimes in which they were placed, particularly regarding the amount of reformatory activity aimed at them.

Obviously it is as necessary to avoid gullible acceptance of all that these writers said about their experience as it is in approaching, say, the enthusiastic claims of prison reformists during the 1840s. However it is also the case that these writings have more value as a historical record than merely being clues to the psychology or attitudes of the writers themselves. They deserve to be inspected for consistent themes as much as any other group of writings about Victorian prisons, and indeed it is worth reiterating that all writers about Victorian prisons had their own axes to grind and tended to frame their subject matter within the boundaries of their own particular beliefs or discourses. The bulk of these prisoners, as will be shown, were quick to point out those actions or instances which contradicted the general bleak picture which they presented and by no means condemned their custodians as universally neglectful of their individual needs.

In the first place, although these men and women were of differing backgrounds, obviously the majority were comparatively well educated. A few were, as indicated earlier, well known Fenian radicals such as Michael Davitt, or critical English political representatives such as Councillor Brocklehurst of Manchester (who refused to pay a fine incurred in connection with an address to a public meeting). Some were sentenced for isolated violent or financial crimes and often protested their innocence. Some were recidivist offenders who had experienced conditions in many different prisons (such as Convict Number 77 or Convict Number 7) and others were people who saw themselves as hitherto of respectable gentlemanly status who had been brought low by vice or folly, such as 'A Ticket of Leave Man' or 'A Merchant'. Some of this body of literature, naturally, was not written primarily as an analysis of British prisons but was concerned with particular political campaigns (Ireland, for example) or a particular alleged case of injustice. Examples in the latter category were Mrs Maybrick, who claimed that she had been wrongly sentenced to death (commuted) for the murder of her arsenic addicted husband, and Susan Willis Fletcher, who represented her conviction for obtaining jewels and clothing by false pretences in circumstances intimately bound up with her being a very active American spiritualist medium against whom was directed particular British prejudice.

These writers did include most detailed accounts of their experiences in British prisons, the majority of them in the time of Edmund Du Cane, which imply from their point of view that the individualist reformatory endeavours of the earlier era were in marked abeyance. Indeed, they shared an almost unanimous view that individual reformatory attempts were absent. There was an unmistakeable impression that they were in the hands of a mechanical, regulated, impersonal prison system in which scant address was made to their own personal attitudes or feelings and in which little effort was made to engage with them on the basis of example or instruction so as to analyse and remedy those circumstances which reformists traditionally believed had brought them into prison. Where individual personal attention was given it was almost invariably described by these writers. Care was taken in recording the identities and words of staff who — whether reformist or not — showed kindness or fairness and justice in dealing with them.[49]

Many of these writers were unsure that any substantial reformist approach was justifiable, and indeed most saw themselves as distinct from the majority of convicts amongst whom they were forced to live. James Mitchel (who served his sentence at an earlier period), in the midst of an Irish revolutionary denunciation of the hypocrisy of 'British Whiggery' which he wished to 'strip . . . bare of . . . treacherous conciliatory liberal lambswool and show gnashing his teeth like a ravening beast' turned on Beccaria, Romilly and Howard as 'genuine apostles of barbarism, ultimately of cannibalism' whose attitude to criminals had resulted in tolerance of those whose skull shapes showed them to be deficient morally: 'I would ventilate the rascals in front of the county jails at the end of a rope.'[50] 'A Ticket of Leave Man' remarked of many of his fellow prisoners: 'four or five thousand of the wretches now confined in convict prisons could be embarked in the Great Eastern, towed into mid ocean and sunk in its fathomless depths [being] vile and filthy . . . cowardly brutes [with] animal instincts . . . [whose] social habits are as filthy inside the prison as no doubt they are in the rookeries which they call their homes [being] reptiles [who commit] hideous and barbarous crimes.'[51]

These therefore tended towards the view that most prisoners were incurably criminal in their conduct and attitude and would never cease from antagonism and calculation in all their dealings with staff, although some were, like themselves, people of intelligence, sensitivity and victims of circumstance whose penalty was not merely prison but disgrace for the rest of their lives. As 'A Merchant' put it: 'I had met with men whose whole life had been spent in constant warfare against society and who had no other intention on regaining their liberty than to continue the struggle to the bitter end — the murderer, cheerful and complacent over the verdict of manslaughter, the professional garotter in whose estimation human life is of no value, troubled only at being so foolish as to be caught . . . with these, the vilest of the vile and also with the hoary criminal who knew no home save the prison . . . I was condemned to mingle.'[52] He believed that over 70 per cent (dedicated and wavering) would return to prison and described in detail the 'thiefological' kingdom of addiction to crime, contempt for all decency, love of the exciting and bizarre situations to which crime may give rise, adeptness in tricking staff and police. Susan Willis Fletcher described the females at Tothill Fields thus: 'It was a curious sight to see this regiment of women from eighty five years old to twelve all dressed alike, but looking so different — a regiment composed almost entirely of drunkards, prostitutes, thieves. One aged prisoner had with her her daughter and granddaughter who, she proudly said, she believed were without exception the best thieves in London because she had learned it "scientific" and taught them in the same way.'[53] However, such an attitude was not shared by others who were influenced by a more optimistic environmentalist view of prisoners as reformable and victims of a cruel world. 'Crime is also the result of lovelessness when it is not a disease and the true curative system should give birth to love in human souls. There is not a man or woman living so low but we can do something to better him or her if we give love and sympathy in the service and have an all embracing affection for both God and Man';[54] 'one of the prisoners in my block was a mere child . . . with feeble and halting step he stumbled rather than walked around the circle';[55] 'the poverty and squalor in which the children of the poor are reared, the next to total neglect of their moral training at the age when ideas of right and wrong ought to be inculcated by means of precept and example and the crowning influence of drunken, depraved or indifferent parents are the sources from which such education is derived and out of which two thirds of the criminal life of these countries has sprung.'[56]

Despite the pessimism about prisoners expressed by many of these writers, a good number of them suggested that the ethos of prisons contradicted the idea that prisoners possessed an innate human value, and they pointed to a general lack of any systematic reformatory theory or practice. Michael Davitt referred to inflexible regulation regardless of individual dignity, violence to prisoners, selective and unremitting punishment of prisoners who had incurred the dislike of officers and subjection to the hardest of labour of men who were actually dying of illness.[57] The 'Merchant' noted an 'indifference to and sometimes cruel neglect . . . of suffering' among medical staff as well as the deliberate infliction of pain to test the genuineness of prisoners claiming to be paralysed, or who might seek certification as insane by 'putting on the barmy stick' as Davitt himself described it.[58]

There was a belief that there existed a general institutional distrust of prisoners, that they were always automatically disbelieved in favour of the officer who reported them for disciplinary offences. It was said that 'if an officer of a higher grade chooses to persecute a prisoner all those of a lower grade will assist him to curry favour.'[59] Individualised reformatory approaches were apparently absent then, and the anonymous author of the widely read *Five Years' Penal Servitude by One Who Has Endured It* remarked to Kimberley: 'There is very little done in the way of reformation'.[60] What remained of earlier approaches was seen to have been undermined by the general ethos of the convict prisons both among prisoners and staff. Indeed it was argued that the residue of reformatory strategy had itself been perverted within many convict prisons. 'A Ticket of Leave Man' carefully described a continuous collusion between officers and habituals who were allowed to be 'the ruling power, the reigning influence, the active spirit'. These habituals became the spies for officers who wanted an easy life on work parties and thus needed agents to warn them of approaching superiors and to compel the novices to complete the work. The habituals also became expert in the officers' 'weaknesses and derelictions of duty' and therefore could betray them at any point. Experienced prisoners and officers at the end of each day agreed together on the precise award of marks to each prisoner. The hardship was borne by terrorised first-timers and prisoners who were outside habitual cabals; the habituals received full marks for policing the system and the officers had to do very little in order to win the high esteem of their superiors for their apparently energetic application of the marks system. Honest officers were speedily discredited by various well tried tactics and all manner of luxuries could be obtained by bribery, the staff being alleged to be characterised by 'morals of the loosest', not 'the slightest regard for truth or honour' and 'everyday language . . . almost as filthy as the filthiest whom they are paid to control', presided over by directors who were 'merely ornamental'.[61]

It must however be emphasised that much of the literature written by ex-prisoners during the 1880s and 1890s, although adverting to individual cases of brutality, was more concerned with the loneliness and despair suffered by prisoners in both convict and local prisons. One man who served twelve months reported in some detail how officers reacted against prisoners who complained to the inspector or governor — ' "you ungrateful young scoundrel, I'll teach you to tell the inspector", then there was the thud, thud of heavy blows or kicks interrupted by a scream of agony . . . sudden shrieks of "Oh don't Sir, don't, don't" intermingled with the gruff voice of the warder hoarse with passion declaring with many oaths that he'd teach the young scoundrel to tell of him . . . "So Number 10's dying is he? That's a good job, we'll teach them to report officers".'[62] But generally the main thrust of the literature was against the steady regulated deterrent discipline. Prison rules never varied: 'they are the same yesterday, today and forever . . . the human element has no place in these establishments . . . feelings, temperament, affection have no place in the lifeless code of rules and regulations . . . the bowels of compassion [are shut up].'[63] Another prisoner whose persistent annoyance of a young woman resulted in two prison sentences remarked on the silence, the absence of any human voice, broken only by the crashing of cell doors and the 'frantic and furious cries' of those who were being flogged,[64] while a female convict remarked: 'the overpowering sensation is one of suffocation. You feel you must and can smash the walls, burst open the doors, kill yourself . . . it is too cruel, it is too fiendishly cruel, the devil himself could invent nothing so cruel as to shut up a woman in a cell to prey upon herself till she breaks down in body and mind.'[65] Another man, whose 'wretched propensity for drink' had led to repeated sentences, complained of the machine-like enforcement of rules which were so absurd as would be 'a disgrace to the prisons of the king of Dahomey'.[66]

The prisons of the late-nineteenth century therefore appeared to them to emphasise a cold, distant, silent response to their inmates: 'a bell rings and my door is again unlocked. No word is spoken because I know exactly what to do. I leave my cell and fall into single file, three paces in the rear of my nearest fellow convict. All of us are alike in knowing what we have to do and we march away silently to Divine Service. We are criminals under punishment and our keepers march us like dumb cattle to the worship of God . . . there is no friendly greeting of good morning nor parting good night within these gloomy walls. The tone is formal and the governor says "How are you Maybrick, any complaints?" and then he passes on . . . the rules were enforced and carried out to the letter. The deadly monotony never varied, all days are alike, weeks, months, years slowly accumulate and in the meantime the mental rust is eating into the weary brain and the outspoken cry rises up daily — "How long O Lord, how long?"';[67] 'a prisoner's life is one of silence and seclusion . . . [it] does its best to reduce its victims to the position of numbered cogs in a mighty juggernaut wheel . . . a machine system woodenly administered . . . [the warders'] faces were continuously covered with an impenetrable mask, cold, hard, chilling, almost dismal . . . the mechanism of their routine duties and the severity of discipline have robbed them of most of the attributes of humanity.'[68]

In such an atmosphere of silence and distance prisoners speculated about one another and acutely observed the human feelings expressed in secret exchanges. Thus one prisoner wrote of a man who whilst intoxicated had killed his son: 'if I lived a thousand years I shall never forget that man's looks out of my memory: the sunken fading eye, the deep lines of grief carved as it were on his face and brow, the sunken cheeks, the hollow broken voice and the large tears scarcely human that coursed down his pallid features as he related to me what he had done and the torments he was now suffering from the awful remorse he felt and from his inability to pray for pardon to his maker.' This writer in poetry expressed the view that he was pent up within a prison by a vengeful state represented by magistrates, 'the great unpaid', hard-hearted executioners and warders who 'in some of the prisons that I have been in . . . pretty near vivisect some of the convicts with the lash'.[69] Another memory (also noted by Ignatieff of separation in the 1840s) to remain with many of them was the sudden breakdown of control, often in the night, the agonised howl of a human in torment. 'The whole prison is awakened by shriek upon shriek, rending the stillness of the night . . . like a savage beast the woman of turmoil has torn her clothing and bedding into shreds';[70] 'one morning I heard a sound which thrilled every fibre and chilled me to the bone. An awful shriek rent the silent atmosphere, a shriek followed by a howl as from a soul in mortal terror';[71] 'suddenly a wild heart bursting cry rang out above the voices of the singers from a convict of some forty five years of age . . . he rushed towards the altar with piercing shrieks while his eyes and face proclaimed the sudden loss of reason and presence of madness';[72] 'I had been there but a few days when about a quarter past five in the morning I heard a poor fellow shout Oh Oh Oh Oh most piteously . . . I heard the screaming of a woman. I listened a minute or so and then I distinctly heard two awful screams as if a poor woman was in the most abject terror and then all was still; soon after the prison clock struck two.'[73] 'The silence, the utter solitude, the isolation from all humane and humanising influences kill one's brain power: the brain loses its life, becomes fettered to monotony of suffering.'[74]

As indicated these writers took pains to relate in great detail occasions when staff did enter into personal discussion, recalling words spoken or actions taken — whether a particularly kind officer,[75] a sensitive clergyman,[76] a 'gentlemanly' governor and firm but fatherly chief warder.[77] Mrs Maybrick observed that the staff were often desirous of closer relationships with the prisoners but were themselves affected by the 'insidious effect of the repressive rules and regulations'.[78] Another, contrasting the approach of a chaplain with the general attitude that prisoners were 'dogs' lamented that this cost the man his job[79] and Susan Willis Fletcher spoke of very strong feelings of compassion aroused among some officers.[80] Similarly Councillor Brocklehurst and 'A Ticket of Leave Man' spoke in detail of acts of personal kindness and the latter mentioned a Portland scripture reader who would 'walk into a prisoner's cell . . . and . . . show him how easy a thing it is for a man, with God's help, to be happy in this world if he is only honest and sober and true . . . such truths spoken earnestly by large hearted men . . . would to all but the most degraded prisoners give food for reflection, preserve them from the extremes of melancholy and inspire them with bright hopes for the future.' Another recalled a prisoner officer's sincerity: ' "here you are", he said, "it's a nice bright cell and you have all the morning sun . . . I am very sorry, really very sorry for you, but you can understand that we are obliged to be strictly impartial here." He spoke with a hearty earnest ring in his voice that told me he really meant what he said.'[81]

Notwithstanding these incidents, almost all these writers recognised a widening gulf between themselves and the society whose acceptance they had once taken for granted. Thus, as his illness grew worse, the merchant felt that he would be an embarrassment in chapel because his bad leg would not allow him to kneel and he 'would have felt while standing there something like a beggar in dirty rags in a fine pew among silks and satins.' He then obtained permission to ask a clergyman of his acquaintance to visit him from outside but the man refused to come. It was at this point that he realised that only 'the sympathy of evil companions' was left and he began to lose expectation of solace or succour, commenting that the 'mild and dignified civility of Sir Joshua Jebb' who had died shortly after his sentence began was not accessible to him, only the imperious 'injustice and incivility' of the other directors.[82] Susan Willis Fletcher sank into apathy when she heard the 'Christmas festivities'[83] outside the prison, while Michael Davitt mourned his lost familiar world as, during the first nine months' separation at Millbank, he listened to Big Ben 'telling the listening inmates of the penitentiary that another fifteen minutes of their sentence have gone by' and to 'the whistle of the railway engine with its suggestions of a journey home'.[84] Another recalled the despair and recklessness created amongst himself and his fellows by the condemnation of a chaplain: 'there was no attempt at showing how the past might be redeemed — no hopes held out to the sorrowing penitent — all God's righteous judgement against persistent impenitent sin was set forth in its coldest and most merciless light while His attributes of love and the infinite mercy that forgives unto seventy times seventy were never even hinted at'.[85]

It is not in this context important that the experience of prison in the Du Cane era seems to have been more severe than that of the earlier period (although in the convict sector and local prisons it is clear that it was, even bearing in mind Ignatieff's strictures on earlier Pentonville separation). The significant change however was that the ideal of reclamation as a central part of penal aspiration was absent in a way which was not the case in the reformatory era with all its inefficiency, idiosyncracy, perversion (as at Birmingham) and enforced separation. The earlier vision of the human value and social inclusion of the offender had therefore become an antiquated ideal seen as irrational and ingenuous in an era in which, in Professor Chadwick's words, 'reason meant Darwin and survival . . . in reason compassion must mean the survival of the least fit.'[86] Thus, however unrealistic in practice, these prisons had been founded long before in the faith that their staff would exhibit qualities of patience, firmness and sensitivity to individual need in respect of those who were not merely strangers to them but social pariahs. As with the lunatic asylums established with many similar aspirations in the earlier part of the nineteenth century, the emphasis came to be upon distant pessimistic regulated containment. Just as the theory of moral management lost ground in asylums, so also the separate cells in which it had been imagined that earnest and hopeful men would seek to illumine the light of religion and true principles of conduct to poor prisoners became tools of an administrative 'Chinese fixedness', essential elements in the pursuit of collective 'uniformity of prison discipline' with prisoners 'mere pieces on a chess board'.[87] Possibly the increased dependence of prisons at all ranks upon ex-soldiers and sailors further invited this, for it could be argued that although in the earlier period many such officers (like Lieutenant Hackett, Governor of Reading) had been noted reformists, there was a natural general distrust among military men for individual approaches to large bodies of men. Their confidence in unvarnished severity had for decades characterised the military prison, and they exhibited a preference for wholesale uniformity of regulation, believing also that the sight of 'cold steel' caused the hearts of the lazy or disobedient to quake. It may also be that a growing discontent within the lower ranks of prison officers at their conditions of service and a strengthening resentment amongst them at their treatment by the state (evident in the 1880s and 1890s) played some part in undermining earlier endeavours.[88] Be this as it may, the era 1865–1895 was unambiguously characterised by a sharp acceleration away from the earlier more optimistic individualised reformist aspirations. The prison system, in any event dragging its fervent reformatory anchors in the late-1850s and early-1860s, thereafter found itself upon a fast-ebbing tide. Furthermore, the architecture and organisation which had been established in the earlier decades proved singularly suitable for use in a new age of distant severe exclusion of human inferiors from the society which they had harmed. It was by no means hard to base the penal structure upon different preoccupations and in so doing the prisons of Edmund Du Cane surrendered a firm commitment to reformation despite the claims of their leading official. In an ethos of collective uniform deterrence all alike must experience disengaged severity as the sufferers of a penality which adhered overall to a pessimistic view of its human cargo and which therefore had little place for their reformation or real inclination to do more than deter all of like character from playing the same dangerous game.

References

1. *RDCP 1864*, PP, 1865, vol. XXV, pp. 116, 88; H. Tomlinson, *Penal Servitude*, p. 142; S. McConville, *English Prison Administration*, pp. 427, 447; J. E. Thomas, *English Prison Officer*, pp. 59–60.
2. *RDCP*, PP, 1880, vol. XXXVI, p. XV; *RDCP 1864*, PP, 1865, vol. XXV, p. 8; *RDCP 1865*, PP, 1866, vol. XXXVIII, p. 30; H. Tomlinson, *Penal Servitude*, p. 142.
3. *RDCP 1872*, PP, 1873, vol. XXXIV, p. vii.
4. *RDCP 1884–5*, PP, 1884–5, vol. XXXIX, pp. XXXIX–XLVI.
5. *27th Report on Prisons in Scotland*, PP, 1866, vol. XXXVII, p. 6.
6. *RDCP 1864*, PP, 1865, vol. XXV, p. 5.
7. *RDCP 1866*, PP, 1867, vol. XXXVI, p. 6.

8. *RDCP 1873*, PP, 1874, vol. XXX, p. vi.
9. *First RCP*, PP, 1878, vol. XLII.
10. E. F. Du Cane, *The Punishment and Prevention of Crime*, Macmillan, 1885, pp. 57, 79.
11. *RDCP 1880*, PP, 1881, vol. LII, p. x.
12. *Third RCP*, PP, 1880, vol. XXXV, p. 16.
13. E. F. Du Cane, *The Punishment and Prevention*, p. 157; see also E. F. Du Cane, *An Account of the Manner in which Sentences of Penal Servitude are Carried out in England*, 1882, p. 20. *First RCP*, PP, 1878, vol. XLII, p. 8.
14. *Third RCP*, PP, 1880, vol. XXXV, p. 16.
15. E. F. Du Cane, *Punishment and Prevention*, pp. 168–70.
16. P. Tibber, 'Edmund Du Cane and The Prison Act 1877', *Howard Journal*, vol. XIX, no. 1, 1980, pp. 9–16.
17. E. F. Du Cane, *Punishment and Prevention*, p. 2.
18. *Report from the Departmental Committee on Prisons*, PP, 1895, vol. LVI, p. 372; *Thirteenth RCP*, PP, 1890, vol. XXXVII, p. 5; E. F. Du Cane, *Punishment and Prevention*, pp. 3, 2–4.
19. E. F. Du Cane, 'The Repression of Crime' in *Transactions of the National Association for the Promotion of Social Science*, Brighton, 1875, p. 301, cited in R. B. Orr, *In Durance Vile: Attitudes towards Imprisonment in England during the Du Cane Regime 1877–1895*, Ph.D., University of Wisconsin, 1968, p. 69, 271; J. F. Saunders, 'Institutionalised Offenders', pp. 264, 266; S. J. Stevenson, 'The Criminal Class', pp. 88–9.
20. E. F. Du Cane, *Punishment and Prevention of Crime*, pp. 190, 6, 2.
21. *Kimberley Commission*, PP, 1878–9, vol. XXXVII, p. 236, xxix.
22. *Report from the Departmental Committee on Prisons*, PP, 1895, vol. LVI, p. 346.
23. Ibid., p. 303.
24. J. Campbell, *Thirty Years Experience of a Medical Officer in the English Convict Service*, T. Nelson & Sons, 1884, pp. 107, 130, 120, 133.
25. *Report of the SC appointed to inquire into the best plan for the control and management of Habitual Drunkards*, PP, 1872, vol. IX, pp. iii, 64, 107.
26. *Kimberley Commission*, PP, 1878–9, vol. XXXVII, Evidence Captain Harvey, p. 77.
27. A. Griffiths, *Memorials of Millbank and Chapters in Prison History*, Henry King & Co., 1875, vol. 1, pp. 120, 121, 119, 138.
28. Ibid., vol. 2, pp. 260, 261, 263.
29. A. Griffiths, *Fifty Years of Public Service*, Cassell & Co. Ltd, 1904, p. 394.
30. A. Griffths, *Secrets of the Prison House*, Chapman & Hall Ltd, 1894, vol. 1, pp. 23, 24, 17.
31. Ibid., pp. 39, 40.
32. *RDCP 1865*, PP, 1866, vol. XXXVIII, p. 252.
33. *Kimberley Commission*, PP, 1878–9, vol. XXXVII, pp. 425, 427.
34. Ibid., vol. XXXVIII, p. 883.
35. Ibid., vol. XXXVII, p. 350.
36. Ibid., p. 439.
37. Ibid., p. 445.
38. H. Hunt, *Investigation at Ilchester Gaol*, Dolby, 1821, Appendix, p. 7; H. Hunt; *A Peep into Ilchester Bastille, dedicated without permission to William*

Hanning Esq., Dolby, 1821, pp. 21–4.

39. *Report of the Commissioners appointed to enquire into the management of Millbank Prison*, PP, 1847, vol. XXX, p. 199.

40. *RDCP 1858*, PP, 1859, Session 2, vol. XIII, part 1, p. 148; *Penal Servitude Commission* Minutes of Evidence 1863, vol. XXI, p. 50.

41. *RDCP 1866*, PP, 1867, vol. XXXVI, pp. 148–9; *RDCP 1869*, PP, 1870, vol. XXXVIII, p. 96; *RDCP 1874*, PP, 1875, vol. XXXIX, p. vii; *Kimberley Commission*, PP, 1878–9, vol. XXXVII, p. 627.

42. *Kimberley Commission*, PP, 1878–9, vol. XXXVII, p. 259.

43. Ibid., pp. 737, 739.

44. Ibid., p. 730.

45. *32 & 33 Vict. Cap 99; 34 & 35 Vict. Cap 112.*

46. *Kimberley Commission*, PP, 1878–9, Report, p. lxi.

47. Ibid., p. lxvi.

48. *Second RCP*, PP, 1878–9, vol. XXXIV: *Kimberley Commission*, PP, 1878–9, vol. XXXVIII, p. 1170.

49. *Five Years Penal Servitude by One Who Has Endured It*, Bentley, 1877, p. 177; No. 7, *25 Years in 17 Prisons*, Robinson, 1903, p. 181; D(onald) S(haw), *Eighteen Months Imprisonment*, George Routledge & Sons, 1883, p. 150.

50. J. Mitchel, *Jail Journal*, pp. 51, 125, 126.

51. A Ticket of Leave Man, *Convict Life or Revelations Concerning Convicts and Convict Prisons*, Wyman, 1879, pp. 13, 14, 15, 18.

52. A Merchant, *Six Years in the Prisons of England*, Bentley, 1868, pp. 42, 125.

53. Susan Willis Fletcher, *Twelve Months in an English Prison*, Dillingham, 1884, p. 326.

54. F. E. Maybrick, *My Fifteen Lost Years*, Funk & Wagnalls, 1905, p. 171.

55. F. Brocklehurst, *I was in Prison*, Fisher Unwin, 1898, p. 93.

56. M. Davitt, *Leaves from a Prison Diary*, Chapman & Hall, 1885, vol. 1, p. 13.

57. *Kimberley Commission*, PP, 1878–9, vol. XXXVII, Evidence, pp. 527, 537, 544.

58. A Merchant, *Six Years*, p. 52. M. Davitt, *Leaves*, vol. 1, p. 142.

59. *Kimberley Commission*, PP, 1878–9, vol. XXXVII, pp. 440, 348.

60. Ibid., Evidence, vol. XXXVIII, p. 992.

61. A Ticket of Leave Man, *Convict Life*, pp. 18, 37, 128, 158.

62. One Who Has Tried Them, *Her Majesty's Prisons: their Effects and Defects*, Gilbert & Rivington, 1883, vol. 2, pp. 173, 115.

63. No. 77, *The Mark of the Broad Arrow*, Everett, 1903, pp. 57, 71, 73–4.

64. Anon, *Pentonville Prison from Within*, Greening, 1904, pp. 165, 167.

65. R.J., *I Was in Prison*, Reeves, 1893, p. 17.

66. Bill Sykes, *Prison Life and Prison Poetry*, Newman, 1881, vol. 1, pp. 87, 109.

67. F. E. Maybrick, *My Fifteen Lost Years*, pp. 69, 70, 199–200.

68. F. Brocklehurst, *I was in Prison*, pp. 21, 17, 56, 83.

69. B. Sykes, *Prison Life*, vol. 1, pp. 54, 71, 135, 164.

70. F. E. Maybrick, *My Fifteen Lost Years*, p. 86.

71. F. Brocklehurst, *I was in Prison*, p. 25.

72. M. Davitt, *Leaves*, vol. 1, p. 173.

73. T. P. Barrow, *A Month in Her Majesty's Prison Leicester and How I Got It*, no publisher, 1882, p. 12.

74. H. Montgomery Hyde, *Oscar Wilde: the Aftermath*, Methuen & Co. Ltd, 1963, p. 87; see also for details of Wilde's experiences at Pentonville, Wandsworth and Reading, O. Wilde, *De Profundis*, Methuen & Co Ltd, 1949.

75. *Five Years Penal Servitude*, p. 177.

76. J. Mitchel, *Jail Journal*, p. 179.

77. B. Sykes, *Prison Life*, vol. 1, pp. 75, 189.

78. F. E. Maybrick, *My Fifteen Lost Years*, p. 202.

79. Anon, *Pentonville Prison from Within*, pp. 53 – 5.

80. Susan Willis Fletcher, *Twelve Months*, pp. 403 – 4, 409.

81. F. Brocklehurst, *I was in Prison*, p. 76; Ticket of Leave Man, *Convict Life*, pp. 202 – 3; One Who Has Tried Them, *Her Majesty's Prisons*, vol. 1, p. 205.

82. A Merchant, *Six Years*, pp. 116, 118, 191.

83. Susan Willis Fletcher, *Twelve Months*, p. 403.

84. M. Davitt, *Leaves*, vol. 1, p. 172.

85. One Who Has Tried Them, *Her Majesty's Prisons*, vol. 1, p. 222.

86. O. Chadwick, *The Secularization of the European Mind*, p. 253.

87. Frederic Hill, *The New Code of Prison Rules*, National Association for the Promotion of Social Science, 1879, p. 14; W. D. Morrison, 'Are Our Prisons a Failure?', cited L. J. Blom-Cooper, 'The Centralization of Government Control', p. 75.

88. For the aspect of prison officers' morale and military background see J. E. Thomas, *English Prison Officer*, pp. 47 – 50, 78 – 103, 111 – 17.

Conclusion

Fin de Siècle

During the late-nineteenth century certain attempts were made to weaken the influence of positivist and social Darwinian theory on general attitudes to groups at the margins of society, and indeed some prison chaplains became embroiled in the debate between biblical revelation and Darwinism. The Irish chaplain, C. B. Gibson, was one of those who sought to turn back on Darwin the ridicule which had been heaped upon the Bible as a true historical account. He exclaimed against the absurdity of the view 'that we were successively marine invertebrates, fishes, reptiles, quadrupeds and apes',[1] arguing that the Bible was indeed literally true but in need of careful explanation. The serpent, for example, did not actually speak words to Eve in the Garden of Eden, rather hissed his temptations to her much as a lamb bleats to his mother or a dog barks to his master. The chaplain of Clerkenwell Prison up to its closure in 1886, J. W. Horsley, argued that innate predisposition was only one of the many influences on conduct and denied that 'these were the only moulding forces of life . . . even thankfully to wonder at their feebleness when confronted with the other forces of free will and grace . . . the materialist has his function and a world of his own in which he may achieve some victories; but it is not the prison world nor has he any gospel for those who for him, but not for our Master, remain the outcast and the lost. He knows but the crucible and scalpel, we know the cradle of Bethlehem, the Cross of Calvary, the empty tomb, the descent at Pentecost'.[2]

However, a more substantial intellectual approach than this also implied opposition to detailed categorisation and institutional exclusion of such groups during the 1880s, although admittedly it was no scientific answer to evolutionist and positivist frameworks but rather proceeded upon the basis of redefinition of Liberal political theory. The original proponent of this new thrust, Thomas Hill Green, was appointed Professor of Moral Philosophy at Oxford in 1877 and delivered a set of lectures two years later which represented 'the most important contribution to political theory of the school of thought sometimes known as the Oxford

219

idealists'.[3] Green maintained that the fathers of utilitarian theory such as Bentham had failed to base their work upon a true conception of human nature and he insisted that man was primarily in reality a being in whom resides God. By application of will and reason man might realise that closeness to God, but this would require the eradication of certain aspects of human life which obscure Him. Religious struggle was therefore the core of man's true destiny and in this struggle the higher self would increasingly draw life, the lower decline and die. The institutions of the state must serve to allow the greatest operation of individual will and reason and they must be based squarely upon a theological conception of man. Amongst the rich, luxury and self-indulgence vitiated the strength of will and reason, as did filth, vice and destitution amongst the poor. Consequently, the concept of citizenship to Green was one of vital voluntary action in which the rich and leisured engaged with the poor towards an enhanced social and moral environment to their mutual spiritual advantage. The state must maintain 'the conditions without which a free exercise of the human faculties is impossible' but moral and spiritual progress would be closely founded upon a voluntarist and passionate dedication among the higher orders, who 'must sacrifice their personal pleasures and atone by social service for the elegant life they lived . . . while so many of their countrymen were denied the chance to realise their potential as human beings.'[4]

Green therefore wished to replace the atomistic political economic base of classical Liberal theory with an unambiguous foundation in theological notions of stewardship, community and shared value in God. This citizenship would be based upon the application of will and reason, ascetic altruism, duty and guilt and mutual spiritual progress towards the inner God amongst all the classes. Scarcely coincidentally, his ideas were formulated at a time when a striking revival of the idea of paternal interventionism was emerging generally out of a sense that the old freedoms of classical Liberalism were an insufficient guarantee of social and economic progress. Through adherence to that framework the poor had been submerged in corrosive urban conditions whose physical and moral consequences to all were abundant. Many Liberals, and some Conservatives, began to place greater emphasis on environment and this had its root in differing concerns. A new 'progressive toryism' strongly defended social measures to maintain the poor so that the empire, monarchy and church would flourish, whilst by 1890 it was clear that among

Liberals had developed a split between the old Gladstonian orthodox political economic base with its promise of continuous progress and those who asserted that their party must 'throw off its indifference to the relations between the classes and the economic issues of the time'.[5] This reawakened commitment to paternalist intervention became evident in many debates about social policy during this decade, such as the split within the 1884–5 Housing Commission between 'laissez-faire theories in support of private enterprise and various proposals for municipal housing and government purchase'[6] and the ideas of Joseph Chamberlain for more forceful state intervention in social problems.

During the 1880s and 1890s a marked spiritual universalist approach to the poor grew up alongside the re-emergence of that unambiguous environmental concern and pursuit of Christian citizenship for which Green had called. The settlements at Toynbee Hall (1884) and elsewhere, and the endeavours by Canon Barnett in the East End of London[7] were well known evidence of this, but a forceful missionary engagement was most noticeable generally and in many ways continued the tradition of Alexander Thomson, Thomas Beames and earlier Wilberforcean evangelicals. Implicit in much of this was a criticism of conventional society for its respectable self-indulgent churchgoing, even its 'unholy wealth — unholy in its origin, unholy in its distribution, unholy in its non-distribution'[8] — and for a declining morality and spirituality allegedly evident in all sections of the community.[9] Numerous critics, often working from a fervent universalist standpoint such as General William Booth, founder of the Salvation Army, severely criticised general urban social conditions.[10] Some of these in particular attacked sentencing and penal practices as a cruel destruction of the future lives of the young, 'worthy only of barbarians and savages . . . [for it was] an agony to Him to see sheep without a shepherd, an unhappy life without another life wiser and stronger to care for it, and His agony became anger when on such fell the blows of virtue instead of the tears of pity.'[11] Lastly, considerable emphasis upon missionary engagement with the outcast and criminal poor characterised the work of many prison chaplains and others who increasingly concentrated on the need to establish close spiritual engagement with prisoners following release from prison. For example, alongside the missionary work of the Salvation Army and Church Army, endeavours were made by individuals such as George Hatton and Susannah Meredith to persuade newly released prisoners to join the temperance movement or to work in protected employment at the Nine Elms Mission in London by means of offering breakfasts to them on release from such prisons as Coldbath Fields, Wandsworth, Holloway and Millbank.[12]

Despite these new concerns, reformism failed to re-enter prison as a strong institutional concern. There were, to be sure, a small number who, like William Tallack, demanded a return to the pure spiritual approach of original separation rather than the treatment of criminals as 'mere brutes to be only punished, deterred and crushed',[13] abandoned to 'a passive deterioration'[14] which allowed little opportunity for purification 'into saintly excellence' by Christ's power.[15] None the less, prisons remained primarily and unambiguously deterrent, although other aspects of penal policy showed the spiritual universalist influence such as missionary probationary supervision of the fallen or the moral paternal tutelage inherent in the borstal system pioneered by Du Cane's successor. Despite all this, the prevalent approach to prisoners remained substantially pessimistic. As a notable American criminologist put it in 1895, 'intellectually and morally criminals are for the most part weak. Their mental feebleness is sometimes so marked as to produce the impression of partial imbecility . . . the criminal is often unable to picture to himself the probable consequences of a criminal action, he does not know how to guard himself against detection. As a child the chances largely preponderate that he was a truant or a dull pupil inclined to mischief and disobedience; stupidity, suspicion and cunning naturally go well together . . . emotional instability is a common characteristic of prisoners; they are easily made to weep or laugh but feeling with them lasts not long enough to be translated into action; they cannot form a resolve and stick to it whether for good or evil. They crave constant stimulation and excitement . . . their attempts at art . . . are for the most part grotesquely crude . . . they are like the insane in respect of their immense egoism.'[16]

The most widely remembered reformist of the 1890s, William Douglas Morrison, chaplain of Wandsworth from 1887 to 1898, based an attack on penal policy on a theoretical analysis which sought to integrate constitutional and environmentalist approaches to criminals. In particular he argued that many young offenders could be reformed in a new type of institution which would replace the prison which 'with its blankness, its silence, its monotony, its almost complete exclusion of the external world and its realities reproduce[s] in a truly marvellous way the blankness, the deadness, the immobility, the lethargy of the prisoner's own mind.'[17] Morrison was convinced that inheritance accounted for a poor physical condition among many criminals and 'a humbly developed mental organisation, whether we call this low state of mental development atavism or degeneracy is to a large extent a matter of words; the fact of its widespread existence among criminals is the important point'. Many adult criminals were 'unfit to take part in working the modern industrial machine; what can be done with them except to seclude them in such a way that they will be no longer able to injure those who can work it',[18] being characterised by an inability to cope with freedom and suited more to a society in which unambiguous compulsion was characteristic.

However, Morrison's analysis also included the notion of progressive deterioration of poor inherited mental and physical ability through environmental influence so that by the interaction between the inherited and the environmental influences the habitual criminal was produced. For the adult criminal he believed that behaviour was substantially unchangeable and thus he argued for lengthy and kindly 'asylum treatment'[19] — being indeed critical of the Du Cane system which sought to inflict severity on those whose behaviour was outside their control. This type was merely the fixed result of the interaction between 'psycho-physical' and environmental factors, having deteriorated into 'a hardened criminal in maturity',[20] whose 'innate congenital qualities of mind', 'defective moral instincts' and 'defective physical capacity' had rendered them most vulnerable to poor domestic and social influence.[21] Morrison argued that it was necessary to intervene before conduct became fixed as a result of this interaction in order that the physical condition could be improved. An artificial environment could be created in which moral and spiritual influence would be brought to bear on those who 'bear within them the seeds of inherited disorders'[22] and who would otherwise inevitably fail to cope with 'the strain and struggle of competitive life'.[23] His vision of a social crusade against slum conditions and his theoretical integration of constitutional and environmentalist theory produced an ideal reformatory treatment of young and still pliable predispositions, but, as far as adult prisoners were concerned, he provided little optimism. Instead his appeal was for long and kindly custodial care of those who, being by early adulthood fixed in conduct, would tend to return to crime on release.

Such considerations influenced the Gladstone Committee which reported in 1895 on the prison system and emphasised the importance of the social environmental approach to crime by 'education, improved dwelling [and] sanitation'[24] as well as the desirability of a prison system which did not inflict more suffering than strictly necessary. This Committee was apparently swayed by a small number of expert witnesses from the Home Office and the Howard League. The paternal tutelary mood now more plainly influenced voluntary and statutory social action and its members rejected the evidence of Du Cane and his colleagues, rather desiring the replacement of hard labour machines by useful instructive occupation, a reintroduction of some at least of the serious moral purpose of early separation, stronger education and greater philanthropic aftercare endeavour, asserting in general that prisoners had been treated 'too much as a hopeless or worthless element of the community'; the present system, 'while admirable for coercion and repression', was 'excessively deficient on the reformatory side'.[25] In particular this conclusion was invited by the evidence of Sir Geoffrey Lushington, for 25 years an Under-Secretary of the Home Office, who asserted that the Du Cane system crushed self-respect, destroyed self-confidence, denied human kindness and submerged the individual in 'continued association with none but criminals'.[26] However, it was plain that he himself actually had little confidence in reformatory strategy as a successful basis of prison discipline, being sceptical even of the success of this in reformatory schools. Despite Gladstone, the abolition of hard labour machines and the introduction of other ameliorations of Du Cane's system during the period of Ruggles-Brise's chairmanship of the Prison Commission, no alteration of primary objective occurred to upset the low importance attached to reformation of adult prisoners. Deterrence and other penal purposes retained their primacy, although of course the Borstal approach to younger offenders established in the Edwardian era was a reformatory application of the ideas of Morrison and others. So far as the last years of the Victorian period were concerned, Oscar Wilde's bitter poetic denunciation of the conditions which he experienced at Reading Gaol in the 1890s[27] ought to have surprised few of his contemporaries who had grown used to collective deterrence as the main basis of their prisons and were, in the main, content that this should be so.

Epilogue

At the end of this long voyage through the prisons of a century during which the Victorians placed prison at the heart of their penal system, one aspect which has never been far from my mind has been the meaning these old events hold for British prisons in the 1980s. As indicated at the outset, the prevailing revisionist view has been widely read and taught. Some have emphasised, after Ignatieff, that Pentonville still stands, a sad monument to the permanence of coercion alongside Brixton, Parkhurst, Dartmoor, Portland, Exeter and so many other relics of Victorian reformation. Others, with Foucault, have more pessimistically believed that modern man, as a fly within a web, is now entrapped within huge rational, instrumental, technical, machine-like organisations (exemplified by modern prisons and their Victorian predecessors). They purport to function, as Max Weber described bureaucracy, upon the basis of imported pure knowledge and derivative method, yet, in reality, sustain themselves by a vast ideological fabrication of information about man, morality and the state. In the conflict of interest, men of power can continue enjoyment of that power, justified by talk of rationality — a kind of subtle replacement of old rights, customs and intimacies in which men flourished as complete beings by a tyranny of disconnecting objectivity.

Yet is there not in such an approach a nostalgic hunger for a garden of wholeness and simplicity, almost as the evangelicals imagined the old pre-industrial world to have been peopled with bucolic labourers, honest squires and kindly parsons? The fact is, the prison was created in its present form in the nineteenth century, it has endured in Britain and indeed has proliferated throughout much of the earth, and it is a reality which to date bears every sign of stubborn survival far into the third millenium. It is not the existence of the prison which is in question (indeed the reverse) but rather the matter of what occurs within it.

It is here that there arise a number of thoughts which have implications for modern prisons. In raising these points it is important to tread gently, cautiously and with humility. Indeed, over-simplification may easily do grave injustice to all who strive and hope for better things whilst working and living in British prisons, and truth may easily be offended by stumbling into the complex system of penal disposal which exists in Britain today — a penal system which is moreover the subject of intense debate,

225

defence and attack. Nevertheless, one might reflect upon the survival of the prison chaplain, for example, and there may even be those who mourn the passing of the evangelical fire of the earlier-nineteenth century. The place of a Christian minister in British prisons is today guaranteed by both state and church; there can be little doubt that his presence within the prison stands at the interface between the power of the state and the self-rejection, despair, bleakness, contempt, anger, even challenge to that power amongst those citizens who are held in growing numbers within prisons. At certain points there may be great tension within that role, as when chapel services are attended by prisoners as a relief from boredom or perhaps as some kind of comic entertainment. The prison staff may come to value the chaplain's organisational function, his roles as reporter, facilitator, conciliator and to pass with little comment over his central spiritual function of bringing the message and meaning of Christ both to staff and prisoners, who in God's eyes are indisputably of equal value to statesmen and sentencers. Indeed, the inherent tendency of the penal institution towards unending regulation and categorisation of prisoners whom it is certainly tempting to define in terms of weakness or badness, manipulation or untrustworthiness, may require of chaplains a high courage in the face of institutional ethos amongst staff and prisoners alike, a great effort of will and faith. This is perhaps more difficult in an age when theological language and religious concepts have ceased to be an important aspect of policy and planning in public and social administrative structures.

At the same time the prison — like so much in the field of British social policy in the twentieth century — has opted for an almost all-inclusive state regulation, apparently thereby decreasing the need for a strong voluntarist presence within it. It is noteworthy that what is currently called 'the welfare function' has been incorporated into the hands of the state-appointed and controlled Probation Officer, who has replaced the old salaried employees of the National Discharged Prisoners' Aid Society, themselves descended from the prison chaplains and the local societies of Victorian times. Whatever overall value one might attach to such a change, a question surely remains as to the degree of the Probation Service's commitment to the prison as a natural, fit and most proper place for the exemplification of the values of social work and the exercise of its skills. On the face of it, numbers of probation officers appear to have had to be dragooned into prison by superiors; there is an almost collective reluctance to embrace the prison. Among many officers there seems to be a sense that such work is of lower importance than that of assessment for courts and field supervision of persons subject to judicial or administrative orders. Despite the existence of prison visitors and voluntary associates, there still remains a question about public access to and knowledge about prisons, implied by Bentham and others. Gone are the days when a Howard or a Neild could secure permanent admittance merely by insistence. Since 1835 the inspectoral and evaluative functions have been steadily and firmly subsumed by the state and prying critical penal explorers and reformers may be excluded at the stroke of an administrator's pen.

Doubtless there are many parallels and distinctions which may be drawn between the Victorian and modern penal experience. The overall shape of the modern prison system has been, like much else in educational, health and welfare administration, profoundly influenced by the Victorian era in which men devoted great thought and energy to such things. Although Victorian reformists unswervingly maintained the necessity for state action to cure the criminal maladies which arose from environmental pollution, they plainly stopped far short of that enormous undertaking, namely the nurturing, planned, tutelary society foreshadowed by Bentham and later by the Webbs. As it eventually emerged in the three decades after the Second World War, it would have provoked the reformists' profound distrust for such gigantic interventionism on the part of the state. However, for their part Victorian prison reformists were a small but none the less influential voice amongst many. They pointed up the risks which they believed had resulted from industrial concentration and thus prepared the way for a new kind of state unknown to them or their forefathers, yet had perhaps been implied by the monopoly over prisons obtained by the central state in 1877.

It is also the case that the Victorian reformists and post-Second World War welfare environmentalist theses (both implying a need for substantial action) each eventually encountered a potent counter-thesis. The former met theirs in evolutionism and positivism, which seemed to validate scientifically so many of Malthus's earlier lugubrious warnings; the latter in a fiercely articulated view of man as an unencumbered entrepreneurial investor of his talents, harvesting economic and social rewards as a result of the competitive use of his acquisitive faculties. Whether that latter change of emphasis of the late-1970s and early-1980s will, as did evolutionism and positivism, strengthen the sense of many that inmates of penal institutions are by their nature unlikely, whatever reformatory endeavours are undertaken, to benefit from or contribute to a society based upon such an ethos remains to be seen. In all likelihood there are implications in this more fragmenting (or less utopian) notion of social and economic reality for the operation of prisons. These may well bear fruit in policy and practice more openly, as the reformatory enthusiasms fuelled by post-war optimism and sociological and psychological theorists pass into the archives of history.

Yet surely the feature of these reformatory prisons of the last century which is of greatest importance to us today is a belief which flickers through the writings of those chaplains, most notably the work of a John Clay or a Joseph Kingsmill. It gave rise to a dominating purpose beyond the mere maintenance of a penal organisation or the mere enforcement of a repetitive obedience to social norms. It is to do with a faith, *together with clear reasons for that faith*, in the prison as the servant of an ideal — in that case spiritual — which places the individual worth of the prisoner close to its centre. That ideal stands in opposition to the chaplain as a mere clerical servant of a mighty and dignified machine of the state, the prison welfare officer as a mere oiler of wheels, the prison officer as mere turner of keys, the governor as mere careerist man-manager, the senior administrator as mere author of memoranda or president over interim policy review subcommittees. Instead, it emphasises their part in a vision of imprisonment which stands four-square against those secretive administrative and judicial cruelties which men, governed by their own fears and self-interests alone, have inflicted in a seemingly endless parade and examples of which litter the ground of the history of the twentieth century.

It is in short the fact that the ethic of shared human value remains of immense importance long after it was emphasised in a penal context by John Howard and his evangelical successors. In particular it matters in modern times that enthusiasm for this ethic be most carefully sustained and fostered by the state, for all prison systems which endeavour to stand upon it must contend with strong attitudes among many that the prisoner is of inferior human worth or even disposable. This is not to argue that sentence length ought to vary in accordance with the predictions of reformists or that prison disciplinarians should rekindle the reformatory claim as a justification for more extensive prison systems, for no fact is plainer in penal history than the overall failure of reformists to achieve substantial permanent alteration in human attitude and behaviour nor indeed would the prospect of such success be necessarily inviting. Nor is it necessary to deny the value of the contemporary 'justice model' which in part emphasises the dedicated pursuit of human dignities within prisons or the importance of firm pursuit of properly planned and led, well co-ordinated, sufficiently resourced non-custodial alternatives to prison. But without some kind of vision or ideal fostered from within the prisons themselves and the departments of state which govern and influence them, the direction of a prison regime towards promotion of the individual human worth of prisoners will be difficult to sustain. Indeed, its absence may lead to a new thrust towards mere incapacitation and bleak pessimism moving into the space vacated by the shrinking of the secular reformism of the later-twentieth century.

Doubtless the reformist aspiration of Victorian prison disciplinarians resulted in forms which at times seem to modern men to have been bizarre and harsh. Doubtless, also, it was lodged, as Ignatieff argued and as one would expect, within the framework of super/subordinate social relationships and direct unambiguous instruction in attitudes and conduct which suited the higher orders. Yet it is also true that many of these proponents of reformism sought to base their action upon a more independent ethic of very high importance, an ideal of social inclusion and human value of prisoners which stood at the heart of many of their endeavours. They preached this consistently and spent much of their lives seeking to promote it. Commentators and historians have been slow to appreciate this, preferring rather to dwell upon the Victorian prison as an example of growing social regulation with reformists as dutiful marionettes of an iron-hearted industrialising society. Nevertheless, contemporary man, who has known the differing manifestations of the power of evil in Dachau, the Gulag Archipelago, Makindye Barracks, Arkansas Prison Farm, and amidst 'the Disappeared Ones', should acknowledge that this particular ethical feature of these reformists' work is of no little importance.

References

1. C. B. Gibson, *Philosophy, Science and Revelation*, Longman, 1874, p. 90.
2. J. W. Horsley, *I Remember: Memories of a Sky Pilot in the Prison and the Slum*, Wells, 1911, pp. 95, 99; J. W. Horsley, *Prisons and Prisoners*,

Pearson, 1898, p. 45.

3. *Lectures on the Principles of Political Obligation* by T. H. Green with an introduction by Lord Lindsay, Longman, 1955, p. vii.

4. Melvin Richter, *The Politics of Conscience: T. H. Green and his Age*, Weidenfeld, 1964, pp. 283–4, 134.

5. Helen Lynd, *England in the 1880's*, OUP, 1945, p. 225.

6. Ibid., p. 150.

7. H. Barnett, *Canon Barnett, His Life, Work and Friends*, Murray, 1919.

8. J. W. Horsley, *Jottings from Jail*, Fisher Unwin, 1887, p. 56.

9. F. Meredyth, *The Decadence of Imperial Britain*, Simpkin, 1893.

10. General William Booth, *In Darkest England and the Way Out*, The Salvation Army, 1890.

11. Rev. B. Waugh, *The Gaol Cradle — Who Rocks It?*, Isbister, 1880, pp. 72, 193.

12. Rev. G. P. Merrick, *Work among the Fallen*, Ward, 1890; R. B. Orr, *In Durance Vile*, p. 157; G. Holden Pike, *Pity for the Perishing, The Power of the Bible in London*, Clarke, 1884, p. 204; G. Holden Pike, *Golden Lane*, Clarke, 1876.

13. W. Tallack, *Defects*, p. 143.

14. F. Scougal, (pseudonym for Felicia Skene), *Scenes from a Silent World, or Prisons and their Inmates*, Blackwood, 1889, p. 85.

15. W. Tallack, *Penological and Preventive Principles*, Wertheimer, 1889, p. 42.

16. W. H. Wines, *Punishment and Reformation*, Swan Sonneschein, 1895, pp. 234–5.

17. W. D. Morrison, *Juvenile Offenders*, Fisher Unwin, 1896, p. 256.

18. W. D. Morrison, *Crime and its Causes*, Swan Sonneschein, 1891, pp. 198, 227.

19. W. D. Morrison, 'The Treatment of Prisoners', in *Humane Society Lectures* (various authors), Bell, 1897, p. 108.

20. W. D. Morrison, *Juvenile Offenders*, p. 107; *The Treatment of Prisoners*, p. 85.

21. W. D. Morrison, *Juvenile Offenders*, pp. 108, 110, 101.

22. W. D. Morrison, *Crime and its Causes*, p. 192.

23. W. D. Morrison, *The Treatment of Prisoners*, p. 108.

24. *Report from the Departmental Committee on Prisons*, PP, 1895, vol. LVI, p. 4.

25. Ibid., pp. 7, 26.

26. Ibid., p. 401.

27. C.3.3. Oscar Wilde, *The Ballad of Reading Gaol*, Leonard Smithers, 1899.

Index

NOTE In this index the term Prison is used generically although strictly the terms Gaol or House of Correction are the correct ones for the period before 1865. To discover whether the institution concerned was a Gaol or House of Correction or both see text.